INDONESIA
BETWEEN MYTH
AND REALITY

Lee Khoon Choy

INDONESIA BETWEEN MYTH AND REALITY

 Nile & Mackenzie Ltd — London

First published in Great Britain 1976 by
Nile & Mackenzie Limited
43 Dover Street
London WIX 3RE

ISBN 0 86031 019 1

Printed and bound by FEP International Ltd.

Foreword

It is not often that one finds the qualities and proclivities of a successful politician, a sensitive writer and fine painter, a versatile musician and enthusiastic sportsman all in one person. It is an even greater surprise to find them in the person of Mr Lee Khoon Choy, Singapore's Ambassador to Jakarta and, by reason of geographic proximity alone, perhaps the busiest Ambassador in the capital city of Indonesia.

It is with great pleasure, therefore, that I comply with his request to write a few words as introduction to this, his most recent 'extracurricular' exploit — a book on Indonesia.

This book is aptly called *Indonesia between Myth and Reality*. For in it, the writer has tried to weave a composite picture of that side of Indonesia by which he seems to be most fascinated — the everyday reality of life cast against the backdrop of legends and myths and spiritual beliefs with which the Indonesian landscape, to use the writer's own words, is so richly endowed.

A glance through the chapter headings already reveals the direction into which the writer intends to lead the reader on this appealing journey through the mystical worlds of the kris and the banyan tree, through Toraja, land of eternal souls, and through what he calls the Badui zone of isolation from civilization.

The racy, and often engaging style of telling the stories belies the obviously thorough and painstaking research through which the writer must have gone in order to be able to present the factual materials he has gathered. Mr Lee himself admits that he has not at all tried to write a learned treatise but that he has deliberately kept the book in a journalistic travelogue style so as not to bore his readers.

But whatever the style, the book shows Mr Lee Khoon Choy to be a keen and sensitive observer of life in Indonesia, an eager student of the variety of religious, social and mystical customs, traditions and beliefs that make up the rich spiritual heritage of Indonesia.

This book also establishes him as a most attractive and intriguing writer of some aspects of Indonesian life and culture about which, I submit, many Indonesians themselves have only a hazy knowledge.

And although I would not recommend this book to those in search of a quick reference to present-day Indonesia, the young, bustling state engaged in an accelerated drive towards overall national development and modernization, I can recommend it to those who, after having been exposed to Indonesian life and culture, may have become interested in aspects of Indonesia which, though off the beaten track, yet still form an integral part of the Indonesian reality.

Adam Malik
Minister for Foreign Affairs
Republic of Indonesia

Acknowledgements

This is a personal report of my observations, impressions, experiences, and study on the Indonesian way of life, derived mainly from my four and a half years' stay as Ambassador and the short periods as journalist and politician. I went to Indonesia to help promote better relations between Indonesia and Singapore. To accomplish this task, I felt that it was necessary to have an open mind and a deeper understanding of the people. It did not take me long to realize that one has to begin from a study of the cultures of the various peoples that make up the great and vast nation. This involved a great deal of travelling to the provinces, visiting interesting, historic places, and talking to prominent people as as well as the commonfolk. In the course of my work, many Indonesians, some well known and in positions of authority whilst others were just ordinary folk, have helped me along the way. Some have helped me to get in touch with people who are not easy to contact, such as the Baduis, the Trungenese and the Torajans. I have also learnt from hundreds of Indonesians from the various regions something about their ways of life, their beliefs, customs and traditions. It is impossible and impracticable for me to mention them all. To each and everyone of them I express my deep appreciation.

I am especially grateful to Mr Mas Agung and Drs Harteadji of the Idayu, an organization for research on Indonesian affairs, and Mr Ananda Sujuno Hamongdarsono of Solo for having kindly arranged for the 'spiritual tour' of Central Java which provided me with the opportunity to have a deeper insight into Javanese mysticism. I would like also to thank Mr Pasila for putting me in touch with useful contacts in Toraja. My thanks also go to Pertamina, Indonesia's national oil company, for the arrangement it made for Ambassadors to visit Wamena, Sorong and Biak in Irian Jaya.

I wish to thank the former Governor of East Java, Mr Mohamed Noor, for having invited me to Madura to see the bull-race which has helped to enrich the chapter 'Sports and Recreation'.

I want to express especially my deepest appreciation to Mr Sumiskum, Vice-Speaker of the Indonesian Parliament, Mr Harry

Tjan of the Centre for Strategic and International Studies, Mr Alex Alatas, formerly Secretary to the Foreign Minister, Mr Adam Malik, and Professor Slamet Muljana for having taken the trouble to read my manuscript and for their valuable comments and suggestions. My great appreciation also goes to Mr Adam Malik for his kind words in his foreword.

A word of thanks to all those who have helped in clerical work and have made the publication of this book possible.

L. K. C.

Contents

Introduction

It may be appropriate for me to start off my introduction with a legend which can be found in a book entitled *Sutasoma* written in old Javanese by Mpu Tantular around the thirteenth or fourteenth century. An ogre king by the name of Purushada (meaning 'eating people') was fond of human flesh for his daily meals. The commonfolk one after another became his victims and they were terrified. A knight by the name of Sutasoma took pity on the people and offered himself to the king to be devoured instead of the people. Purushada was furious with Sutasoma for trying to interfere with his eating habits which he considered quite normal. He attempted to kill Sutasoma but in vain. A bitter struggle took place. Lord Siva entered the body of the king, and Lord Buddha entered that of the knight. It was an endless feud in which supernatural powers were invoked. Neither party could defeat his adversary. Then the Brahmins came, appealed to both warriors to cease fighting, and reminded them that though their appearances were different, they were virtually one. In the old Javanese language, the words which the Brahmins used to drop the hint that Siva and Buddha were one in different forms were *Bhinneka Tunggal Ika*. Siva and Buddha, realizing the oneness in them, left the bodies of the two warriors. Purushada gave up his habit of devouring people and began to lead a normal life.

The words *Bhinneka Tunggal Ika* mean 'unity through diversity'. This statement now speaks for the flexibility of the Indonesian people to syncretize and to blend the various religious beliefs, traditions and cultures — some of which are conflicting in the eyes of foreigners — into one to suit local conditions. In India, for instance, where Sivaism (Hinduism) and Buddhism originated, Siva and Buddha were irreconcilable opponents in the past. In Java, Sivaism and Buddhism not only flourished side by side, but were syncretized into a religion called Siva-Buddhism by King Kertanegara of the East Javanese kingdom of Singhasari (father-in-law of Prince Wijaya, founder of Majapahit). When the king died in 1292, he was buried in a Siva-Buddhist temple which he had founded. Today, there are thousands of Siva-Buddha followers in Java and Bali.

When the Indonesian people achieved independence they chose *Bhinneka Tunggal Ika* as their national motto and inscribed it on their state crest. From a religious symbol, it became a political one and has become the guideline for the now 120,000,000 people. It reminds them of the necessity and virtue of the spirit of tolerance and accommodation in a multi-racial, multi-religious, multi-cultural and multi-lingual society. The Republic of Indonesia comprising 13,677 islands is indeed a nation of diverse peoples. Although Bahasa Indonesia has become the national language to unite the people, the dialects, customs, dresses, traditions and religious beliefs vary from one end of the country to the other. There are some 250 dialects and a number of major languages not understood by people of different groups: Javanese, Balinese, Ambonese, Bataks, Dayaks, Minangkabaus, Menadonese, Sasaks, Buginese, Timorese and Papuans.

This book is an attempt to touch upon the diversity in the way of life of the various peoples who form the Indonesian nation. The diversity of the peoples and their different characteristics are reflected in the differences in dress, temperament, dances, music and games.

I have chosen the title *Indonesia between Myth and Reality* for various reasons. The impression which the outside world has about Indonesia is a myth in itself. Many people, including foreign dignitaries, have the misconception that Indonesia is an Islamic state or that it is made up of one race and culture. Not too long ago, the same error was repeated in a speech made at Istana Negara. Many Indonesian leaders told me later that they were surprised that many people still thought that Islam was the state religion of Indonesia. There is also a widespread misconception that the 120,000,000 Indonesians are of the same race, speak only one language, and have one religion. It was the wisdom and brilliant foresight of the founders of the Indonesian state to have chosen Malay, a minority language spoken in the Rhio Islands, as the official and national language. It has helped to unite the people. But to talk of one language, one culture, and one people is still a myth. The use of *Bhinneka Tunggal Ika* as the national motto is a clear enough suggestion that the people are a diverse group, striving towards unity. In other words, diversity is a reality and unity still an aim — or shall we say, a myth. The important factor is that the spirit of tolerance which is enshrined in the motto has made it possible for a people of different languages, religions, and cultures, in such a vast country, to unite into one nationality called the Indonesians.

Another reason I have chosen this title is that in my personal experience, I have realized that in this country, myth and reality are sometimes so blurred that even Indonesians themselves find it difficult to draw a dividing line between the two. To the Western-oriented mind, a kris is a weapon used for cutting or for battle. To most Javanese and Balinese and, for that matter, all Indonesians who possess a kris, it is more than just a piece of metal. Behind every kris is a story or a myth; it is a *pusaka* (heirloom) in which a certain spirit dwells, and at least once a week, due respect is given to it in proper ceremonial formality. The kris is a weapon which everyone can see. But the myth which lies behind it, which the human eye cannot see, only the owner of the kris is able to understand.

Again, a Javanese puppet-show or shadow-play is more than a form of public entertainment. The leather puppets are not just pieces of material to be manipulated by the *dalang* (the man who operates the puppets from behind the screen) and to be discarded when they are worn out. They are more than just dispensable material to most Javanese. Till this day, the antique puppets that are kept in the *kraton* (palaces) in Central Java are brought out at least once a year for a bath. It is a solemn occasion and the water which has caressed the bodies of the *wayang* (puppets), believed to contain mystical powers, is brought home to be poured on the paddy-fields for a good harvest. The puppets are real and the show, too, is a reality. But a chain of myths and mystical practices which are concealed to the uninitiated eye and not easily comprehensible to the Western-oriented mind surrounds them. The shadow plays an important part in Javanese philosophy. It is something one can see but not touch. It is real, yet a myth.

In the following chapters you will find in the customs, traditions, and religious beliefs of the people, not necessarily confined to the Javanese, many aspects that lie between myth and reality. As it is not possible in so vast a country to speak of all of them, the spotlight in this book is on those rarer ones which are seldom heard of in the outside world, as well as on the undercurrents of thoughts and beliefs that prevail in the minds of a large proportion of the Javanese, who constitute 60 per cent of the Indonesian population. The different stages of development of the Indonesian culture is revealed in the striking gap that exists between the Stone Age *koteka* dress of the Dhani tribe in Irian Jaya and the highly sophisticated Javanese cultural refinement or Minangkabau modernization.

In a country like Indonesia, particularly in Java, the fertile soil of spiritualism absorbs all kinds of religions and then acculturalizes them into beliefs and practices which have unique features and characteristics of their own. Nothing remains pure, and orthodoxy is not necessarily considered a virtue. In Indonesia, too, nothing is absolutely black or completely white. It is always grey and, even then, in different shades and tones. Take the spread of religions, for instance. The Islam that is closer to the shores of the Indonesian archipelago, such as in Demak, Cirebon or Aceh, has stronger Arab influence and is more orthodox probably because Islam came by the sea through the Straits of Malacca. As it got deeper and deeper into the hinterland, it was gradually watered down and underwent the process of synthesis because of strong Hindu and Buddhist influences there. Islam became more Javanized and fused with some elements of Javanese beliefs and traditions, as well as Hindu beliefs. Most Javanese Muslims in the interior believe that Semar, the ugly but supernaturally powerful clown in the *Mahabharata*, is the guardian spirit of Java. All of them wear a kris which invariably houses a spirit. They also pay respect to ancestors' tombs or even try to invoke the spirits of their ancestors.

Similarly, Christianity has been Javanized in many areas of Java. I have met Indonesian Christians who believe in mysticism and follow Javanese traditions and customs which can be regarded by orthodox Christians as rather unchristian. For instance, many Christians in Toraja still follow the old customs of burying their beloved dead in rocks and cliffs and slaughtering cows for the funeral feast. In the southern part of Jogjakarta, there is a Catholic church where *gamelan* music is played instead of the organ. The hymns are sung in Javanese accompanied by the *gamelan* to Javanese tunes. Not far away is a Prambanan-type of church which is decorated with two statues, one having the image of the King of Madura and the other, the face of the wife of Arjuna, one of the five Pandawa heroes of the *Mahabharata*. The King is regarded as a personification of Jesus Christ, and the wife of Arjuna, that of Mary. Somewhere north of Jogjakarta, a Christian *Romo* (father) by the name of Senjaya of Muntilan was killed in 1947. Till today many of his Christian supporters go to his grave to invoke his soul for spiritual guidance. His belongings such as shirts, shoes and slippers have become *pusaka* and are used for curing the sick.

In Central Java, East Java and Bali, Sivaism and Buddhism have merged into a syncretized religion called Siva-Buddhism. There are thousands of Siva-Buddhists — in fact, most Balinese are Siva-Buddhists. Whenever a religious ceremony takes place, such as the purification of a temple or a cremation, it is jointly officiated by a Hindu priest and a Buddhist priest.

At the Borobudur temple, I met a learned Indonesian official guide who said he was a Buddhist as well as a Muslim. He believed in Prophet Mohammed and Allah, but he also practised the Buddhist way of meditation and the Buddhist way of life, a compromise which is unimaginable anywhere else in the world.

In most parts of Asia, a Buddhist is a Buddhist, a Taoist a Taoist, and a Confucianist a Confucianist. But in Java, the three religions have become one, known as *Sam Kow* in the Fukien dialect. Inside the temple of Sampo Kong in Semarang, Central Java, you will find symbols of Buddhism, the picture of Confucius, and relics of Taoist mysticism. The temple was built in commemoration of Admiral Cheng Ho who visited the South Seas seven times with sixty-two treasure ships. To add to the mystery, Cheng Ho was a Muslim eunuch. The temple is today taken care of by Javanese Muslims of Chinese descent.

This spirit of tolerance and syncretism has made inter-marriage between persons of different religions a common affair. It is not unusual to find an Indonesian family in which many religions exist side by side. I have a friend in a high position who is a Muslim. His wife is a Catholic, and his children are either Muslims or Catholics. One of them even practises *Kebatinan* (an indigenous Javanese religious movement) with a strong mixture of Buddhism. In this country, nobody tries to force another to adopt his religion. There is mutual respect so that all can live in harmony.

The Javanese spirit of syncretism is not confined to religion alone. The former President Sukarno, being a Javanese, tried to syncretize nationalism, religion and communism into a state ideology under the name of Nasakom. Although it might appear to observers that the basic tenets of the three politico-religious concepts contain fundamental contradictions which are irreconcilable, he was tempted to give it a trial run. Nasakom ended on the rocks. The failure, according to some Javanese leaders, was caused not so much by the irreconcilability of the three concepts but because one of the three forces tried to impose its will on the others by the use of force. It thus infringed the spirit of tolerance sacredly inscribed on the Indonesian state crest, *Bhinneka Tunggal Ika*. Once the rule is broken, the balance of the scale is tipped, and the whole idea collapses.

It was a good lesson to most people, and the spirit of tolerance as symbolized by *Bhinneka Tunggal Ika* is being institutionalized. Professor Mukti Ali, the Minister for Religious Affairs who is a Muslim, told me that one of the functions of his Ministry is to preach and implement the spirit of tolerance which is vital to the survival and harmony of a multi-religious, multi-cultural, and multi-racial society like Indonesia. According to him, the Ministry is in the process of arranging for periodical dialogue among the leaders of the various religions to seek common ground in the spirit of tolerance.

The slogan *Bhinneka Tunggal Ika* may be comparable to the biological term 'symbiosis', meaning 'relying on one another for survival'. The more popular phrase in everyday use is 'to live and let live'. The Indonesian Minister of Information, Mr Mashuri, described the Indonesian way of life as an example of the Eastern concept of symbiosis in human relations as opposed to the Western concept of 'survival of the fittest'. Expounding the theory of the basic difference between the two concepts to me one day, Mr Mashuri said the symbiotic approach is to treat one's fellowmen as an interdependent part of the whole human society whose survival is conditional upon mutual help for mutual benefit. On the other hand, the Western concept of 'survival of the fittest' makes humans treat one another as separate, antagonistic units. They attempt to eliminate one another in order to survive, in the same way that big fish eat small fish and small fish, the shrimps. Based on this concept, the strong try to dominate the weak and impose their will on them. This is the root of all the trouble in human society, according to Mashuri. Unless people learn to live with one another instead of following the concept of 'survival of the fittest', the world will always be plagued with tension, chaos and friction. The failure of the Nasakom ideology can also be interpreted as a clash between the spirit of 'symbiosis' and that of 'survival of the fittest'. One of the proponents of Nasakom tried to apply the theory of 'survival of the fittest' on Indonesian soil, but failed because traditionally the soil was saturated with the *Bhinneka Tunggal Ika* spirit.

The failure of the Nasakom ideology has brought Indonesia back to its philosophy of Pancasila originated by Sukarno but reemphasized under the New Order. This philosophy was, in fact, promulgated in the early days of the Indonesian revolution in 1945, and was crystallized by the Investigating Body for the Preparation of Indonesian Independence. The present government is making efforts to revive this philosophy which consists of five principles: Belief in one God, Humanity, Sovereignty of the People, Social Justice, and Democracy. The day the six generals and one soldier were assassinated and thrown into Lubang Buaya (Crocodile Hole) has become, officially, Pancasila Day. Thus, every year the first day of October (the day after the disastrous Gestapu coup of 30 September 1965) is a day of national mourning.

To revive further the spirit of the 1945 revolution and the struggle for independence, a Pancasila monument was erected at Kalibata where national heroes are buried. The monument comprising five towering pillars representing the five principles of Pancasila was officially declared open by President Suharto on 11 November 1974. The monument was to commemorate the millions of unknown Indonesian soldiers who had sacrificed their lives for independence. An actual funeral ceremony took place when the remains of an unknown soldier, dug out from one of the graves in Surabaya, were reinterred in the underground pavement of the monument. The ceremony was conducted solemnly and with pomp under the supervision of President Suharto in the presence of national and foreign dignitaries.

Nobody knows who the soldier was whose remains are now interred in the Pancasila monument to represent all unknown soldiers. Nobody knows what religion or race he belonged to. In the spirit of tolerance, the ceremony was conducted without too much fuss. The important thing was to pay respect to the dead souls and to make the monument a source of inspiration for future generations to maintain the spirit of the revolution for the development of the Indonesian nation and for the welfare of the people.

The first principle of the Pancasila Democracy is 'Belief in one God'. Nowhere in the world do we find a country in which religion plays such an important role in the lives of the people.

The Indonesian people believe in the existence of God, be he in the image of Buddha, Jesus Christ or Mohammed. Whether they are Christians, Buddhists, Hindus, Muslims, Confucianists or Taoists, they have to believe in one God. There is no place for atheists. A non-believer is always viewed with suspicion that he may be a communist.

Notwithstanding the diversity of religious beliefs, the Indonesians have one thing in common: they pray to their ancestors. This tradition of ancestor-worship has been in existence since the Stone Age. In Wamena, the Dhanis still pray to their mummified squatting ancestor. The Bataks in North Sumatra build pagoda-type monuments to house the ashes of their ancestors and, like the traditional Confucianist Chinese, would feel uneasy if they did not visit such sacred places once a year. The Torajans in the northern part of South Celebes bury their dead in rocks and throw a big feast to send their souls to heaven. The Balinese have an ancestors' shrine in every temple and invoke the souls of their ancestors to partake of a feast on their birthdays. The Baduis in West Java, the Tenggerese in East Java and the Trungenese in an isolated valley off the Kintamani Valley worship their ancestors in different fashions. In Central Java, it has become a tradition for Javanese to visit the graves of their ancestors and pay homage. Ancestor-worship seems to me a common trait in all the traditional cultures of Indonesia. It is also characteristic of most Asian cultures.

The average Indonesian believes in the existence of the soul. He believes that death is not the end of everything and that there is such a thing as a soul, or you may call it superconsciousness, which can be contacted by well-trained mystics. There is nothing new or strange in this concept, for the greatest discoveries in every field of knowledge have had their origin in the intuitions of men of genius. Through intuition they see, sometimes in a flash, things not seen by other men. Through it, they perceive relations between apparently isolated phenomena which others have missed. Through it, they attain knowledge which could have been attained in no other way. The insights of intuition often have the appearance of something given, a sort of revelation coming from something outside oneself. The mind often in a state of passivity makes a sudden leap. What has been obscure before is integrated and takes on a pattern. You will find in the following chapters many instances of this practice of contact with the superconsciousness which is referred to as God, the soul or by other different names. The Javanese mystics even contact the souls of their leaders or ancestors.

This aspect of the psychological make-up of a large proportion of the Indonesian people, particularly the Javanese, is something which the Western-oriented mind finds difficult to comprehend. Call it mysticism or superstition if you like, but an understanding of this aspect of the Indonesian mind is necessary if one wishes to have a better understanding of the Indonesian society. Without this understanding one may be like a blind man groping in the dark.

The word 'mystic' is not an Eastern invention. It has its origin in Greek mysteries although the East had plenty of them in different terms earlier than the Greeks. A mystic was one who had been initiated into these mysteries through which he had gained an esoteric knowledge of divine things and had been 'reborn into eternity'. The object of the mystic was to break through the world of history and time into that of eternity and timelessness. Mysticism has its fount in what is the raw material of all religions and the inspiration of much philosophy, poetry, art and music, a consciousness of something beyond. Mystical experience or speculation is not limited to one religion. In Christianity alone, many have claimed to have had mystical experiences. Catholic mystics such as St Teresa and St John of the Cross, the Venerable Augustine Baker, St Francois de Sales, Madam Guyon and Father Pierre Caussade, to mention only a few, were all considered mystics. As Christianity came to Indonesia rather late and did not flourish until the Dutch occupation, its mysticism was not felt in this part of the world. Thus, much of the mysticism in Indonesia was derived from Hindu and Buddhist origins. The mysticism of Sufism and even Chinese Taoism also left its traces in the rich spiritual soil of Indonesia. Today, it is not difficult to find Indonesian translations of the *Tao Te Ching*, the bible of Taoism, in the bookshops of Jogjakarta.

I went to Indonesia to promote better understanding between my country and our big and great neighbour. To fulfil my duties, it was necessary, first of all, to have a deeper understanding of the country and the various aspects of Indonesian life. The world today challenges everyone to understand culture. Modern science and technology have made the world shrink in terms of distances. Human contact has become much easier and more frequent because of radio, television, tourism, foreign relations and technical assistance programmes. The impact of the Western materialistic concept of life left behind by past colonial rulers makes the peoples of South-East Asia take for granted that they are all the same. Rarely does one realize that although the people may wear coat and tie, eat with fork and spoon and speak a common language such as English, French or Dutch, behind their minds lurk a thousand shadows of differences that divide them. This applies also to people of the same country. Modern technology is inadequate to deal with cultural diversities. Experts who go abroad to advise developing countries on how to cut down population growth, increase food production, or set up modern factories are not geared to understand how the problems with which they must deal are rooted in foreign ways of life. Guide-books tell tourists precisely what monuments to see and what to buy, but stop short of explaining the life styles they will encounter abroad. More than ever before, it is hazardous for people of different cultures to live together with inadequate understanding of each other's culture and sense of values, especially those which affect decison-making.

The aim of this book is to help bring about a better understanding of the Indonesian people who have inherited not only one of the richest natural resources of the world but also a rich, diverse cultural heritage. My book was written without scholarly pretensions. I was not afraid now and then to introduce my own personal impressions and reflections on the course of events. Nor did I shy away from prying into purely personal relationships. I have deliberately tried to give an account of what I saw or heard in a journalistic style. I realize that the specialists who may read my book will probably discover certain defects. To some extent this is inevitable. For instance, I have not touched on the rapid progress made by the Government under the New Order in the field of industrial development.

To be frank, I was amazed by the progress Jakarta had made when I revisited the city as Singapore's Ambassador in 1970. I last visited it as a journalist in 1955 when I went to attend the Bandung Afro-Asian Conference. Indonesia may in time to come develop into an industrial nation. Modern Western technology may help to change the surface and image of Indonesia's various towns into bustling cities of booming economy, industrial pollution, skyscrapers, and traffic jams. Western influence may change the face of Indonesia and make her appear Westernized. But I doubt that it can penetrate the minds and hearts of the Indonesian people who, I venture to guess, will remain Indonesian. The Japanese remain Japanese and have stuck to their traditional way of life despite their success in modernization. It is a matter of maintaining a balance between modern technological advancement and traditional values. And the fundamental philosophy of the Indonesians is to strike a balance between material and spiritual happiness. Having watched the Indonesian situation for some years, I am inclined to believe that, like the Japanese, the Indonesians will continue to retain their traditional ways of life, customs and beliefs even when Western technology has caught up with the country's industrial development.

This is yet another reason why it is necessary to have a better understanding of the socio-cultural and spiritual background of the Indonesian people. It is my sincere hope and desire that this book will help contribute towards this purpose.

1 The Landscape

"Come, Dewi Srengenge! A kingdom awaits you. You will regain your beauty and live forever," a voice from the watery depths beckoned the princess who was to become Queen of the Indian Ocean.

Indonesia is a paradise for artists and writers. The landscape itself is a treasure-house of mysticism, culture, religion and mythology. A mountain can mean different things to different people. To the painter, it is a scene of beauty; to the writer, it will have a story to tell; to the mystic, it will offer serenity for meditation. Similarly, rivers, lakes and the roaring waves of the Indian Ocean (referred to as the Indonesian Ocean in Indonesian geography books) inspire different people differently. A cave, a waterfall, a banyan tree or even a mysterious rock will have a story to tell. There is, therefore, an abundance of legends, known as *dongeng*, relating to landmarks throughout Indonesia.

Some legends are mere fantasies, others are about humans or animals and their places in the cosmic world. Sometimes, the humans are endowed with supernatural powers. There are legends which have a moral to teach. They concern feelings of love, hatred, suspicion, jealousy or greed, usually between father and son, husband and wife, or between mother-in-law and daughter-in-law. These legends form part of a cultural heritage which has been passed from generation to generation by word of mouth. At family gatherings or village get-togethers, the elders will relate interesting tales to the children who are always willing listeners. The influence of such stories on young children is not to be passed off lightly.

I have chosen to relate four legends concerning rather remarkable and revered landmarks in Indonesia: the Indian Ocean, the volcano Tangkuban Prahu, the river Banyuwangi and Lake Toba. As an introduction to the spiritual and cultural significance of the landscape in Indonesia, the legend of the Queen of the Indian Ocean explains the relationship of the Queen to the royal family of Jogjakarta and Surakarta (better known as Solo). This legend still influences the thinking of many people today. Indonesia is a country of volcanoes, and a visitor to West Java would never miss Tangkuban Prahu (meaning 'volcano of the capsized boat') situated near the beautiful city of Bandung. A visit is so much more interesting if one knows the history or legend of the place. A legend sometimes even reflects the thoughts and feelings of the people of the region.

The river which one has to cross on the way to Bali from the eastern tip of Java is called Banyuwangi (meaning 'the river of perfume'). How can one cross 'the river of perfume' without wondering about the origin of its name? Lake Toba in North Sumatra is fast becoming a tourist attraction, and yet so few realize that the local folk still believe that the lake is ruled by the Dragon Queen, also known as Baru Saniang Naga. The legend reminds people not to break a promise.

In Indonesia, especially in Java, it would be an exception if someone had not heard of Lara Kidul. Queen Lara Kidul is not only a legend; to most Javanese she is also real. She dwells in the rough sea off the southern coast of Java. From Samudra Beach, I had a glimpse of the angry sea where Queen Lara Kidul is said to reside. The rocky cliffs that surround the recklessly winding coastline and the luxuriant vegetation are a feast for the artist's eye. The constant murmur of the sea and the roar of the rolling waves, now and then interrupted by the shrieks of giant birds, are an inspiration for the composer. The atmosphere is full of excitement and mystery, particularly for those who know the legend of Queen Lara Kidul.

Nyai Lara Kidul's maiden name was Dewi Srengenge, or Sun Maiden. Her beauty was unsurpassed. The King of Banyumas, in Central Java, fell in love with her and made her his favourite wife. This made one of his other wives, Dewi Kundati, jealous of the beautiful Dewi Srengenge. So she employed an old wizard who used his magical powers to turn Dewi Srengenge into an ugly and frightening creature. Dewi Srengenge was so distressed that she ran away. As she wandered, she met a kind-hearted old man who listened to her story and took pity on her. The old man reported her story to the King, who immediately sentenced Dewi Kundati and the wizard to death. But no one could give back Dewi Srengenge her beauty. In her sadness, she roamed from village to village, until she finally reached the southern coast of West Java. At the beach near Samudra, she heard a voice calling, "Come, Dewi Srengenge! A kingdom awaits you. You will regain your beauty and live forever. Come!" Lured by the voice, Dewi Srengenge entered the sea and from then on was known as Nyai Lara Kidul, Queen of the Indian Ocean.

It happened that Nyai Lara Kidul had a beloved sister who had been searching for her. It was not long before her search led her to the same spot where Lara Kidul had entered the sea. Grieving over the loss of her sister, she stood there sobbing when suddenly a voice made itself heard, "You need a fish's tail if you wish to join your sister." Thereupon, Kidul's sister was transformed into a mermaid and she swam into the ocean to join her Queen sister in her watery palace.

This legend also serves to explain the origin of the mermaid called *air mata duyung*, meaning 'longing tears'. Today, there is a kind of fish called *ikan duyung* which seems to have tears.

However, the story of Lara Kidul does not end here. It is said that Senopati, King of the Mataram Empire, once went to the southern beach to meditate. Nyai Lara Kidul came to know of it and appeared before the King. A romantic version of the legend says that he was at once struck by her beauty, fell in love, and married her. Thus was established the tie between Queen Lara Kidul and the great royal house of Mataram. Another more prosaic version says that Lara Kidul promised to come to the aid of King Senopati and his royal descendants whenever they wanted her service.

The deep, spiritual significance of the union of Queen Lara Kidul and the King of Mataram can be witnessed during the Labuhan Ceremony still celebrated annually at the water's edge. The ceremony, which takes place one day after the birthday of the Sultan of Jogja, is to honour Queen Lara Kidul and to ask for her blessing on the Sultan, his court and his people. Offerings are brought from the Sultan's palace to Parangsumo on the southern coast facing the Indonesian Ocean. The offerings include money, petals, and female garments such as a shawl and lengths of batik. There are also cuttings of the Sultan's hair and clippings of his fingernails. The offerings are first brought to the village of Kretek on the western bank of the river Opak early in the morning. They are then carried across the river and down to the village of Parangtritis

Offerings to Lara Kidul, Queen of the Indonesian Ocean, are brought to the water's edge at the village of Parangtritis.

at the water's edge. This is where Senopati, the sixteenth century Mataram ruler, was said to have met Lara Kidul. The offerings are then placed on a bamboo raft and are cast out to sea by *kraton* officers. An enthusiastic crowd watches as the raft is tossed by the waves, throwing the offerings into the sea. When the offerings are eventually washed back to shore, spectators scramble to collect them, believing that they contain supernatural powers. The Sultan's hair and fingernail clippings, however, are buried in the sand in a special walled-in spot on the beach. These, too, are eventually dug up by spectators and kept as sacred souvenirs.

A ceremony of this nature was held on 21 June 1971 in conjunction with the celebration of the 61st birthday of Sultan Hamengkubuwono IX, who is now Vice-President of the Republic of Indonesia. The offerings included a complete set of clothing for a princess — a sarong, a *kebaya* (blouse), a *selendang* (shawl) and an umbrella, in addition to food. Some people are prepared to pay high prices for these items of clothing or other offerings retrieved from the sea if the finders are willing to part with them. It is commonly believed that possession of these objects brings material as well as spiritual good fortune.

Today, the legend of Queen Lara Kidul is still very much a part of the local traditions and beliefs. Whenever a swimmer is swept away by the treacherous waves along the Samudra Beach resort at Labuhan Ratu in West Java, local folklore has it that the Queen has taken another to join her entourage. Some years back an Ambassador from an East European country went for a swim there and never returned. During violent thunderstorms, villagers of nearby Sukabumi lock their doors and fasten their windows, as they fear Queen Lara Kidul's display of her temper. On special occasions during court festivities, Queen Lara Kidul is again venerated in a palace dance called Bedoyo Ketawang.

The story of the capsized boat, which turned into a volcano, is very popular among the Sundanese who live predominantly in West Java.

Long, long ago, the country of Priangan in West Java was covered with forest where wild, native animals were free to roam. There lived a powerful king called Raden Sungging Perbangkara. This king had an unusual relationship with a wild-boar which gave birth to a beautiful daughter named Dewi Rara Sati. Dewi loved to sit in the mountainous forest knitting while she admired the scenery of lush valleys below. One hot day, as she was knitting at the top of a mountain, she dozed off, and one of her knitting needles fell into the valley. As she treasured her knitting, Dewi Rara Sati promised to marry whoever could retrieve the needle. A dog by the name of Si Tumang heard of Dewi's pledge and rushed into the valley to look for the needle. After a long search, he found it and returned it to her. In order to keep her promise, Dewi was obliged to marry Si Tumang. A year later, she gave birth to a son who was named Sangkuriang. Mother and son lived happily together, and Sangkuriang never knew the identity of his father, Si Tumang the dog, or his grandmother, the boar.

Dewi was very proud of the boy because he was a good hunter and often brought home the heart of a mouse-deer for dinner. One evening Sangkuriang could not get a deer, but instead wounded a wild-boar which happened to be the mother of Dewi. Fortunately for Dewi, her boar-mother escaped into the forest. Sangkuriang then asked the dog Si Tumang to chase after the wild-boar, but Tumang stubbornly refused. In great anger and desperation, he shot Tumang instead and brought home Tumang's heart, and lied to his mother that it was the heart of a deer. His mother soon discovered that it was the heart of Si Tumang, her husband and the father of Sangkuriang. She went into a fit of rage, took a *tongkat* (walking-stick) and hit her son on the forehead. He left the house with a bleeding wound, not to return for many years.

Sangkuriang grew into a fine young man. One day he happened to come by a mountain, not recognizing that it was his birthplace. There he saw a beautiful woman and fell in love with her. It was Dewi Rara Sati who had managed to keep her youth. When they were about to marry, Dewi accidentally discovered the wound on the forehead of the young man and immediately recognized him as her son. She did not disclose her identity, but secretly determined not to marry him. So she told him she would marry him only if he could fulfil one condition to prove his worth. Thinking that it would be an impossible task, she asked him to dig a lake out of the mountain and build a boat before sunset so that they could sail on their honeymoon. Love worked wonders, and when Sangkuriang had almost accomplished the task, Dewi became alarmed. So she used her magical powers to change the colour of the sky from blue to crimson, and sunset soon turned to twilight before Sangkuriang could finish the boat. He, in turn, was so angry that he turned the half-completed boat upside down. As he did that, the earth shook and trembled, and the mountain erupted, the fiery lava sweeping both Dewi and Sangkuriang away in the volcanic streams. Today, the live volcano looks like a capsized boat.

Whenever I visit Bandung, I never miss the opportunity to visit

Tangkuban Prahu which is also known as Sangkuriang. My first visit there was in 1955 as a journalist to the Afro-Asian Conference. It is one of the places I like to visit, not because I like the smell of sulphur which pervades the atmosphere, but because it is cool, pleasant and gives one a feeling of calm, despite the hot, bubbling lava in the volcano below.

I often think of the legend of Sangkuriang and ponder over its significance — the relationship between a king and a wild-boar, then that between a beautiful princess and a dog, and later between mother and son, a remarkably strange but interesting legend which seems to me to have a theme. There is throughout the story a conflict between fulfilment of desire and keeping it a secret. The king keeps a secret about his wife who was a wild-boar, the princess about her relationship with her dog-husband, and finally the mother tries to keep the secret of her identity from her son. Secret relationships and hidden truths lead to human tragedy.

There is nothing extraordinary about the town that bears the name Banyuwangi, 'the river of perfume'. The water of the river itself is not clean, nor is it at all fragrant. But the legend lends the town a certain degree of romance as well as fame.

In East Java, there once lived Sidapaksa, who was Prime Minister to King Sindwaja. Sidapaksa married a beautiful woman whom he loved so much that even his own mother became jealous. She was determined to break up the marriage because her daughter-in-law was a commoner and she wanted her son to marry into royalty.

Now the Queen of Sindwaja had been seeking a magic flower that could give her eternal youth and beauty. When Sidapaksa's mother heard about this, she saw it as an opportunity to break up her son's marriage. She convinced her son that, as Prime Minister, he should please the Queen and go to Mount Ijen in search of the magic flower. At first, Sidapaksa was reluctant to leave his wife who was then pregnant, but finally he departed.

In his absence, his wife gave birth to a son. When the baby was only three days old, the mother-in-law quietly snatched him away and threw him into the river. When Sidapaksa's wife discovered her son missing, she rushed about the *kampong* (village) searching for him in vain. She soon fell seriously ill. Meanwhile, Sidapaksa had succeeded in finding the magic flower for the Queen and was highly commended for his noble deed. He rushed home to share his happiness and success with his wife and new baby. But before he reached home, his mother had poisoned his mind with rumours that his wife had been unfaithful to him and that she had thrown the baby into the river. In a mad fury, he went to his sick wife and drew his kris ready to stab her. Denying the allegations, she pleaded with him to bring her to the river to witness the truth for himself. When she reached the river, she jumped into it and disappeared. Sidapaksa was shocked yet disappointed that he had still not learnt the truth. At that moment, two pure white lotus flowers — one large and one small — appeared on the surface of the water. The bigger lotus spoke, "Let your own son tell you the truth." The smaller lotus followed, "Pak, it was your mother, my grandmother, who threw me into the river." The two flowers then disappeared into the waters of the river, leaving behind a fragrance which permeated the air throughout the village. And this explains the origin of the name of the river Banyuwangi.

There are many Indonesian legends and tales with similar themes of jealousy. The 'perfume river' legend also reflects the tensions that existed in the society of the region where the legend originated. There was class consciousness in favour of royalty as opposed to the commoner, the desire to remain eternally young, the feeling of jealousy and rivalry between mother-in-law and daughter-in-law, and the driving force of love and suspicion. Such legends still play an important role in Javanese society, particularly in the moulding of the young mind.

From Java, let me take you to the north of Sumatra where we come upon Lake Toba. The lake looks more like a vast sea surrounded by volcanic mountains. I love the serenity and cool mountain air. It gives one a feeling of contentment and peace of mind. Lake Toba is easily the largest mountain-lake in Asia. How big is it? The Protocol Officer of the Governor of North Sumatra, who was my guide during my first visit, gave me a hint. Pointing to Pulau Samosir in the middle of the lake, he said, "Do you see the island before us? It is bigger than Singapore." As we travelled in a motor-boat towards Samosir, dark clouds began to hide the sun, and a strong wind suddenly disturbed the tranquillity of the lake. The boat began to rock. Anxiety crept over the face of our aged boatman. "Let us hope that Baru Saniang Naga is not losing her temper," said the boatman to his colleague. Baru Saniang Naga, the Dragon Queen, is said to rule Lake Toba.

Batak folklore has it that, once upon a time, there lived a farmer at the foot of Dolok Rihit, a huge mountain that once towered over Pulau Samosir. The farmer liked to fish in a stream near by. One sunny morning, he caught such a heavy fish that it took all his might to land it. To his surprise, his catch turned out to be a beautiful maiden. The farmer fell in love with the beautiful girl, who was called Saniang, and asked for her hand in marriage. She agreed to marry him provided that he swore never to disclose her identity to anyone. She warned him that there would be great calamity if he ever broke his promise. He happily agreed and married her.

It was not long before Saniang gave birth to a son. One evening, when the farmer returned from the fields, he discovered that his son, who was then a growing boy, had eaten all the dinner, leaving nothing for him. The father, impulsive and hot-tempered by nature, scolded his son loudly, "You uneducated son of a fish!" On hearing this, Saniang was furious and angrily accused her husband, "You have broken your promise and now all is ruined." Almost immediately, a volcano erupted causing Mount Rihit to tremble. A violent storm followed and flooded the whole valley, turning it into a lake. All that was left of Dolok Rihit was the mountain top, which is now known as the island of Samosir. Saniang returned to the water, never to be reunited with her husband and son again. Since then, whenever a storm threatens Lake Toba, the local folk remember Saniang, the Dragon Queen, who they believe expresses her displeasure by disturbing the calm waters of the lake.

By the time our boat reached Samosir, the threatening storm had subsided. The old boatman said it was because he had quietly dropped some *sirih* (betel leaf) and *pinang* (areca nut) into the lake to pacify the Queen. It is the custom of boatmen and fishermen to give offerings to the Dragon Queen before they set sail. Sometimes, when small boats capsize or when a travelling car is blown into the lake during a violent storm, the village elders would imply that Baru Saniang Naga caused the mishaps because she had not first been appeased.

2

The Koteka
of the
the Stone Age

Morning star, greatest of all stars,
Come and be my herald and make me a
hut of leaves
In the east, in the east of Judaca.

a *koreri* hymn

It is difficult to believe that a flight of only six hours from Jakarta
to Irian Jaya via Makassar will bring us back to the Stone Age.
Our Fokker Friendship 28 landed on a small airstrip in the village
of Wamena, situated on a huge plateau 650 metres above sea-level,
in central Irian Jaya — the land of *cenderawasih*, birds-of-paradise.
As guests of Pertamina, our group of thirty foreign Heads of Mission
was to be taken back hundreds of years in time to the Stone Age.
It was a fine day; the weather was cool and refreshing when we
arrived. As we stepped out of the plane, many of us were at once
quite taken aback by what we saw. Gathered along the barbed-wire
fence at the perimeter of the airstrip was a group of wide-eyed but
almost naked Dhani natives. The men wore only a rather strange
horn-shaped covering over their penes. This covering, called
koteka in Bahasa Indonesia, or *holim* in the local Dhani dialect,
juts out from the penis but is held in place by a string tied to the
end of it and connected to the waist. The womenfolk were equally
naked with just a skirt of beads tied round their waists and dangling
down over their bellies. Around their heads were long fishnet-like
scarves hanging down to their buttocks. Characteristically, the
Dhanis have curly hair, large mouths and square jaws. Generally,
they appeared strong-limbed and rugged.

As we disembarked from the plane, we wondered whether the

Dhanis had come to welcome us or were simply curious to see us. They probably considered us equally conspicuous in our clothing. They made no gesture of welcome or protest, nor did they make any noise. Silent, with mouths agape, they stared blankly at the steel giant and the visitors. Until very recently, they regarded the rarely-seen planes as some fantastic, foreign animal. Being followers of the cargo cult, they worshipped whatever was new and strange to them. It was very difficult for them to understand how such a huge and heavy thing could fly like a bird without supernatural powers. It must have been a divine creature to them. All these thoughts flashed through my mind as I looked at their charmingly innocent faces. While some of the foreign dignitaries avidly snapped photos, one of them turned to me and said, "It is unbelievable that in this modern age, there are still people living in the Stone Age. Am I walking in a dream? I just cannot believe it."

Believe it or not, the facts are there for everyone to see. The Dhani tribe, which lives on the remote plateau of Wamena, has been isolated from the outside world for centuries. But what did the Dutch colonizers do to them or for them during the three centuries of colonial rule? This was the question that immediately came to our minds. Despite their primitive way of life, the Dhanis are a friendly and gentle people who number about 200,000 throughout Irian Jaya. They are soft-spoken and pleasant-looking. Most of them speak a smattering of Bahasa Indonesia. They tried their best to please the visitors by posing for the photographers. Simply one word *nayak*, meaning 'thank you' in the Dhani language, was enough and they went off with a smile. Not a single native asked for a tip. Perhaps the materialistic values of modern civilization have not caught up with them yet. Perhaps they did not know that they were being exploited by the visitors.

First we were taken to see the hamlets of the Dhani tribe in Wamena. Each hamlet is about 300 metres from the next and is surrounded by a tall bamboo fence. Inside each hamlet, at the far end of a long yard, is the men's hut facing the entrance. The hut is characteristically circular with a diameter of approximately 4 metres, and had a domed, thatched roof. To the right of this are several women's huts — the number of huts depending on the size of the family — and to the left is the cooking area. Surrounding these living quarters is a garden in the shape of a horseshoe.

We were invited to visit a male hut and as the entrance to the hut was only waist high, we had to crawl in. It is pitch black inside. The daylight that manages to creep in through the doorless entrance enables one to see the fireplace in the centre of the hut. At night, a fire is necessary to keep the hut warm. The smoke that is produced from the burning of the wood helps to drive away the mosquitoes. How it is that the occupants are not suffocated by the smoke is a mystery as there is not a single window or any other sort of ventilation on either the ground floor or upper floor which are separated only by a bamboo platform. All the occupants sleep on the upper floor, which can be reached by a ladder. One has to climb up, groping one's way in the darkness. We noticed that on the ground floor there were neither chairs nor tables, but when we saw the upper floor, one Ambassador asked, "What do the Dhanis use for pillows?" But the Dhanis had never heard of a pillow. We also noticed that there was no bathing area, because the Dhanis do not bathe. Instead, they rub their bodies with pig fat to keep themselves warm. At a height of 650 metres above sea-level, the nights are often extremely cold.

Despite their nakedness, the Dhanis do have a sense of modesty and moral standards. Their yardstick for modesty is in a way more conservative than Confucius' teachings. Confucius only preached that a man and a woman should not get too close to each other if they were not married. In the case of the Dhanis, even married couples have to live apart. Privacy is a luxury. A husband and wife have to make appointments to meet; at an allocated time they would meet near the fireplace in the woman's hut when no-one else is around. After the wife has given birth, the couple will not have a rendezvous for the next three years.

It is difficult to say whether this is the Dhani way of family planning. It has certainly led to many social tensions and problems such as rape, stealing of wives, and so on, which are considered immoral acts and which result in fights, and even in killings. Nature has not been kind to the Dhanis. Any additional birth means another mouth to feed. Produce from the land is limited because of the primitive tools still being used. Stone axes, bows and arrows, and spears are the order of the day. Ropes are made by twisting bark fibres. Weaving is known but rarely practised. A number of fairly elaborate methods of plant netting and knitting are known and used in the manufacture of bags and armour. Pottery and basket-making are unknown. Carving is worked only on arrows used for fighting. Because of the difficulty in making a living, a new child is often not welcome. Abortion is common. The woman would take a kind of leaf grown locally as medicine to bring on an abortion. It is often successful but if it should fail, then the aid of a 'medicine-man' would be sought to perform the abortion with his bare hands.

In each hamlet, the cooking area is just an empty space where bunches of vegetables are scattered here and there. By striking together two pieces of flint, a wood fire is started and sweet-potatoes are baked. The sweet-potato is the staple food of the Dhanis. The daily meal is the same, day after day, the monotony sometimes broken with extras such as cucumbers or beans. Occasionally, the Dhanis will bake fish caught from the river. Although the pig is a domestic animal in Wamena, pork is rarely eaten except on ceremonial occasions such as a wedding or tribal festivals. Pigs are reared by Dhani men for marriage dowries and as a symbol of wealth. A person's wealth is therefore assessed by the number of pigs he possesses.

The Dhanis are fond of dancing and singing. They dance in circles on moonlit nights. The men first drink a kind of spirit made from palm-juice, similar to Indian toddy, as they like to get drunk before they dance. The Dhanis of long ago would chant hymns to communicate with departed souls, for they believed that one day their ancestral spirit, called Anggena, would return, and life would be easier and food plentiful. However, during the past few decades, the Dhanis have responded in large numbers to evangelism and have become Christians. But there are still those who practise ancestor-worship. The Dhanis believe that spirits, particularly the spirits of their own ancestors, influence their lives. In war, the support of such spirits is vital for victory. A man only becomes a leader if he wins a war and ancestors' support can only be received by brave descendants. So bravery is essential before one can secure the support of the ancestors by performing a secret ritual. The ceremonies are performed by men only and carried out in great secrecy, as women and children are not allowed to witness the proceedings.

On the slope of a mountain about four hours' walk from the airstrip is a small hut where the mummified body of one of the Dhanis' first ancestors is kept. This hut is considered by the Dhanis to be the centre of ancestor-worship. The mummy is in a squatting posture and is well preserved. It is hard to understand how a people who still live in the Stone Age could have learnt the technique of mummifying a corpse. In my opinion, there is a similarity between the ancient beliefs of the Dhanis and those of the Chinese or Egyptians, that the soul of a dead person would return to the body if it was well perserved. In that way, a person could have eternal life after death. But perhaps, like the ancient Egyptians, the Dhanis realized that mummification did not bring eternal life. And thus the hillside mummy is the only one left.

The present burial custom of the Dhanis is to cremate the body. But they can hardly afford an elaborate Balinese type of cremation. For them, it is a simple affair of putting the body into the flames of burning firewood.

It is apparent that with time, Dhani customs and traditions are slowly changing. The Dhanis still dance and sing on moonlit nights, not to invoke the return of the souls of the dead, but to keep warm and have fun. Old customs and habits did not help to bring about a better life for the Dhanis. Missionaries have therefore been able to change their beliefs and there is now a fairly large Christian church in Wamena which is well-attended on Sundays.

The most significant changes in Wamena came after the visit of President Suharto in 1970. A special committee was formed to monitor the development of the Dhanis and now a task-force is run by young, energetic and idealistic Indonesian officials. They are at work to educate the Dhani people. The task-force has set up a centre to teach farming and to carry out various types of community work. I learnt from one of the officials that when President Suharto visited Wamena, he started a fund for rehabilitating the Dhani people. According to the scheme, anyone who donates 6,000 rupiahs can 'adopt' a Dhani child by becoming his or her godfather. The money would be spent on educating the child. There is also a silent campaign to discourage the Dhanis from wearing the *koteka* which the authorities consider indecent in modern times.

But traditions die hard — more so in an isolated, unsophisticated society such as that of the Dhanis. During my visit there, I found that some Dhanis who live in modern houses still put on the *koteka* for a walk in the garden. We were told that the authorities are trying to ban the sale of *koteka*. On hearing this, some diplomats in our group felt rather disappointed, fearing that they might not get a *koteka* to bring home as a souvenir. However, when we visited the market-place we found *koteka* still being sold openly in the market and surrounding shops.

The Wamena market is an interesting place to visit. It is a congregation of different tribes of Papuans, all of them naked except for the men's *koteka* and the women's strings of beads. The womenfolk huddle over their vegetables — sweet-potatoes, cucumbers, beans, and fruits such as bananas. The men hawk spears, bows and arrows, polished green stones wrapped in dried banana leaves (to be used as weapons or blades), stone axes and cowrie shells strung into long chains called *jao*. Until recently, the *jao* was still highly valued, as one cowrie shell was accepted as one day's wage.

The *jao* could be used to purchase pigs, but nowadays is more commonly worn as jewellery. Bargaining is a problem for foreign visitors because the Dhani hawkers are still unaccustomed to the various denominations of Indonesian currency. It is easier if the buyer has a hundred rupiah piece. Otherwise, bargaining is a painful affair and usually the seller refuses to accept anything other than a hundred rupiah note. A middle-aged Dhani offered me a pair of pig's teeth for only 5 rupiahs. I thought he must have made a mistake and told him it was too little. He then increased the price to Rp. 500. I gave him Rp. 200 and the Dhani was very, very happy to part with the pig's teeth. A generous Ambassador paid Rp. 5,000 for a stone which was first offered to him for only Rp. 500.

At the market-place, I saw an old woman selling vegetables, who had lost all her fingers except the thumb. Through an interpreter I asked what had happened. She replied that she had chopped them off as a symbol of mourning for her husband who had died a long time ago. Another explanation which I got from an old Dhani near by was that her fingers had been chopped off because she had stolen something when she was young.

The market-place is an excellent place to study faces. There were two Dhani men who had their faces painted black from the eyes down to the mouth. They wore horns on their heads. I was told that they were brothers and that they were mourning for their mother who had just passed away. They looked stern and serious.

The most interesting character that I met during the trip was a short, limping, elderly Dhani called Joe, whose face looked like a chimpanzee's. He was one of the very few who were dressed in khaki uniform and wore hats. He spoke a little Bahasa Indonesia and followed our delegation from place to place. An Ambassador, who was busy taking cine pictures, discovered that Joe was a willing porter, and so asked him to carry a bunch of *koteka* and other souvenirs he had bought. When the party reached the hotel, the Ambassador was still busy taking pictures when I saw Joe selling the *koteka* to other Ambassadors for Rp. 1,000 each. When the time came to board the plane, the Ambassador asked Joe where his bunch of *koteka* was. Joe replied that they were all in the plane. The Ambassador boarded the plane but found no trace of the *koteka*. It was too late for him to get off the plane to question Joe. Meanwhile, Joe made a dash for the plane and was acting as if he wanted to hand over something to the Ambassador. When he was told to move back, he became furious and started to shout and quarrel with an officer on the airstrip. He then ran around the plane several times to see whether he could get in, but in vain.

As the plane took off, through the little window I saw Joe looking very miserable and angry. The question which remains unanswered is why Joe sold the *koteka* when he was supposed to look after them. Did he try to make some money out of them? If that was the case, he could have just disappeared instead of waiting till the plane took off. In fact when the Ambassador asked, he said that the *koteka* were in the plane. What did he try to explain? Was he trying to do the diplomats a favour by selling them the *koteka* or was he showing off his salesmanship to the Ambassador who had entrusted him with the *koteka*? Was he trying to return the money he obtained for the *koteka* to the Ambassador when he tried to dash onto the plane? The meaning of the whole melodrama remains a mystery.

The Pertamina plane took us back to Biak, an island off the mainland and a resting terminal for oil-drillers and civil servants who work in Irian Jaya. The Biak people, who belong to one of the Papuan tribes, are comparatively more civilized than the Dhani. Nearly every Biak Papuan is clothed. Most of the Biaks have become either Christians or Muslims, so that in Biak there are both churches and mosques. In order to provide entertainment for the oil company employees and civil servants, there are cinemas, restaurants, bars and nightclubs, a far cry in terms of modern materialistic civilization from that of near-by Wamena.

However, the Biak people are still influenced by ancient Biak mythology. Many still believe in ancestor-worship and the cargo cult. A major element of Biak mythology concerns treasures and ceremonial valuables. In the past, Biak pirates went to the Moluccas to get their spoils, and thus valuables of foreign origin became an increasingly important factor in Biak mythology. The emphasis on material goods is fully expressed in the myths and in the various movements termed cargo cult.

Biak is an island of wonderful and strange myths. There is the myth of Ori, the sun, and Paik, the moon, both of whom lived on the earth as brothers. Their father hid them in a cave and in the night Paik served as a light. One day Ori betrayed Paik's hiding-place to the humans. The people took him away, hung him on a tree and shot arrows at him. Slowly Paik rose into the sky until finally he stood still in the heavens. Ori and the people went after him but in vain for they could not reach him. I wonder what the Biak people have to say about this myth now that man has managed to reach the moon.

There is also a myth of an old, double-headed snake called Karu-budawi, who lived in a cave and managed to entice a young pregnant woman to his lair. The snake brought up the woman's child as his grandson. Karubudawi was soon discovered by the real father who made six attacks on him and finally succeeded in liberating his son. The old snake then changed his body into a canoe and set out to find his grandchild. He went to the near-by islands of Biak, Roon, Numfor and Gebe, passing Salawati and Manokwari, until he was eventually recognized by his grandson. The real father also recognized old Karubudawi as his own father-in-law and decided to give him presents to make peace. He gave him a slave, cotton cloth, dishes, and bracelets made of steel and silver. After great rejoicing, the boy returned home with his parents, and everyone lived happily ever after.

Myths often express the psychological tensions that exist between the individual and society, between personal ambitions and cultural limitations. They also mirror the dynamic forces inherent in a culture, reflecting personal crises caused by hunger, sickness and death. The myth of the old, double-headed snake illustrates the Biak social organization. The father was not entitled to his child until his wife's dowry had been paid to the old father-in-law. As soon as this was done, the father-in-law turned from being a rival to a feast-giver and tensions were soon eased.

There is the myth of Ropokai which is about a dragon swallowing people and their houses. A young man named Amboni disguised himself as an old man to get close to the dragon and kill him. He then revived all those who had been swallowed. All the dragon's bones turned into people. Amboni then provided the people with sago, wood and goods in abundance.

Many Biak myths refer to the resurrection of the dead. Two of such myths tell of resurrection through the love of relatives, by singing a lament for the dead. The songs are called *kayob* (lament for the dead). The Biak people's belief in the resurrection of the dead was so strong that it developed into a sort of movement called *koreri*. *Ko* in Biak language means 'we' and *reri* means 'change' or 'transform'. They believe that some day a Messiah, called Manseren Manggundi, will appear and will bring with him permanent happiness and prosperity so that the people will not have to sweat and toil any more. The first reference to the Messianic figure occurred in a publication in 1854 which speculated that Manseren Manggundi would return some day to establish an earthly kingdom of peace and plenty. The *koreri* movement began to grow and became a dynamic force in Biak and other neighbouring islands such as Numfor, Manshiham, and Wandamen. Supporters of the *koreri* movement would perform the ceremonial rites on moonlit nights.

The men would get drunk on palm-wine and dance in circles until they collapsed. They would sing the songs of lament which they believed would hasten the arrival of their saviour and resurrect their dead ancestors. The Biak people are talented singers and have a gift for creating songs of lament. One of the best known *kayob* goes something like this:

> Morning Star, greatest of all the stars,
> Come and be my herald and make me a hut of leaves
> In the east, in the east of Judaca.

The belief in *koreri* became so strong and widespread that, from time to time during the last century, many impostors tried to exploit the myth by claiming to be the saviour. Some even attempted to resurrect the dead. Most of these were medicine-men who indulged in black magic. The movement gathered momentum and even became a political weapon. The movement changed character sometime in 1938 when a woman by the name of Angganitha Menufaur was its leader. She was born in about 1905 and, through her ancestress Inserensowek, was related to Manseren Manggundi. She tried to create a myth that she was the reincarnation of the Messiah, Manggundi, who was supposed to come one day to save the people. Angganitha was married and had three children. She had a reputation as a poet and a composer, her songs being used mainly for dancing to invoke the return of ancestors and better days. The *koreri* dance ceremonies gradually became more intense. Sometimes the gatherings turned into mass meetings of over 6,000 people. They would sing with excitement and would try to overcome their disappointments by increasingly drastic means such as magic, medicines and magic wands. Some fasted, whilst others drank palm-wine. They wanted to see visions and thus forced their tired bodies to perform the strangest exercises. In a frenzy, they would believe any rumour and would shout for the spirits of the deceased, reel over the graves and finally collapse.

It became an arduous task for the authorities to restrain the movement from getting out of hand, for sometimes the ceremonies led to fights and general disorder. In 1942 an Ambonese policeman was killed when he clashed with participants. When the Japanese took over West Irian, they tried to put a stop to the movement and had the leaders arrested. Consequently, the movement developed into an anti-Japanese and independence movement, with the *koreri* army having its own blue, white and red flag. The supporters used *karbere* (club) and spears, hatchets and arrows as weapons against the Japanese. They also used magic powers said to be endowed upon them by their ancestors.

At one stage, the Biak-Numfor armies tried to liberate the whole of New Guinea from the Japanese. It was a hopelessly vain attempt for the masses, who were inspired by the *koreri* beliefs that they were invulnerable and that Manermakeri, their god, would turn their clubs into rifles and the bullets of the enemy into water. The struggle for freedom became a holy war. However, in 1943, many leaders went over to the Japanese and one of them became a policeman. The remaining *koreri* disciples fled to Numfor.

When the American bombers came to attack the Japanese in Numfor, supporters of the *koreri* movement thought that Manermakeri was leading the Americans to liberate them. It must have been quite an experience for the *koreri* supporters when the bombs dropped on their land. The whole business of modern warfare must have appeared as an apocalyptic monster to these simple-minded people. Could they be thinking that Manermakeri himself had descended in the light of the flames, the forerunner of a hell of fire and pain and large-scale destruction? When the news came that the Americans were constructing a naval base in Biak and that hundreds of ships were unloading supplies on the shores of Meokwundi, the very island of the Messiah, the Biak people shouted themselves hoarse. The Americans generously distributed clothing and food to thousands of natives. To the Biak people, the *koreri* ideal had materialized. All that had been prophesied had been fulfilled — except the return of the dead.

Since then, the *koreri* myth has gradually died — perhaps because of the end of wars, the advance of modern civilization and the introduction of Western technology. Most of the Biak population are now either Christians or Muslims. Yet songs of the *koreri* era can still be heard, though only as entertainment. As I sat in a seaside hotel in Biak admiring the sunset, I heard a boy and a girl singing a beautiful *koreri* tune, as they fished leisurely amongst the rocks. Indeed the sun had set for the *koreri* movement.

Although many of the Papuans in Wamena and Biak still live in the Stone Age, they can be considered somewhat civilized when compared to the headhunters who still inhabit the jungles of southern and western Irian Jaya. One of the headhunting tribes, called Marind Anim, occupies a vast territory stretching along the coast in the Merauke district. They are one of the relatively few Papuan peoples who have a name of their own to denote their tribal identity. The word *anim* means 'men', while *marind* is a distinctive native, tribal name. The Marind Anim is one of the headhunting tribes in Irian Jaya of whom a study has been made.

It is not easy to get a guide to tour villages of headhunters, for who could guarantee the safe return of the visitors, particularly when they are diplomats? According to stories derived from books and from indirect interviews, we have a rough idea of how, where and why headhunting is still being practised in many parts of Irian Jaya.

To the Marind Anim, headhunting is not just an act of warfare, self-defence or the human desire for conquest. The prime motive of the Marind Anim in organizing a headhunting expedition is to gather names for their children when the supply of names has been exhausted. To the Marind Anim, it is necessary to have a separate 'head' name for each individual child. It is a sort of status symbol. Every child is named after a victim who has been beheaded. Before the victim's head is chopped off he is asked to spell out his name. Whether the name uttered is correct is immaterial so long as a sound is heard which resembles a name. Thus, when a child is born, the parents need to hunt for a head in order to inherit a name. Some renowned warriors have names saved up like a name bank. Sometimes they give them away to relatives as presents, or give their own children more than one name.

Before a hunt begins, a feast-house called *kui-aha* is erected in preparation for festivities following a successful expedition. The expedition is not confined to men only. More often than not, women and children join in, together with their pigs and dogs. Only the old and sick stay at home. The habit of brutality and cannibalism is thus implanted in the minds of the young at a very tender age.

Headhunting usually begins during the rainy season, for it is mythologically associated with thunderstorms. It is a festive occasion, a sort of sport which even the women and children look forward to. They sing *ayase*, the headhunters' song, which has mythical significance, accompanied by the beating of drums. Amidst singing and dancing, the men have promiscuous intercourse with the women in order to become hot and courageous, which they term *yaret*. At day-break, the headhunters raid the appointed village, yelling at the top of their voices. They seize their victims — men, women and children — and loot whatever they can lay their hands on. It is an opportunity to acquire new canoes, stone clubs and provisions. Childless couples kidnap a child or two to take home and raise as their own. When the plunder is over, it is time for festivities. The heads of victims are chopped off for names. In some cases, the legs and arms are cut off to be eaten. However, the practice of cannibalism, I was told, is confined mainly to medicine-men who need human flesh as an ingredient for their magic. They mix human flesh with a sago preparation for the sick.

After beheading a victim, the headhunters clean the skull by first skinning it neatly. The brains are then removed and the eye-balls thrown away. A rattan nose is stuck on, and the eye sockets and nasal openings are stuffed with sago palm leaf, while the cheeks are padded with clay. The skin is then sewn back onto the skull with rattan fibre and hair is put on so that the skull once again resembles a human head. These heads are eventually suspended from trees which look like fruit-bearing coconut-palms.

The home-coming after a headhunting expedition is an occasion for merry-making. According to research made by ethnographers, headhunting rituals may have cosmological implications. To the Papuan headhunters, the ceremonial feast is a grand affair. It is an occasion to demonstrate the greatness of the past, and the might of the present. The feasts are meant to preserve a certain mythical cult connected with the soul. The provision of human heads may be one of the prerequisites for a successful celebration. Here again is a case of myths affecting the realities of life of a people who still live in the Stone Age.

With the discovery of oil in Sorong on the eastern tip of Irian Jaya, modern technology has moved into an area which was inhabited by other groups of people whose cultural development stagnated way back in the Stone Age. When the Pertamina plane brought us to the oil-fields off Sorong, we heard stories of the difficulties faced by engineers and contractors who had to stay near such primitive communities. There was always the fear of headhunters or the dangerous malaria mosquito. However, the Papuans' knowledge of the jungle helped engineers immensely when it came to clearing the thick forest. Some Papuans were even absorbed into the work-force as crew on oil rigs. Apart from oil, Irian Jaya is also producing nickel and copper. Consequently, large areas of forest are being cleared in many parts of the island. The sudden appearance of modern machines and equipment for the exploitation of the rich natural resources is bound to make an impact on a population who are handicapped by such a wide cultural gap. It is essential that development and industrialization go hand in hand with an understanding and appreciation of the Papuans, if the reality of modern science is to avoid a clash with Stone Age myths and superstitions. The success of technological advancement depends a lot on the support and co-operation of the people being affected by the changes. In this respect a great deal more is needed to be done in the field of anthropology and sociology.

As a nature lover, I went to Irian Jaya with a secret wish to see a *cenderawasih* for which Irian Jaya is famous. I did not see one. The noise of oil-drilling machines may have driven the birds deeper into the forest. Instead, I saw the *koteka*. Will it, too, disappear with the advance of modern civilization?

3

Toraja, Land of Eternal Souls

He goes where the sun descends,
There shall he to Heaven rise.

from a Toraja hymn

There is no easy road to Toraja, the 'Land of Kings'. It is about 400 kilometres north of Ujung Pandan, the capital of South Sulawesi, from where I started out on my rough trip to Toraja. Accompanied by my wife and three acquaintances, I hired a jeep which turned out to be a real boneshaker. For eight hours, we rumbled along a rocky road, feeling most uncomfortable. Although the trip was tiring, the scenery was indeed rewarding. The green paddy-fields on the way to Pare Pare were dotted here and there with tall Bugis houses on long stilts. Near Enrekang, the undulating hills made us feel as if we were riding the waves of a rough sea. It was late in the night when we eventually reached Rantepao, the spiritual centre of Toraja.

Toraja is a land of rocks. Rocks are seen not only along the banks of the rivers, but also scattered over the paddy-fields. And the most fascinating feature of the Toraja landscape is that in Rantepao the rock-cliffs have 'eyes'. Near the top of Toraja's highest mountain, Mount Sesian, there is a place called Lokomata which literally means 'the eyes of rocks'. We inspected a massive rock which was as tall as a coconut tree and as long as an ocean liner. There are square 'eyes' all over it. These 'eyes' are, in fact, large holes dug into the rock-cliffs. They are covered with wooden flaps painted and carved with beautiful Torajan designs. Inside are the corpses of royal families or prominent and wealthy Torajans buried there long ago. The 'eyes' command a panoramic view of the orderly, sloping paddy-fields and the breathtaking scenery of Rantepao below. Although Toraja means 'Land of Kings', I prefer to call it the Land of Eternal Souls. According to the Torajans, the souls of those who were interred into the rocks still mingle with them as they go about their daily activities. They help to keep an eye on the rice-fields and ward off evil spirits that might try to harm their people.

The Torajan tradition of burying the dead into rock-cliffs is unique to the religion of *Sa'adan Toraja*, 'the cult of the dead'. It is only practised in Toraja, where the majority of the people still believe in animism, although a large number of them have been converted to Christianity and Islam. In many instances, even Christians bury their dead in rock-cliffs and perform the elaborate rites which are essential to ensure that the souls go to heaven, according to their traditional belief. A ceremonial burial is often a very expensive affair for it entails the slaughtering of animals such as buffaloes and pigs for a continuous feast, sometimes lasting for a month.

Lokomata can be considered the highest and most exclusive place for rock-burials. It is about 30 kilometres from Rantepao village. On rainy days, the roads are so bad that Lokomata can be reached only on foot. To carry a coffin 30 kilometres through rugged mountains requires a strong will, courage and dedication. But before a funeral can take place, a hole must be dug and the elaborate funeral rites properly performed. To chip a hole into hard rock sometimes takes one, two or even three years of manual labour. The task becomes even more difficult when the hole has to be dug at the top of a giant rock-cliff. It means erecting a wooden staircase and a platform for the rock-carver. So far, the use of drilling-machines is still unknown to the Torajan rock artisans, whose work is done entirely by hand. Every piece of dust from the rock is dug out with sweat and blood. The process is therefore an expensive one, beyond the reach of the average Torajan. The expenditure includes the feeding of the whole family of the rock-carver for the duration of his work plus a reward of three buffaloes when the work is completed.

In olden times, when the Torajan society was more feudalistic, only royal families and prominent, wealthy citizens were allowed to be buried in the rock-cliffs. In any case, the ordinary people could hardly afford such a luxury.

A stone's throw from the Lokomata burial rock-cliff, we saw

many tall rocks with their sharp peaks pointing skywards. The tallest one reminded me of Cleopatra's Needle, an obelisk which soars between the trees that line the Thames Embankment. I used to admire Cleopatra's Needle when I strolled along the Thames on Sundays during my student days in London. The Torajan rock also reminded me of the obelisk which I saw in the Karnak Temple of Egypt. Although the obelisks which I saw in Toraja were pygmies compared to those which I have just mentioned, it is significant that the purpose of erecting an obelisk both in Egypt and Toraja was the same. In ancient Egypt, the Pharaohs erected the obelisk so that their achievements could be carved on the sides. In Toraja, it was a status symbol to have an obelisk erected after one's body was interred in the rocks, but there was no carving on it. Even without any carving, the erection of an obelisk was an expensive matter for it involved the search for a sharp-pointed rock, then its transportation by human effort to the desired place. A big feast was always arranged to celebrate the occasion.

On another burial rock-cliff, called Lemo, about 9 kilometres from Makale, a town near Rantepao in Toraja, we saw a row of well-clothed, wooden puppets perched high on a terraced rock-cliff, enjoying a bird's eye view of the surrounding scenery. These wooden puppets were actually the same as the Si Gale Gale puppets which I had seen on the island of Samosir in Lake Toba. In Batak land, the Si Gale Gale puppets perform dances, whereas in Toraja, they serve as replicas of the deceased and are placed on terraces near the rock-graves. Offerings are made to them from time to time and their clothing is changed as a sign of respect for the ancestors. The similarity between the wooden puppets of Samosir and Toraja is not a coincidence, for the Bataks and the Torajans are, after all, cousins. They belong to the same stock. The wooden puppets and the boat-shaped roofs of their houses remind the Bataks and the Torajans that they once shared the same civilization.

Like the obelisks, carved wooden puppets were once restricted to royal families. It used to be the practice to assemble the wooden images of one family all together on one terrace. From afar, they look like humans looking out over the vast land below them. They serve as reminders to Torajans of the permanent presence of their ancestors' souls and they also exert a certain amount of psychic influence on the people.

The Lemo cliff appeared to me much steeper than that of Loko-mata. It is difficult to imagine how the rock-carvers managed to dig holes into a sheer cliff-face using only primitive hand-tools.

It must have involved tremendous effort. I learnt that in ancient times, the Torajan feudal society divided the people into four categories: the rajas (kings), the relatives of rajas, the free men and the slaves. Perhaps in those days, slaves were forced into the risky job of chipping graves out of rock-cliffs for the feudal lords.

Since the cutting of a rock-grave is an expensive affair, one might wonder how less fortunate souls reach Bambapuang, the gate of heaven. But nature has been kind to the poor by providing a natural cave in Rantepao. The huge limestone cave of Londa has become a public burial ground for those who cannot afford the expense of a rock-cliff grave. When we visited Londa, a number of boys and girls were playing with human skulls scattered indiscriminately at the entrance of the gruesome cave. The skulls were placed on top of discarded wooden coffins. Over the entrance to the cave is a terrace where some wooden puppets, replicas of the deceased, seemed to be keeping an eye on visitors. The cheerful children, holding fire torches in their hands, showed us the way into the cave. A sense of eeriness pervades the air. At every corner of the cave are human skulls separated from their bodies. We passed deeper into the cave where thousands of skeletons and skulls were dumped together like victims of Hitler's concentration camps. The cave is big enough to accommodate thousands and thousands more corpses — free of charge. The only requirement, according to custom, is the sacrificing of one or two pigs during the ceremony outside the cave to facilitate the passage of the deceased's soul through the gate of heaven. On our way out of the cave, we noticed, near the entrance, a new coffin containing a wrapped up corpse which could not have been there more than a week. To me, it was indeed a horrifying yet pitiful sight, but the children seemed to have got used to corpses. They even played games with skulls, sometimes using them as footballs!

Why do the Torajans bury their dead in rocks? When did it all start? These questions were uppermost in my mind as I toured Toraja. The custom of rock-burials is not new to me for I have seen similar practices in Egypt. The early rulers of Egypt regarded the pyramid as a kind of celestial step-ladder leading the dead king upwards to his eternal home in the sky. An early Egyptian text states clearly that "a staircase to heaven is laid for the Pharaoh so that he may ascend to heaven thereby". The pyramid of stone was considered holy. In ancient Egypt, the ordinary folk had a vested interest in keeping alive the memory of their ancient kings. The spiritual influence of a good Pharaoh continued even after his death. The king was as valuable an asset to his subjects when he was dead as when he was alive, continuing to be a source of psychic power. That was why the Egyptians buried their Pharaohs with such loving care and in such fantastic tombs as the pyramids. After the twelfth dynasty, kings and noblemen were no longer buried in pyramids but in cut-rock tombs such as those I saw at Beni Hasan. Later, the Theban autocrats of the New Kingdom decided to construct their cut-rock tombs in the celebrated Valley of the Kings to secure maximum secrecy as a precaution against tomb robberies.

I thought of the Egyptian pyramids and cut-rock graves of the Valley of the Kings when I saw the rock-cliff graves in Toraja. Could there be any connection between the two and, if so, how did it come about? Not being an anthropologist, I tried to look for a quick answer. I talked to a few experts on Torajan culture, one of whom was Mr F. K. Salongalo, the Vice-Speaker of the Parliament of Toraja. I also tried to read whatever books I could lay my hands on. Literature on Torajan culture is, unfortunately, very scarce in the English language. More of it is written in Dutch. So I only managed to get some clues to the origin of rock-cliff graves.

There is a Torajan legend which says that in olden times there was a staircase connecting heaven and earth. Once upon a time, there was a man called Pong Sumbung Sarepio (meaning 'the man with a loin-cloth made of patch-work') who climbed to heaven by the staircase and stole the gold flint belonging to the Lord of Heaven. He was so excited that he stumbled down the staircase, which suddenly turned into rock.

Another legend has it that Pong Maratintin climbed the staircase to heaven to seek the Lord's advice on whether a boy could marry his sister. The Lord split an areca-nut and told Pong Maratintin that marriage between people so related was forbidden. The Lord then split both halves of the areca-nut to indicate that cousins, too, should not marry each other. A further split of the quarters was made and the Lord explained that at this stage, marriage of distant relations was permissible. Pong Maratintin, however, was so eager to contract the marriage with his sister, that when he returned to earth he deliberately told a lie, saying that the Lord had approved of his marriage. When the marriage took place, the earth sank into the ground and the staircase tumbled down and turned into scattered rocks.

The ancient Torajans obviously believed that there was a rock staircase connecting the earth and heaven. The only link that now remains between earth and heaven is therefore the rocks which have tumbled down. Could it be that the Torajans chose to bury their dead in towering rocks so that the souls' passage to heaven would be easier?

It is interesting to note that both the Torajans and the Egyptians had similar beliefs concerning a staircase connecting earth and heaven. Both peoples practised the cult of the dead by burying their deceased in rock-cliffs. Was there any connection between these peoples in the past? This question again cropped up in my mind just as it did during my visit to Pulau Samosir where I saw the stone tomb of King Sida Buta which closely resembled an Egyptian sarcophagus. Indonesian writers have written stories of Arabs who came to Lake Toba about 2,000 years ago. However, to my mind, they were not Arabs but Egyptians who came to Lake Toba, for Islam came only 1,000 years later. If the ancient Egyptians, who had built the pyramids, had reached Lake Toba, they could also have reached Toraja and brought with them certain aspects of their culture such as cut-rock graves.

Another significant aspect is the similarity in shape of the roofs of Batak and Torajan houses and the ancient Egyptian papyrus boat. The Egyptian craft of ancient days had a low, curved prow and a high stern. The ends of both prow and stern were often curled into the form of a papyrus flower. The Egyptian ship also had a mast as long as the vessel itself, with a cross at the top, and usually located in the centre of the ship. The roof of a traditional Torajan house has a shape similar to that of the Egyptian papyrus ship. The only difference between the two is that the long mast, which was used to carry the sail on the ship, is transformed into a long pillar, part of the foundation of the Torajan house. Again the cross at the top is retained, with a few more beams to support both sides of the curved roof. The Torajans themselves believe that in ancient days Mount Sesian and other lofty mountains in Toraja were surrounded by sea, and the land of Toraja could only be reached by boat. Consequently, they believe that their ancestors arrived by boat. According to historians, the ancient Egyptians ventured out into the Atlantic beyond the Pillars of Hercules and may even have circumnavigated the African continent. Could it be that they had also come to the East?

While visiting Toraja, I met a Muslim Torajan businessman by the name of Sampe Tobing who has a keen interest in the history of Toraja and who has written an article called *Tanah Toraja*, 'The Land of Kings'. During our conversation, he remarked that when he was a child, he used to roam about in the surrounding mountains, visiting the various rock-graves where ancient Torajans were buried. In a rock-cliff some four hours from Rantepao, he once found some skeletons which had exceptionally long limbs and huge skulls. He indicated that the ancestors of the Torajans might have been giants compared to the present population. I wondered about this and was therefore disappointed that I did not have the opportunity of examining the large skeletons myself. The mountain rock-graves had been neglected and the approaches to them were almost overgrown with thick jungle, so it was impossible for me to visit them. However, I was told that there were very few large skeletons left anyway, as they had mostly been removed for research by Western anthropologists. Nevertheless, I could not help wondering whether the large bones belonged to travellers from distant lands, such as sailors from ancient Egypt, where the people were in fact extraordinarily large. There is indeed a wealth of history and culture yet to be discovered in Toraja land. Is it not interesting to note that there is a village in Toraja called Kairo — a name sounding very much like Cairo, the capital of Egypt?

The traditional Torajan house, with its boat-shaped roof and tall pillars, is a masterpiece of architecture. It would surely puzzle Western architects, for the whole building, including the roof, is like pieces of a jig-saw puzzle, put together without using a single nail. A large part of the boat-shaped roof is made of bamboo knitted together. The other materials are hardwood for the pillars and timber for the walls. In almost every Torajan house, there are invariably three important symbols — the sun, the cock and the bull, beautifully decorated and painted on the front pyramid-shaped wall. The cock standing on the sun is usually at the top of the wall. According to Torajan culture, the sun represents the source of life and provides heat and energy for all living creatures. The cock is a symbol of strength, pride, patriotism and virility. In every Torajan house, there is at least one cock. The horns of a bull are a symbol of courage and bravery. They are either painted on the wall or the actual horns are mounted along the pillar that holds up the roof. The more bull horns the pillar bears, the richer and braver the owner of the house is. We saw on the pillars of a certain Torajan house, dozens of bull horns. It meant that the owner was so rich that he could afford to slaughter that many bulls for funeral ceremonies. It is interesting here to note that in ancient Egypt, the people worshipped the sun-god, Ra, and his gentle and much beloved wife, the goddess Hathor, who had the head of a cow.

The cock symbol may have evolved from Torajan mythology

which considers the cock to have magical powers. According to a Torajan legend, there was once a beautiful lady who was pursued by strangers one evening as she was going through the woods. She tried to deter the strangers by distracting them with trinkets which she scattered along the way, but to no avail. She soon came against a huge tree blocking her path, so she climbed up the tree. But the strangers chopped the tree down, causing the woman to fall to her death. At that moment, a cock came along, solemnly chanted some magic prayers and brought the woman back to life. She then escaped to the moon. Nowadays, on the seventh day of the seventh moon each year, folks look to the moon to see the figure of a woman who spends her time weaving.

Strangely enough, this Torajan legend is very similar to a Chinese legend about a shepherd and a maiden who weaves on the moon. The Chinese celebrate a festival related to their legend and this celebration takes place on the seventh day of the seventh moon each year. It would be very interesting to discover the origin of both the Torajan and Chinese legends.

The traditional Torajan residential unit comprises a house for the whole family, a storage-hut for paddy, known as *lumbong padi*, and a community house, known as *tongkonan*. The boat-shaped roof of the house always points from north to south and the main door must face east in order to ensure peace, security and prosperity. In the olden days, the Torajan house with a boat-shaped roof was built only for kings and noblemen. The houses are often built in a row, all the roofs pointing the same direction. Torajans believe that their ancestors came from the south and moved towards the north. According to folklore, the ancestors sailed along the River Sa'adan from the sea and landed at Bamba Puang, north of Enrekang, which became the centre of culture in those days.

The *lumbong padi* is a place where the Torajans store their rice. At harvest time, it is the custom to perform a small ceremony to ensure abundant harvests in future years. A rope is tied to the *lumbong padi* and stretched to the rice-fields. Four to six girls, carrying torches, walk to the fields to sprinkle pig's blood over a few rice stalks heavy with grain. These few rice stalks are then cut, tied together into sheaves and then taken to the *lumbong* for storing. They are not to be eaten. Torajans believe that these sheaves will then protect and preserve all the rice stored in the granary. The *lumbong padi* also serves as a community centre for villagers to hold meetings, to chat over coffee, or generally to entertain guests.

The third type of Torajan house called *tongkonan* is a sort of community house, the function of which is similar to that of Singapore's former Sago Lane 'death-houses'. We visited one belonging to Sampe Tobing. The exterior is the same as the two other types of houses. The interior, however, is divided into three levels. The first compartment on the highest level is meant for praying, the second for sick persons who are receiving medical treatment, and the lowest for the dead. The patient is quite free to choose between treatment by a Westernized doctor or a medicine-man, either a Chinese *sinseh* or a Torajan *dukun*. When a patient dies, he is removed to the lowest compartment where he awaits burial. Thus, the *tongkonan* serves as a church, a mosque or a place of worship for any religion, a hospital and a 'death-house'.

The Torajans make up a tightly-knit community because of their spirit of *gotong-royong* (mutual help). *Gotong-royong* is clearly manifested at burial ceremonies. Whenever a family has to conduct a funeral, not a single person in the village fails to turn up with a gift, which can be a bull, a pig, a chicken, a bamboo container filled with *tuak* (a sort of liquor made from palm seeds) or just some rice. A funeral ceremony can last one day or one month depending on the family's financial resources. The biggest funeral ceremony ever held was for the burial of Raja Sangalla, a prominent nobleman of Toraja, in October 1970. Funeral ceremonies, big or small, must be held only at harvest time, when everyone is free to take part. A funeral ceremony is not only to bury the dead, but also to appease the deceased's soul so that he will ensure abundant harvests for his survivors and descendants.

In Toraja, it costs more to die than to live. A full funeral ceremony is not only expensive, but also extremely elaborate. In the case of a prominent person, it would mean slaughtering many full-grown buffaloes and pigs, and providing food and shelter for all those who turn up for a whole month. The average Torajan regards a perfect and proper funeral ceremony as the most important thing in his life. He believes that without a proper funeral ceremony, his soul will not ascend to heaven. The Torajan concept of a human's spiritual nature is that man has a *sanga* or life-force as well as *sumana* or consciousness present throughout his life on earth. A man also has a *bombo* or a personal spirit. The *bombo* can leave a man's physical body when he is still alive. A seer can actually see a person's *bombo*, can manipulate it and direct its action through black magic. It is believed that when a person dies, his *bombo* becomes restless and frightened and can no longer be controlled or manipulated. After the *bombo* leaves the body of the dead person it goes to the buffaloes or pigs that are slaughtered for him and takes away the spirits of these animals. They then wander round the village or gather under the *tongkonan* where the dead person awaits burial. The spirit of the dead person can proceed to the Land of the Souls only after the entire death ritual has been performed. Until then, the spirit will continue to roam about and feed on *kambola* fruits. A spirit can also manifest itself as ants which take to plants called fly-traps, known in the local dialect as *duka bombo*. When the ants die, they become clouds which later turn into rain to make rice grow.

The traditional belief in the necessity of having a complete burial rite is so strong in Torajan society that even those who have been converted to Christianity or other religions continue to perform the ritual. Sometimes, the corpse of a person is kept in the house for a long period until sufficient funds are collected. When we were in Rantepao, we met a family who have cared for a corpse for twenty-five years. The body of their deceased father could not be interred in a rock-grave because of a dispute over the distribution of his property. During the twenty-five years, someone in the family had to touch the dead body of the father every day. This will continue until the funeral rite is performed.

The elaborate Torajan funeral ceremony starts when the *To Mebalam*, the expert who knows the secret of embalming corpses, is called in. He belongs to a class of slaves and usually wears a hat made of areca palm. As his main role in society is to prepare corpses, he is considered unclean and may never enter the houses of other people. In the past, like the Egyptians, the Torajan corpses were mummified. How it was done remains a secret. I was told that in Toraja, the roots of the *pinang* fruit-tree are chopped off when the tree begins to flower. The roots are later pounded into a fine powder and applied all over the corpse. In certain cases, a minor operation is done on the dead body to allow the fluid of the intestine to flow through a bamboo pipe into a bucket. Toraja is a country with many hills of limestone which, we know, the Egyptians used for the mummification of their corpses. Perhaps lime was also used by the Torajans.

Once the corpse is properly embalmed, it is wrapped in plain white cloth which may run into hundreds of yards, depending on the wealth of the deceased. Finally the body is wrapped in a beautifully-designed red cloth. When completed, it looks like a huge, red tree trunk, ready to be transported to the chamber of the *tongkonan*. A pig is killed to mark the occasion.

Meanwhile, a wooden image of the deceased is placed in front of the *tongkonan* where the corpse is kept. A stage is then erected and decorated with colourful buntings, to be used to display all the gifts of food from relatives and friends who begin to gather outside the house. When a gong is sounded, the usher, who is usually an old man with a walking-stick, would welcome the guests family by family, village by village. Strict protocol is observed in the procession of incoming guests. Those with the most expensive gift of buffaloes lead the way, followed by those with pigs, then chickens and other gifts such as *tuak*, rice and other foodstuffs.

For the entertainment of the guests, a bull-fight is arranged. In Toraja, a bull-fight takes place in the open paddy-field. The bull-fighter, often called *tukang bunoh* (one who kills), is usually a *dukun* who has magical powers. He needs no slaughter-house. With a long knife in his right hand, he catches the bull by the horn with his left hand, mumbles some chants as he looks up towards the sky and, in a single stroke, slashes the throat of the bull. The buffaloes must be killed with only one stroke, otherwise it is an omen of bad luck.

As soon as the bull falls to the ground bleeding from the throat, young men and children holding long bamboo rods with sharpened ends rush forward to thrust their rods into the throat of the bull to collect its blood. These blood-filled bamboo rods are then baked over a fire, sometimes with raw meat. The cooked dish, which is a delicacy for the Torajans, is called *papiong*.

After a sumptuous evening feast, a gong is struck to signal that the guests may begin to sing hymns or *Ma'badong* in praise of the dead. In the hymns, the names of Mount Bambapuang, Mount Kalesi, and Enrekang are often mentioned, for it is from these places that the great spirits usually ascend to heaven. There are many versions of these hymns which are normally sung in unison. One of them goes like this:

> And then onwards south he passed here,
> Beyond the eyes' sight did he go —
> But looking hard, south might just be seen.
> He sits now with his ancestors
> His seat is with his forefathers.
> South he stands, a coconut palm
> A sugar palm, high over all,
> Then westward does he pass from view;
> He goes where the sun descends,
> There shall he to Heaven rise,
> There in the all-enfolding dwell.
> A deity shall he there become
> The all-enfolding shall he be.

The Great Bear holds him in its arms,
The Pleiades clasp him unto themselves,
The shining stars encompass him.
We look for him to bless the rice,
When time it is to sow the seed
When we would scatter it about.
May you prosper, may we prosper,
May each of us good fortune have,
May you have children, may we all.

Such hymns, which are sung into the early hours of the morning, are all in the Torajan language.

At dawn, it is time for the *Ma Parempe* ceremony of bringing the body to the cut-rock grave. This is the turning point of the funeral when the solemn mood of mourning turns into gaiety and light-heartedness. After all, ought one not to be gay when a soul is about to ascend to heaven? When the corpse is placed onto the wooden stretcher, people rush forward to give a helping hand. The journey to the cut-rock grave resembles that of a Balinese cremation procession with the difference that on top of the Torajan stretcher there is no pagoda-type structure or sacred cow, only the beautifully decorated red bundle containing the corpse. The bearers carry the stretcher all the way to the grave on their shoulders. They rock the corpse like a baby in a cradle as a sign of affection for the one who has departed. They wind through the mountains and across rivers and streams, making merry all the way until they finally reach their destination. Then comes the last solemn moment when the corpse is about to be interred in its rock-grave. The family of the dead pay their last respects by weeping loudly as they caress the dead body.

In the evening of the same day, a final feast is laid out for the guests. All the buffaloes, pigs and any other livestock brought by the guests are slaughtered. The next morning, the guests take their leave and go back to their respective *kampong*. Every gift, big or small, is recorded by the organizing committee. Nothing is omitted for it is important to remember the gratitude one owes to everyone. The guests are always politely treated. They have to be received, provided with accommodation, and served with food and drinks. To organize a camp-in for thousands of guests for a week or, even worse, for a month, is not an easy task. Rarely does a villager fail to turn up for a funeral ceremony, for to do so without sufficient reason would mean self-isolation or ostracism from the community.

The funeral ceremony does not end when the corpse is interred in the rock-grave. Three days later at 2 a.m., a final ceremony is performed to guide the soul to heaven. In this ceremony only the womenfolk may participate. Led by a priest, the women walk silently in a row towards the forest. The eldest in the family, who leads the way, pretends to carry the soul of the dead on her shoulders. When they reach a certain distant spot in the forest, all of them utter the words "Ee, Ee" continuously to indicate to the soul that he should now leave the village to ascend to heaven. The womenfolk may not look back on their way home.

Throughout the funeral ceremony, the female members of the family wear a black band round their heads. When the last ritual is completed, a white thread is tied round their arms and a yellow band round their heads to indicate that the rituals are over. At the funeral, the closest relatives wear grey jute cloth similar to that worn by the Chinese or Vietnamese for a Taoist funeral. The eldest in the family holds a bamboo pole with a piece of jute cloth hanging from it. This practice is again similar to the Taoist tradition, but it is difficult to trace the origin of this custom to find out whether it was actually influenced by Taoism. There are many stories about mysticism and magic connected with Torajan funerals. I was told that during certain burials in the past, *dukun* with magical powers could make a corpse jump and climb mountains and then finally retire into its cut-rock resting-place. This was done by chanting magical formulae at a distance from the corpse. Is it not strange that the Taoists also had stories of frozen corpses rising from the coffin and jumping from place to place? Even today, Torajans still believe in the *dukun's* powers of black magic.

The Torajans also believe that God has bestowed on them a special breed of bull called the *tedong* which is meant only for funeral rites. The *tedong*, which is not found in any other part of Indonesia, has white skin with black spots and stripes. This very much sought after bull is worth at least half a million rupiahs each, so that only the rich can afford it. The *tedong* belongs to an albino class which cannot be scientifically bred; it is the product of an accident of nature. The flesh of the *tedong* is very tender and the horns are most valuable. Despite the large number of bulls slaughtered each year, there is no trade in bulls' horns because the Torajans consider the bull's horn sacred and therefore keep them for display at home. Even though the owner of many horns may be poor, he would not part with them because of pride and also the superstition that selling the horns might bring bad luck.

Conducting all the proper rituals for a Torajan funeral ceremony means a great deal to the family of the deceased in terms of prestige.

However, it has an adverse effect on the economy of the family, as well as the village as a whole. The younger generation, particularly those who have been converted to Christianity and Islam, are beginning to feel that grand funeral ceremonies take away the lives of too many buffaloes which are necessary for ploughing the paddy-fields. In order to discourage indiscriminate slaughtering, the authorities have now imposed a tax on each bull that is killed. The younger generation feel that something more should be done to restrict the number of bulls slaughtered for each funeral ceremony so that production of rice is not affected by the shortage of bulls. Here one finds an undercurrent of opposition resulting from the generation gap. The older generation feel that the performance of a full funeral ritual is vital to ensure the blessing of their ancestors who will in turn give them good crops; therefore killing a few bulls is insignificant when compared to the abundant harvests the sacrificial offerings will bring. The younger generation, on the other hand, feel that it is the number of buffaloes ploughing the rice field that proportionately decides the output. In most agricultural and rural societies, tradition dies hard. In Toraja, one can only hear personal grievances, but no one dares to organize a campaign to discourage expensive funeral rites for fear of being condemned as an offender against tradition. Social pressures at present are still on the side of the religion of *Sa'adan Toraja*.

In Toraja, just as the funeral rituals bind the community together, so do the rituals of a traditional marriage ceremony. A Torajan marriage is not a private matter between two persons in love. Before a marriage contract is signed by the bride and bridegroom, there is a family meeting between the two parties. At the meeting, both parties solemnly pledge to God that should there be any separation, the sinner has to pay a certain number of buffaloes as compensation. In order to exert a moral obligation on the couple, a large number of buffaloes, such as twelve or twenty-four, is mentioned as the price for compensation. The interesting point is that not only the bride or bridegroom but every member of the family is responsible for the payment of compensation. Thus, whenever a dispute or quarrel occurs between the couple, every member of the family makes an effort to put pressure on both parties to settle their differences amicably. They will generally keep an eye on the behaviour of the bridegroom and bride so that he or she does not commit adultery or go astray. This custom helps families to remain closely-knit, but it is probably family pride and the fear of 'losing face' in having to admit to a mistake, as well as having to compensate, that enforces the custom. Thus the divorce rate, I was told, is rather low

47

in Toraja. There is, however, traditionally, an escape route for the sinner if he or she is prepared to wash away his or her sins and if such a compromise is acceptable to the party who has been wronged. The sinner must sacrifice a cock, a bull and a pig and mix the blood of the three sacred animals in a porcelain plate. He should then dip his first finger in the blood and smear it on both his palms, his cheeks and his 'third eye', the place between the eyebrows. This will clear him or her of all sins, and bygones will be bygones.

The Torajans are a proud race. They originally withdrew to the distant mountains because they refused to be converted to Islam when the Muslims invaded the southern part of Sulawesi and converted the Bugis. Long ago, they guarded their religion so tenaciously that when the first Dutch priest came to preach Christianity, he was killed by Torajan animists. Later in 1913, however, the preaching of both Christianity and Islam was tolerated.

The Torajans are also a brave people. They still remember their martyred hero, Pong Tiku (1846–1907), who refused to surrender to the Dutch in a gallant defence of Toraja land. They erected a monument to commemorate the hero on the site where he was killed. Pong Tiku was the leader of an underground movement which fought against the Dutch; he swore "never to surrender from the bottom of my feet to the top of my head". He was finally captured by the Dutch and shot. Today, Pong Tiku is somewhat of a national hero to the Torajans.

When I was visiting the public market near the town of Rantepao, I met an old man who claimed that he was nearing ninety. His face was heavily wrinkled. Despite the cold climate he wore a thin, torn shirt and shorts. With the help of a walking-stick, he had come on foot from a village near Lokomata, the distance being easily more than 16 kilometres. I was curious about his age and wanted to know how he got his stamina, so I struck up a conversation by offering him a cigarette. Through an interpreter, he told me his secret, "I get my strength and inspiration from Pong Tiku, our hero, who was also my friend and comrade." Relating stories of the struggle against invaders, the old man remembered the spears and the *labo* (a native weapon) which Pong Tiku had used to fight the Dutch. He also remembered the baffalo-horn-shaped *songkok* or helmet which was used to protect the head. He also spoke of *tirik lada*, a sort of red pepper which was used to spray into the eyes of the enemy at close range. The name of Pong Tiku has become a legend. Some Torajan intellectuals are trying to persuade the Government to include Pong Tiku as one of the *pahlawan* (national heroes) of the Indonesian Revolution.

4

The Gateway
to Heaven
and Batak Land

"*Horas, horas!*" greeted my host when I first arrived at Prapat, a cozy town at the edge of Lake Toba, the largest lake in South-East Asia and also the highest above sea-level. *Horas* is the word used by the Bataks to welcome a guest and is often followed by the throwing of rice and flowers on visitors of special importance. *Horas* was also the first word I learnt when I visited the home of the world famous 'Sing-Sing-So', a song which is now popularly sung in many languages and countries far from Sumatra.

Where did the word *horas* come from? I asked many Batak friends, but few could give me a satisfactory answer. The word kept ringing in my ears until much later when its significance suddenly occurred to me. Of course, it was the god Horus whom I had read about in Egyptian mythology. But how could there be any connection between the word *horas*, which the Bataks use as a greeting, and the god Horus in Egyptian mythology? Had the Egyptians been to Batak land in ancient times and left behind traces of their culture?

Whatever the explanation, the resemblance of certain aspects of the two cultures is striking. Egyptian mythology tells of how man is admitted to heaven by first passing a stern test to prove his worth and honesty. For this test, one had to face the Goddess of Truth who would place the heart of the deceased on one pan of her scales and the magical feather, which was her sacred emblem, on the other. In attendance was the dog-headed god who would record the result of the test on his papyrus scroll. If the heart and feather balanced exactly, then the jury of forty-two assessors would allow the person to pass into the next world. The god Horus was the one who would then step forward to welcome the person who had passed the test and would usher him to the gate of heaven. Is it not interesting to note that the Bataks of Sumatra use the word *horas* to welcome guests?

The god Horus in Egyptian mythology was half-falcon, half-man. In Batak mythology, there are also stories of half-man half-animal creatures walking in hell on their hands instead of their feet. Batak *lontar* (ancient writings on palm leaves) tell the story of one Si Aji Sambola, a half-man half-animal, who was on his way from hell to heaven when he saw men doing the reverse of what they did when they were alive — they were walking on their hands instead of their feet, a sign that they were sinners. Some of these people were also balancing *kerbau* (buffalo), pigs, chickens, dogs or other things which they had stolen during their lifetime. Others were walking upside-down with long tongues hanging from their mouths right down to the ground. The god Horus would not welcome such people who had sinned.

The Bataks could not have found a more appropriate word than *horas* to welcome visitors to Lake Toba, which can easily be considered the gateway to heaven with its beauty, refreshingly cool climate, and atmosphere of tranquillity. The lake, a picture of serenity, is situated at the top of a volcanic mountain far away from the hustle and bustle of city life. If the ancient Egyptians had reached the shores of the lake, they would have exclaimed, "How beautiful the water is!" The Egyptian word for 'beautiful' is *toi* and for 'water' it is *ba*; thus the exclamation would have sounded *toi ba*! Can it be that the Egyptians did come to Lake Toba and that the exclamation *toi ba* gradually became Toba? Whether the origin of the name Lake Toba has any Egyptian connection or not remains a subject of historical, anthropological and etymological studies.

But the words *horas* and *toba* are not the only traces of possible Egyptian influence in Batak land. When we crossed the lake, we came to the island of Samosir which incidentally sounds like *mesir*, the Arabic word for 'Egypt'. Like other tourists, we were taken to the burial ground of Raja Sida Buta, the King of Samosir, who is said to have died about 400 years ago. It was less than five minutes' walk from the shores of the lake. The moment I set eyes on the tombstone, I noticed its striking resemblance to the sarcophagi of Egyptian Pharaohs which I had seen in Cairo Museum. It was customary for the ancient Egyptians to carve an image of the Pharaoh on the top of his coffin. Similarly, King Sida Buta had his own image carved on the stone coffin in which he was buried. His melancholic eyes were mysteriously penetrating and he wore his hair long—like the present-day hippies. Below the King's image was a carving of a determined-looking, bare-chested man. Our tourist guide, who claimed to be a descendant of King Sida Buta, explained to us that the man, Tengku Mohammed Syed, was the King's *panglima besar* (military commander-in-chief) and also his personal bodyguard. As a brave general, Syed had helped the King to defeat all his enemies. Although the King was an animist, he trusted and loved the Muslim general so much that he ordered Syed's image to be carved on his coffin before he died. Syed's image was also meant to provide continued protection to the King in the next world.

The lady carved on the back of the coffin was the King's sweetheart, Anteng Melila Senaga, who was the loveliest maiden in Samosir. The romance between Sida Buta and Melila lasted ten years. When the King eventually asked for her hand in marriage, Melila refused. It is said that she was charmed by the black magic of another suitor who was a rival king living near by. Sida Buta became so angry that he, in turn, used black magic to turn Melila into a mad girl, whereupon she ran aimlessly into the jungle, never to appear again. Till the time of his death, Raja Sida Buta was still in love with Melila and so he ordered her image also to be carved on his coffin. Spattered over the carved tombstone was a red liquid—not red paint, but human blood, I was told. It is said that in the days of tribal battles, the Bataks used to commemorate Raja Sida Buta's death by killing prisoners from rival tribes. The blood was thrown over the King's coffin and the hearts of the enemies were devoured during a feast lasting a week. Animists believed that the heart was sacred and that by eating the heart of an enemy one became brave, and the enemy's soul would be destroyed.

The resemblance of Raja Sida Buta's stone coffin to those of the Egyptian Pharaohs further strengthens my belief that Egyptian influence must have crept into the Batak culture. But how did this come about? I kept asking myself. I finally got a clue from an Indonesian book *Sejarah Kebudayaan Suku-Suku Di Sumatera Utara*, written by Dada Meuraxa. Quoting research sources, the book claims that more than 2,000 years ago, the Arabs had come to trade with the Bataks. They came for *kapur barus*, a sort of

The tombstone of King Sida Buta on Pulau Samosir. Below the image of the King is his military commander-in-chief, Tengku Mohammed Syed, who was also his bodyguard.

camphor which was necessary for mummifying the dead. I am more inclined to believe that the traders who came to Lake Toba were Egyptians who brought with them ancient customs and traditions, such as carving images on stone coffins.

Whenever I visited the tomb of Raja Sida Buta and pondered over the strange similarity between the Batak and Egyptian customs, my attention was always drawn to the gigantic banyan tree that provides permanent shade to the tomb. Tourist guides usually explain that the tree is as old as the coffin, because the king's mourners were said to have planted it. But I have my doubts as to its real age; it could indeed be more than 400 years old. A combination of beauty and mystery surrounds every branch that hangs down and takes root again in the earth. Because of its spiritual significance, the banyan tree, or *waringin*, is generally treated with reverence and respect by Indonesians. To the Bataks, the banyan tree is the origin of life.

According to Batak mythology, in the beginning there was a god called Ompung Tuan Bubi na Bolon, the only God. God Ompung (meaning 'great grandparent') is omnipresent and omnipotent. He makes the rain, creates the waves and determines favourable or unfavourable harvests. As he leaned against a huge banyan tree, a decaying branch cracked and fell into the sea. From this branch came fishes and all living creatures of the vast oceans. Not long afterwards, a decaying branch fell to the ground and from this originated crickets, caterpillars, centipedes, scorpions and insects. A third branch cracked into huge pieces which turned into deer, tigers, boars, monkeys, birds and all animals that live in the jungles. A fourth branch crumbled over the plains and turned into *kerbau*, horses, goats, pigs and all other domestic animals. The marriage of two of the newly-created birds, Patiaraja, the male, and Manduangmandoing, the female, bore eggs from which human beings were brought forth into the world during a violent earthquake. This is how Batak mythology explains the origin of all living creatures.

The banyan tree is considered the tree of life in more ways than one. In every Batak home you will find a family tree in the form of a diagram of the banyan tree. The family hierarchy is represented by the branches moving downward, showing close and distant relations, often dating back several generations. Whenever Bataks meet, the conversation invariably leads to comparison of the family trees. It is not difficult for each person to determine quickly his position of seniority in the hierarchy and to assume his place and manners appropriate to his status.

As the banyan tree is considered the tree of life, it is not surprising that much Batak philosophy and culture revolves round it. I have chosen to relate the legends explaining the origin of two Batak customs and illustrating how the tree is still very much a part of the culture of Bataks today. The legends concern Si Gale Gale, a puppet, and the *tunggal panaluan*, a walking-stick—both objects traditionally carved from wood of the banyan tree.

Si Gale Gale is a puppet-show with a difference. It is a dance— a one-man show—and is quite unlike the Chinese puppet-shows I have seen in Singapore and Malaysia or the Javanese puppet-show. It is purely of Batak origin, untainted by any foreign influence. Carved from wood of the banyan tree, the man-sized puppet is a replica of a Batak youth in traditional costume. He wears a red turban, a loose pyjama-type shirt and a blue sarong. From his shoulders hangs a red *ulos*, a cloth traditionally used to wrap round new-born babies and also used to place round the shoulders of a bride and bridegroom to bless them with harmony, unity and fertility.

The prelude to the dance is a musical introduction by a flute, a wooden *gamelan* orchestra and drums. Then the *dalang* manipulates Si Gale Gale to roll his eyes and raise his hands which display long, gracious fingernails. The puppet continues to dance to the sound of rather monotonous but rhythmic music, sometimes standing, sometimes sitting, as directed by the *dalang* from behind. Manipulating several strings at a time, the skilful *dalang* guides every movement of Si Gale Gale. In some more elaborate performances, Si Gale Gale can be made to shed tears or even smoke a cigarette!

But what is the origin of the puppet-show, Si Gale Gale? One source says that once upon a time, there lived on Pulau Samosir a very loving couple who had no children. When the husband suddenly died, his wife felt very lonely. So she made a wooden puppet in her husband's image. Whenever she felt lonely, the widow would employ a *dalang* to make the puppet dance and a *dukun* to communicate with the soul of the husband through the puppet. The ritual of communicating with a soul in this way soon became part of Batak culture. Si Gale Gale was therefore performed at funeral ceremonies to revive the souls of the dead and to communicate with them.

Another source explains the origin of Si Gale Gale with the following legend. Once upon a time, in a moment of inspiration, a skilful wood-carver fashioned a statue of an unusually beautiful maiden from a banyan tree-trunk. She looked so real and charming that she captivated a dress pedlar who offered to dress her up in beautiful clothing. A passing *dukun* suggested that she be given herbs. Naturally the wood-carver was overjoyed with his master-piece and hurried home to show the statue to his wife. Imagine their surprise when the maiden suddenly came alive! As they had no children, the couple named the girl Nai Mangale and raised her like a daughter.

Word quickly spread that Nai Mangale was not only a rare beauty, but also a talented dancer. It was not long before both the dress pedlar and the *dukun* came to claim Mangale for their own because of their contributions towards her beauty and existence. The ensuing dispute was settled by a wise chief who suggested that the carver remain as the girl's father, the *dukun* as her godfather, and the dress pedlar, her brother.

Soon, a prominent young man, Datu Partiktik, came to ask for Nai Mangale's hand in marriage. As she refused, she was forced by black magic to marry him. Many years passed, but no child was born. One day, Mangale became ill and died. Her dying request was that a wooden replica of herself be made, so that she could return to her original source.

The Si Gale Gale puppet dance became popular long before the advent of Islam and Christianity to Batak land. It reflects the ancient Batak animistic belief in the existence of souls and spirits in nature, such as in trees, rivers and mountains. Like other races in Indonesia, Bataks believe that the souls of their ancestors survive after death and that they can be contacted to give continued guidance and advice to those who are still living. Whatever the origin of the Si Gale Gale dance, the puppets provide a means for the Bataks to communicate with the souls of the dead.

Like the Balinese who often spend their fortunes on cremation ceremonies, the Bataks who died rich but childless often spent all their accumulated wealth on Si Gale Gale ceremonies, which sometimes lasted seven days and seven nights. As the Bataks believe that many children bring prosperity, a childless marriage is often construed as a curse. The Si Gale Gale myth is perhaps a reflection of the fear of being childless and the desire to have many children. To ensure many children, the Bataks in the past practised polygamy; one Batak king, Raja Simalungun, had fourteen wives and seventy-two children!

During a Si Gale Gale funeral ceremony, all personal possessions of the deceased would be used to decorate the puppet. To the accompaniment of music, the *dukun* would invite the deceased's soul to enter the wooden puppet as it danced on top of the grave.

At the end of the dance, the villagers would hurl spears and arrows at the puppet while the *dukun* performed a ceremony to drive away evil spirits. Several days later, the *dukun* would have to return to perform another ceremony, sometimes lasting 24 hours, to chase away evil spirits again.

However, with the growing influence of Christianity, the Si Gale Gale funeral ceremony is gradually disappearing. Nowadays, the Si Gale Gale is mostly performed simply as a puppet-show, but the vertical hand-waving movements of the puppet to the accompaniment of monotonous, yet rhythmical music has become part of a Batak dance performed during wedding ceremonies.

When Singapore's Prime Minister, Mr Lee Kuan Yew, paid an official visit to Lake Toba, he was presented with a walking-stick by the *bupati* (regent). The Bataks regarded the visit as a rare honour because Mr Lee happened to be the first Prime Minister in the world to visit Lake Toba. The walking-stick, *tunggal panaluan*, a symbol of great honour, is not exactly a walking-stick in the Western sense of the word. The *tunggal panaluan* is an *alat* (instrument) of authority which is said to possess mystical powers. On it are carved three men, a pair of twins, a dog and a serpent. Sticks of this nature can be bought in tourist shops. But like the *kris*, the *tunggal panaluan* has more value when presented by someone than when purchased in a shop.

Once again, one asks what is the origin of this tradition? What was the original function of the *tunggal panaluan*?

A long time ago on the island of Samosir, there lived a priest, Guru Hatiabulan, who was better known as Dato Arak di Pane. He had a wife called Nom Sindak Panalueon. For many years they had no children, but when his wife finally became pregnant, her pregnancy lasted longer than usual and coincided with a long drought which beset the village. The superstitious villagers started to blame the prolonged pregnancy for the natural disaster. There were even arguments leading to skirmishes over the strange phenomenon. When she finally gave birth, Sindak Panalueon delivered twins—a boy and a girl. Surprisingly, the rains came and ended the long drought.

The parents were very proud of the twins and named the boy Si Aji Donda Hataburan and the girl Si Boru Tapina Uason. They celebrated the happy occasion by inviting friends and relatives to their home. At the party, a *dukun* advised the parents to separate the boy and the girl in order to prevent disaster — one should go west and the other east. (Bataks believe that unidentical twins bring misfortune to the parents.) The parents ignored the warning.

One day during her childhood, Si Boru Tapina went for a walk in the woods where she saw a tree bearing juicy fruit. It was the *piupiu tanggule* tree, the trunk of which is covered with long thorns. Si Boru Tapina climbed the tree to pluck some fruit, but was eaten up by the tree. Her twin brother, Si Aji, went looking for her and saw her head protruding from the tree. He immediately tried to save her, but he, too, was swallowed up in the same way.

Their anxious parents sought the advice of a *dukun*, but he was also devoured by the tree, as were two more *dukun*, a passing dog and a serpent. Finally, the parents consulted a *dukun* called Datu Parpanna Ginjing who suggested chopping down the tree. When that was done, the protruding heads of the five persons and two animals disappeared. The *dukun* then ordered the tree to be carved into a stick with the images of those who had been devoured. With his magical powers, he invoked the separate souls into the respective images carved on the wooden stick which then began to speak. It was the voice of the boy, Si Aji, who told his father that he could use the stick to bring rain, to cure sickness, to command respect and to fight enemies. The *tunggal panaluan* thus became a mystical instrument of authority and is considered a prized and honourable possession by Bataks today.

The *waringin* or banyan is regarded as a sacred tree not only by the Bataks, but also by the Javanese, the Balinese, and, for that matter, most Indonesians. It is a symbol of protection. In the ancient days of feudal Java, a petitioner who had a grievance would put on a white jacket and sit under a *waringin* tree near the *kraton* to attract the attention of the Javanese king. If lucky, he would catch the eye of the king and would be given an audience. Even today in the grounds of all the Javanese *kraton*, there is at least one banyan tree. In Bali, all temples are invariably shaded by a banyan tree. The banyan tree has become so deeply entrenched in Indonesian culture that it even found its way to the state crest when Indonesia achieved independence. The banyan tree is also the symbol of Golkar, the functional group comprising military and non-military organizations which won more than seventy per cent of the votes during the 1972 parliamentary elections.

The banyan derives its name from Hindu traders who used the shady area under its branches as a market-place. In Indian folklore, the banyan tree is a representation of the god Siva, and anyone who cuts one down will be punished with the annihilation of his family.

Tahitian (Polynesian) mythology explains the shadows on the moon as the branches of a huge banyan tree. Tahitian folklore says that once, while clambering in the tree, Hina, a goddess, accidentally broke off a branch with her foot. It flew through space to Earth, took root and became the first banyan tree in the world.

I have chosen to relate more about the banyan tree in this chapter about the Bataks, although it is generally treated with respect by all Indonesians, because Batak mythology considers it the origin of all creation, and much interesting folklore is woven round it. If one links the Tahitian and Batak (both are Polynesian) myths about the banyan tree, it would appear that the branch of the banyan tree which fell from the moon might have taken root in Batak land and thus became the origin of all earthly creatures. This was just an interesting thought which entered my mind when I was admiring the huge banyan tree which shades the tomb of the Batak King, Sida Buta.

Let us go back to the banyan tree and the trinity concept mentioned earlier — the tree represents the universe divided into the upper, middle and lower worlds. This concept of three levels does not apply only to spiritual matters, but is also visibly apparent in the daily lives of Bataks. A visitor to Batak land will first be struck by the style of architecture peculiar to that region. A Batak house looks like the long-house of the Dayaks, except that the former is divided into three levels. The lower floor, which has no walls, resembles a farm-yard. It has some fencing and is, in fact, meant for rearing domestic animals such as cows, pigs, goats and sometimes chickens. Animal excretion is conveniently used as fertilizer. The middle floor is for human habitation and is reached by wooden steps supported by bamboo poles. It is usually an unpartitioned, community sleeping-hall. Privacy is nobody's privilege. The roof which has no ceiling represents the highest level.

One of the biggest Batak long-houses which I visited was once used by Raja Simalungun to accommodate his fourteen wives. It is now preserved as a museum. It was actually part of the King's residential complex. The long-house is flanked by the court-house, a VIP guest-house, a community meeting-place and a special house for pounding paddy. With the support of a thick bamboo pole, I climbed up the seven steep steps leading to the King's hall. It was bleak and dark inside. Not a ray of sun could penetrate the mysterious, unventilated chamber. On the pillars facing the entrance hung a glorious display of bulls' horns representing the changes of dynasties. My guide showed me to a small, dark room situated near the entrance of the huge sleeping chamber for the

fourteen wives. It was the King's private room which was deliberately made dark. The fourteen wives slept in the larger, adjoining
chamber in two rows of seven, each with her own cooking-stove
and utensils. The King's hobby was to organize cooking contests
for the wives once a year. King Simalungun was the last descendant
of a line of thirteen kings. When the Japanese came, the villagers
took the opportunity to kill him because he collaborated with the
Dutch and went against the interests of the people. Nobody knows
what became of the wives and children.

The Bataks also built special houses to preserve the ashes of the
dead of each clan. These houses, called *tugu*, also have three levels.
The upper level is meant for the ancestors, the middle level is
reserved for the present adult generation, and the lower level is
for their children. A dead person is first buried in the ground until
the body decomposes. Then it is exhumed and burnt so that the
ashes can be stored in the family *tugu*. All members of a clan must
contribute to a *tugu* fund, and rich clans build bigger *tugu*. Once
a year, there is communal worshipping of ancestors, somewhat
similar to the annual Chinese Cheng Beng.

The trinity concept extends even further into the lives of present-
day Bataks. To a Batak, life itself is divided into three stages —
childhood, puberty and manhood. An interesting Batak custom is
the teeth-filing ceremony when a child reaches puberty. Like the
Balinese, the Bataks believe that if one's teeth are not properly
levelled by filing, it would be difficult for one to enter the kingdom
of heaven. In olden days, it was difficult for one to get a marriage
partner if the teeth were not filed. There were special *tukang*
(artisans) for filing teeth and they were supported by a *dukun*
who gave his blessing. The teeth-filing feast was one of joy for the
family, for it meant one's offspring had grown up and had learnt
the Batak *adat* (customs).

Another important aspect of the trinity concept is what the Bataks
call Dalihan Natolu, a sort of clan system stipulating the hierarchy
of inter-family relations. *Dalihan* is an earthen burner used for
cooking. *Natolu* means 'three-legged'. The *dalihan* which used to
be a vital cooking utensil — an instrument of survival in ancient
days — had three legs so that it could stand firmly on the ground.
The philosophy of survival and stability of the Batak society evolves
from the earthen tripod burner. Each of the three legs has a name:
one leg is called *dongan sabutuha* (*dongan* means 'friend' and
sabutuha, 'stomach'), referring to friends and relatives; the second
leg is called *hula-hula*, representing the family of the bride; and
the third is called *boru*, representing the groom's family to which

the bride is given. *Hula-hula* has a higher status than *boru* because it is the family that gives away the bride. The bridegroom's family or *boru* is considered inferior in status. This is the way the Bataks fix the hierarchy of inter-family status even today. Wealth and power are not the criteria in determining family status in society. However rich and powerful a Batak family may be, it has to pay due respect to the *hula-hula*, the bride's family, however poor or humble it may be. When a couple marries and the *ulos* is placed round their shoulders, parents and elders utter the words, "May you have sixteen sons and seventeen daughters."

To the Bataks, the Dalihan Natolu is a triangle-democracy according to the law of nature. Thus, although the Batak society is a patriarchal one, the birth of a girl is never regretted for it gives the family a chance to be *hula-hula*. This may be interpreted as the matriarchal aspect of a patriarchal society. The principle of triangle-democracy is applied in all family functions relating to birth, marriage and death.

5

Trungen, the Cradle of Balinese Culture

Life on earth is temporary,
The world beyond is eternal.
Each action has a reaction;
You will reap what you have sown.

a Balinese proverb

The world has perhaps heard more about Bali — the beauty of the island and the exotic culture of its people — than about the rest of Indonesia. Attracted by this picture, many tourists come to Bali expecting to find bare-breasted Balinese women walking along muddy roads, balancing heavy offerings on their heads. They find, instead, sun-tanned Western hippies lying naked on Kuta Beach in the bright sunshine, surrounded sometimes by curious Balinese boys. Fortunate are the tourists who happen to be in Bali when a cremation ceremony is on, for Bali is the only place in Indonesia where cremation has become an official custom. It has become so deeply rooted a tradition in Balinese society that people tend to associate Bali with cremation. Few realize that, long before the Hindu believers brought their religion to Bali, the Balinese had a religion of their own which is still preserved by small groups of people who now live in isolated parts of the island, such as in Tenganan to the east of the island, Sembiran to the north, Trungen on the eastern shores of Lake Batur, and also in Seludung, Batukaang and Catur. These are known as Bali-Aga villages, where there are still traces of ancient Bali culture. Of all the Bali-Aga villages, Trungen is perhaps the oldest and can be described as the cradle of Balinese culture.

I was eager to find out about the original culture and religion of the Balinese, now known as Bali-Aga. Through the help of friends in the Idayu (a research institute on Indonesian culture) and Dr Murdowo, a doctor, painter and university lecturer, I made a fruitful visit to Trungen. It was fruitful because we were fortunate to meet an Indonesian anthropologist, James Danandjaja M.A., who was doing research on Trungen culture. This made our task easier in the hurried search for knowledge.

The trip to Trungen was not at all smooth. We went down the valley of Kintamani on horseback, followed by an hour's boat ride across Lake Batur. The Batur volcano near by still shows traces of its wrath on the terraced slopes. The darkish lava emitted from the crater thickens at the foot of Gunung Batur and still perspires its white, smoky heat. The blue Batur lake, however, seemed unruffled by the fury of the neighbouring volcano.

From a distance, the Trungen village looks like any other fishing village except for the pyramid-shaped roofs of the huts. Several fishermen in their primitive dug-outs were casting their baited hooks. Dark-skinned villagers clad in *sarong* and wearing *kupeng* (the Balinese headgear) on their heads came to the shore barefooted to welcome us. The village was so quiet and serene that we could hear the voices of school-children parroting lessons in Bahasa Indonesia in the near-by school, the only one in the village, constructed not long ago. The *merah putih*, Indonesia's national flag, fluttered from a flagpole outside the school. The modern school seemed rather out of place in the surrounding of dilapidated shrines and long-houses constructed centuries ago, the relics of Trungen culture. The long-houses were meant as community centres for the distribution of food during festivals. The one and only thoroughfare of the Trungen village was virtually deserted. Two hungry-looking, skinny brown dogs were dozing under lonely, wooden benches in front of a *warung kopi* (coffee-shop) where flies were the only customers of the exposed food. Most of the villagers had gone up the mountains to toil on the farms; the Trungenese generally have a hard life. When the school-bell rang for recess, we were immediately surrounded by a crowd of children begging for alms.

We could not have had a better guide than James the anthropologist, who was not only kind but enthusiastic. He had received his Master's degree from Cornell University and was doing research on Trungen culture for his doctorate. The house where James had rented a room was the brightest in the whole village for it was the only one with windows. The other attap huts with pyramid-shaped roofs had none. They reminded me of the

Serene Lake Batur with angry Gunung Batur towering over it. The Bali-Age village of Trungen lies on the eastern shores of the lake. The Trungenese live in attap huts with pyramid-shaped roofs.

Papuan domes I saw in Wamena, Irian Jaya, where the interior of the huts was gloomy even in bright daylight.

In the entire village of Trungen, there was not a single Hindu temple or stone image of Brahma, Vishnu or Siva. Nor were there any Buddhist temples. The Trungen sacred place of worship was simply an old square compound surrounded by a brick wall and shaded by the luxuriant leaves of a giant banyan tree. Inside the compound stood two ancient shrines. We visited the smaller one which was built for Pinggit, the Queen, who is said to have descended from heaven and was the first Trungenese. There was nothing spectacular about the square, brick shrine—in fact, it was in a state of decay. It was about five metres high, built over a deep hole which was believed to be the place where Pinggit had landed from heaven. Legend has it that when Pinggit descended, she was the only woman in Trungen. One day, as she was bathing in Lake Batur, she was caressed by the sun and became pregnant. She gave birth to twins, one a *banci* (neither male nor female) and the other a beautiful girl. As the girl grew up, her beauty was further enhanced by a perfume scent emanating from a *kemenyan* (incense) tree which stood in the compound. The fame of her beauty and the perfume attracted a prince from Java. The prince, Dalam Solo, fell in love with the princess and asked for her hand in marriage. When she refused, he raped her and she produced many children. These were the ancestors of the Trungenese.

The word *trungen* could have been derived from the words *turunan hiang*. *Turun* means 'to descend' and *hiang* is 'goddess'. The Trungenese therefore regard themselves as the descendants of the heavenly goddess, Pinggit, mother of the beautiful girl who later bore so many children.

The larger shrine in the compound was built to commemorate the prince who was later known as Batara Pencering Jagat. The word *jagat* means 'world' and *pancer* 'the centre'. The Jagat shrine, built of aged red bricks, is tiered like a pagoda. Inside the shrine is hidden the stone image of Batara Jagat. He only shows his face once a year on 1 October when the dilapidated wooden gates leading into the shrine are opened. Fortune was not on our side when we visited the shrine, for the doors were locked. No one would dare unlock the door, except on the auspicious day, for fear of punishment. Since I missed the opportunity of seeing the monument of Jagat, my eyes lingered on the worn-out wooden doors. This led to a pleasant surprise, for I found two Chi-ling, one on either side of the door. A Chi-ling is a mythical Chinese creature. In Chinese mythology, the Chi-ling was the symbol of *yang* (male or good), producer of rain and the element of fertility in nature. It was also the symbol of the emperor, and its image decorated the royal standard, postage stamps and the coin of the realm. The Chi-ling has the head of a dragon, the antlers of a deer, the eyes of a rabbit and the ears of a cow. Its neck is serpentine while it has the belly of a frog, the scales of a carp, the talons of a hawk and the paws of a tiger. On each side of its mouth are whiskers, and a beard hangs down from its chin. The Chi-ling which I saw on the doors of the shrine resemble those on Chinese porcelain and stamps. I became familiar with the Chi-ling when I took up collecting Chinese figurines and porcelain as a hobby. Among my humble collection are two greenish Chi-ling made of bronze.

The discovery of the two Chi-ling on the wooden doors of the Jagat shrine was really exciting, particularly for James, my anthropologist friend. They might help to throw some light on the history of Trungen culture. How did the wooden doors engraved with the two Chi-ling come to be in Trungen? How did the Chinese influence come about, and in which period of Chinese history? The mythical Chi-ling had figured in Chinese tradition for countless centuries before the Ming dynasty, although it became popular only after the late Ming and Ch'ing periods. How did the Chi-ling gain prominence in Chinese history? This was a subject which many learned people made studies of. The Chi-ling was once qualified as a species of the dragon. In the Hsia dynasty (2205–1557 B.C.), dragons and Chi-ling were associated with ancestor-worship and fertility. According to legend, one of the kings collected foam from the mouths of two ancestors who appeared at his palace in the form of Chi-ling. He put the foam in a box and never opened it. No descendants of his dared open the box either. At the end of the reign of the tenth king of the Chou dynasty (1100–221 B.C.), the box was opened and the foam spread through the palace. The King made his queen appear naked before it. The foam turned into a black lizard and entered the woman, causing an extraordinary pregnancy. Since then a dragon or Chi-ling became the symbol of the emperor; it even appeared on the Chinese flag. It symbolizes the essence of *yang*, or masculinity.

Could it be that the ancestors of the Trungens had some knowledge of the Chinese mythical beast and had adopted it as a symbol of their king and ancestor to whom the shrine was dedicated?

On the lower part of the beautifully-carved wooden doors was an ugly face with big, round eyes, a nose of three circles, and a huge mouth with two Dracula-like teeth protruding downwards. It looked like Yama Raja, the ruler of the underworld and judge of all souls after death. The full figure of Yama Raja is usually shown in the centre of the magic circle of the universe. Yama Raja has a lotus on his chest and carries eight emblems of the gods pointing in the eight main directions of the compass. He has a frightening face and hair that stands on end. He has reddish eyes and holds a club and a ploughshare in his hands. He looks like a multi-coloured giant with a big belly, but dwarfed limbs. Yama Raja is surrounded by his goddesses who, mythologically speaking, are stronger than he. (Incidentally, in Trungen, the womenfolk are senior in hierarchy to men because their original ancestor was Pinggit, a goddess.)

Yama Raja is mentioned in Buddhist scriptures, such as the Purvaka Veda Buddha which contains various *mantra* (mystical chants) for reciting on different occasions. These *mantra* are often recited by Buddhist priests for self-protection or at funeral ceremonies for deceased Buddhist Brahmins. The Yama Raja *mantra* are also recited by Brahmin priests in Trungen, and the Balinese recite them in corrupted Sanskrit or Archipelago Sanskrit at public rituals. Those who are well-to-do in Bali often seek the aid of the priest to recite these *mantra* during a critical period of their life such as marriage, sanctification, pregnancy, birth, the falling-away of the umbilical cord, the celebration of a baby's first six months or 210 days, teeth-filing, the first menstruation or death. Some *mantra* of Yama Raja can also be used for black magic and sorcery.

An interesting aspect of one Yama Raja *mantra* is found in the verse referring to death caused by smallpox. The *Babad Arya Tabanan*, the annals relating the history of west Bali, tells of Prince Pamade, alias Ki Gusti Nurah Made Kaleran, who died of smallpox. The annals stated that after the prince died, he returned to the heaven of Buddha. As the death was due to smallpox, the Yama Raja *mantra* was chanted to neutralize 'evil death' so that the soul could go to heaven. The Yama Raja *mantra* also stipulated that the bodies of all who died of smallpox should be left exposed as their souls would return to the heaven of Buddha anyway.

I have tried to tell briefly a little more about the Chi-ling and Yama Raja because I think they are significant to the customs and religion of the Trungenese. They may even be clues to the origin of the Trungen burial custom of leaving dead bodies exposed on top of their graves.

Apart from the Chinese Chi-ling and the Buddhist Yama Raja deity on the Jagat shrine, I was also attracted by an altar near the Pinggit shrine. On the altar was a simple, upward-pointing stone, symbolizing the male phallus, surrounded by four round stones, denoting points of the compass. The stone phallus is a representation of the male organ called the *lingga* encountered in the earliest known Indian art (during the Indus-Valley civilization of the third millenium B.C.) and still very commonly worshipped throughout India by the Hindus. This was perhaps the clearest indication of Hindu influence on early Trungen culture. The *lingga* is associated with Lord Siva, symbolizing the male creative energy of the god and thus the generative force of the universe. In the myth relating the origin of the *lingga*, the gods, Vishnu and Brahma, encountered each other in the primeval universe and argued as to who was the progenitor of all beings. As they were arguing a huge, fiery *lingga* rose up and penetrated the infinite space like a crystal mountain. Brahma, with his supernatural power, transformed himself into a kite and flew upwards and upwards looking towards the peak of the crystal, which continued to grow taller and taller. Vishnu transformed himself into a bore and burrowed deeper and deeper into the earth, but could not reach the base of the crystal. Thousands of years went by, but the end seemed as remote as ever. Finally, the giant phallus burst open, revealing Siva within who proclaimed himself the origin of all things; so Brahma and Vishnu bowed before him.

The four round stones surrounding the stone *lingga* on the Trungen altar were supposed to be portals radiating the energy of the *lingga* to the four corners of the universe. The *lingga* is frequently combined with the *yoni*, symbol of the female creative energy. The two convey various concepts associated with Siva and his goddess — symbol of procreation of the world, of divine parenthood and unity of opposites and therefore harmony.

This was not the first time that I came across the *lingga* and *yoni* while travelling around Indonesia. I have chosen to mention it in this chapter because the *lingga*, which I found in Trungen, was in its primitive form and might well be the first *lingga* ever introduced to Indonesia. In fact, the symbols of the *lingga* and *yoni* can be found in every part of the country. In Jakarta, the National Monument towering sky-high in the heart of the city is a symbol of the phallus. The square below the monument is a symbol of the *yoni*. The glittering flame, made of 34 kilograms of gold, on top of the *lingga* corresponds to the ray of sunlight symbolizing the virility of the Indonesian people. The whole monument represents the strength, virility, unity and harmony of the Indonesian nation.

In Jogjakarta, the symbols of the *lingga* and *yoni* can be found on the roofs of many Muslim mosques. Anyone who has been to the *kraton* of Surakarta must have noticed the symbol of the *yoni* bearing a baby on the right-hand side of the entrance and the symbol of the *lingga* on the pillar in the left-hand corner.

In central Java, not very far from Solo, is an old temple called Candi Sukuh which was built primarily for the worship of the *lingga*. Very little has been written about this mysterious temple which seems to be crumbling away. At the entrance to the temple, a stone carving of the *lingga* and *yoni* in a state of harmony is laid right across. It was mainly used by villagers to decide whether a wife had been faithful to her husband, or whether a prospective wife was still a virgin. The woman had to wear a sarong and stride across the symbolic statue. If the sarong tore during the stride, her infidelity was proven.

Again, inside the Prambanan temple in Jogjakarta, the *lingga* is present in the form of Siva, who is shown standing on a huge lotus. Here Hinduism, which is symbolized by Siva, has merged with Buddhism in the form of the lotus to become a religion called Siva-Buddhism. There are many Siva-Buddhists in Indonesia, particularly in central Java and Bali.

The Trungenese are a proud race. They regard Trungen as the centre of the earth. They believe that their sacred land is the safest place under the sun and is also invulnerable. When the powerful Gaja Mada invaded Bali, Trungen remained unscathed. When the Majapahit Empire fell and Islam penetrated into the hinterland of Java, an exodus of Hindu believers retreated to Bali, but few intruded into Trungen. In 1953, when Gunung Agung erupted and burning lava devastated many parts of Bali and several parts of Trungen, the sacred shrines of the Trungenese remained undamaged. Given this sense of security, the Trungenese have no urge to migrate. They also refuse to be influenced by the customs and rituals of the rest of Bali. The most striking example of tradition peculiar to the Trungenese is their burial custom. Geographically, Trungen is part of Bali and it comes under the jurisdiction of the Kabupaten of Bangli. But the Trungenese never adopted the custom of cremating the dead. In Trungen, a deceased person is first stripped naked and bathed with holy water. A tiny precious stone called *musika*, which looks like a pomegranate seed, is put into the mouth. The Trungenese believe that it will help to preserve the body. White cloth is used to wrap up the naked body, which is then put into a canoe decorated with a small pagoda. A procession of canoes carrying mourners, the priest and *gamelan* players proceeds to the cemetery further down the shores of Lake Batur. The convoy of canoes soon reaches the final resting place of the Trungenese. The corpse is taken out of the canoe and laid under a tree near the shore of the lake, as the priest climbs a few steps to the Trungen cemetery. It is a small plot of land with only seven graves. Old corpses are scattered about for they are not buried in the ground. The priest goes to the centre of the row of seven, removes the bamboo pyramid covering the last corpse, pushes the corpse aside, and levels the earth for the new arrival. He throws seven Chinese coins onto the earth as a fee for the guardian spirit for the plot of land for the new visitor. Strangely enough, Chinese coins, which are round in shape with a square hole in the middle, used in China during the Ming and Ch'ing dynasties and which went out of circulation long ago, have become the 'spiritual currency' for the Trungenese and Balinese. After the coins are deposited, the corpse is brought to the spot and properly dressed in his favourite clothing. The precious stone is taken out of the mouth and the corpse is left exposed except for the covering of sharp-pointed bamboo sticks. No tombstone is erected. He will soon have to give way to whoever treads the ultimate path next. Consequently, bones are left scattered all over the place. Skulls, arranged in a row by children, make the atmosphere more eerie. Some tourists took away the skeletons as souvenirs.

The small pagoda, which accompanied the corpse in the canoe, is thrown into the lake on the way back after the ceremony. It is not burnt with the corpse as the Balinese do with their pagodas in their cremation ceremonies.

The Trungenese divide their death rituals into three categories. Only adults who die a normal death are entitled to the ceremony which I have just mentioned. For unnatural deaths, such as murder and suicide, the corpses are buried elsewhere without burial rites. Babies are believed to be sacred and need not go through the rituals which are meant to pave the way to heaven. Children are buried under rocks near the lake.

Why are there seven graves? Why do the Trungenese leave their dead exposed? James, the anthropologist, posed the same question to many village leaders. However, nobody seemed to be able to give an acceptable answer. They merely said that they had been following the custom for centuries and there seems to be no record of the origin of this custom. Some suggested that perhaps it was meant to make the bodies smell so as to counteract the fragrant smell of perfume which had attracted the Prince who came to rape their princess. Or was it due to the Buddhist belief, which I mentioned earlier, that those who died of smallpox could leave their dead bodies exposed because they would go to heaven anyway?

Could it be that at the dawn of civilization in Trungen an epidemic of smallpox took many lives; the many corpses were laid to rest according to the Yama Raja *mantra* and from then on it became a custom? Perhaps after further research, James might be able to throw some light on this strange custom. The Trungen burial custom reminds me of the death rites of the isolated Badui tribe in West Java. The similarity between the two is that neither bothers to erect tombstones for the dead. The Baduis bury the body but at the same time deliberately make it difficult for future descendants to find it. The common characteristics are that both the Trungenese and Baduis regard the dead bodies as waste matter and that the souls of the dead which ultimately join the souls of their ancestors are most important. The Baduis have the Arca Domas, the sacred burial ground of their Batara Tunggal, the final destination of all Badui souls. The Trungenese believe that the souls of all Trungenese will find their way to Pancering Jagat, the sacred land of their ancestors.

Unlike the Torajans of Sulawesi, who are forced by moral pressure to attend every village funeral ceremony for fear of being ostracised, the Trungenese funeral is a private affair for the family concerned. The only similarity between the two is the custom of wrapping the dead in white cloth. They differ greatly in the treatment of the dead body — the Torajans preserve the body whilst the Trungenese treat it as dispensable waste. One aspect of funerals seems to be common to the Torajans, Baduis, Trungenese, Balinese and, for that matter, even the Bataks and other races of Indonesia — that of ancestor-worship. The Trungenese have special shrines dedicated to their ancestors to whom they pray on certain days and on anniversaries. They also give offerings to their ancestors as they do to their gods. The essential offerings are the ancient Chinese coin, known as *kupeng*, and *gula kelapa* (palm sugar). The *gula kelapa* is coloured red, by adding the blood of a pig or chicken, and white, by cooking it in coconut-milk.

The use of *kupeng* as offerings in both the Trungen shrines and Balinese temples is most fascinating. At the funerals of either the Trungenese or the Balinese, the *kupeng* has become almost indispensable. It is hard to imagine how the priest would perform his duties without it. At a Trungen funeral, the *kupeng* is used to buy the passage to heaven, whereas at a Balinese funeral the priest scatters them in abundance as offerings for the spirits. The *kupeng* is also used at other spiritual ceremonies. It is even more intriguing to find that, besides their usefulness in the spiritual world, the *kupeng* can still be used to buy ice-cream in Denpasar or a packet of rice in Trungen. Made of copper, most of these coins found in Trungen and Bali might have been minted during the Ch'ing dynasty by Emperor Kang Hsi when Chinese art reached the zenith of its fame. With a little luck, one might also get a *kupeng* of the Ming dynasty minted during the time of Emperor Yung Lo who was responsible for the despatch of Admiral Cheng Ho's expedition to the South Seas about 600 years ago. Not very long ago, the Chinese coins were shipped in bulk to Tokyo and other Western ports because they were considered antiques. These Chinese coins have been out of circulation since Dr Sun Yat-sen defeated the Manchus and established the Republic of China. Least did the Chinese emperors of the Ming and Ch'ing dynasties expect that their coins would be used in the far-away land of Bali as currency of the spiritual world.

Why did the Trungenese and Balinese use the Chinese coins as spiritual offerings? And what happens when the *kupeng* disappears from circulation? What will the priest and worshippers use instead? Neither the Trungenese nor the Balinese could give me a rational answer. Their replies only helped to further mystify matters. The Trungenese and Balinese believe that the *kupeng* in fact descended from heaven and were not brought from China. It is the goddess of money, called Mercu, who sends down these *kupeng* from time to time. When the *kupeng* fall from heaven, one can see dragons flying in the sky and hear thunder. Goddess Mercu also sends down other types of coins which the Balinese call *pis*. There are *pis bolan* which bring luck to the possessor in affairs of love. There are *pis kuda* which enable the holder to walk as far as a horse. There are also *pis Arjuna* (the hero in the *Mahabharata*), *pis Hanuman* (the Monkey-god) and *pis Kresna*, all of which can bestow the possessor with the magical abilities of the respective characters.

The Chinese coins were used as legal tender throughout Java and Bali from the Majapahit period until the Dutch colonized the country. The Hindu kingdoms then did not produce any coins of their own, so it became a Hindu custom to use the *kupeng* at spiritual festivals.

Besides the funeral ceremony, the wedding ceremony of the Trungenese also differs from that of the Balinese. The Trungenese wedding usually takes place on a moonlit night, the ceremonies being picturesque and colourful. The bridegroom has to pass through three stages in a marriage ceremony before he can be admitted as a full-fledged member of the clan. The first stage is the most interesting as the ceremony compels the bride to bend her body downwards until both hands are touching her toes whilst the bridegroom bends his body over her spine. In olden days both bride and bridegroom had to be naked. In that position, holy water is sprinkled over them and *mantra* are pronounced by the priest. The second stage of the ceremony is held on the threshold of the family shrine and the third inside the shrine. As each stage involves a feast, not every bridegroom can afford to have the three stages on the same occasion. Once the three stages are performed, the bridegroom becomes a full member of the clan and is entitled to certain privileges, such as the right to vote and to receive his share during the distribution of food offerings. When the son of a family becomes a full member, the father has to retire and forego his privileges.

The Trungenese are united through the spirits of their ancestors and practise a sort of primitive socialism. They have their own peculiar way of choosing the name for a new-born baby. As a matter of fact, they believe that the spiritual guardian of the baby chooses its name. When a baby is born, three joss-sticks, each bearing a name, will be burnt at the altar. The joss-stick that burns off last will accordingly be used to name the child.

Except for the attempt of the government to educate the population of 1,500 Trungenese in Bahasa Indonesia, modernization has not affected the villagers. They still climb the mountains to till their land every morning, trudging along a rugged road made of huge stone slabs. One wonders how the villagers managed to place the heavy stone slabs in position at such a height, as it must have involved a great deal of effort. Actually, the Trungenese believe that the rugged road was built single-handed by a 'Tarzan' named Kebo Hiwa, a sort of Hercules or Seet Jin Kooi of the T'ang dynasty. In Bali, we often hear of famous people like Kebo Hiwa, a kind-hearted, strong man, whom even Gaja Mada feared to confront. Kebo Hiwa was famous for his kind deeds not only in Trungen but throughout Bali. To know about the hero, one has to turn to legends and folk-tales — after all, Bali is a treasure-house of myths and legends.

At the *pendopo* (entrance) of a small village *pura* (temple), called Penopengan, at Belah Batu, a descendant of the royal family of Klungkung Gusti Made Jelantik told me the story of Kebo Hiwa's encounter with Gaja Mada. When Gaja Mada invaded Bali, Kebo Hiwa resisted. He was so strong and powerful that Gaja Mada had to devise a plan to trick him. Knowing of Kebo Hiwa's weakness for pretty girls, Gaja Mada invited him to the Kingdom of Majapahit and promised to get him a pretty princess. When Kebo Hiwa reached Java, he was asked first to demonstrate his strength by digging a deep well. He was told that a deep well was necessary because the poor people were dying of thirst. Being susceptible to flattery and sympathetic to the poor and underprivileged people, Kebo Hiwa immediately went into action. The well was soon dug and he found himself at the bottom of it, when suddenly large rocks and boulders began to pour on him. With his mighty hands, he threw them back to the top one after another. He knew then that he had been tricked and said to Gaja Mada in a loud voice, "If you wish to kill me, you need not do this. Just sprinkle *kapur* (limestone powder) on my eyes and I will perish." This was done and that ended the life of Kebo Hiwa.

I have visited Bali many times and each time I have heard new legends and folk-tales. Bali is a myth in itself. The Balinese generally live in a world of their own. They are fatalistic by nature. They go about their daily life in harmony and with poise, never distracted by what happens in the world outside. They attend to their farms from sunrise to sunset, but when evening approaches, the farmers transform themselves into completely different roles. They become dancers, dramatists or musicians. Some drown themselves in the jerky, chinking sounds of the *gamelan* orchestra. Others become either Barongs (mythical lions) or Rangdas (witches) or, in a trance, try to pierce themselves with sharp krises. Many take part in the spectacular dance drama, called Kecak, where the *Ramayana* hero, Rama, and his heroine, Shinta, dance their story accompanied by an orchestra of voices. Little Balinese girls dance the traditional Legong, delicately fluttering their slender fingers as they weave about gracefully to welcome visitors. The more experienced dancers would attempt the fire-dance in a trance. In the past, dancing was an evening pastime — the Balinese simply danced for pleasure. As more and more tourists flock to Bali, money becomes the incentive to dance. The same applies to painting and sculpture, for which the Balinese are talented and famous. The real artists fear that greed for money may cause the quality of the dances, paintings and sculptures to deteriorate. For the Balinese, however, money may be an incentive, but it is not often used to buy the pleasures or comforts of the materialistic world. Money is sometimes accumulated to pay debts inherited from parents who overspent on elaborate Balinese cremation ceremonies.

Generally, the life of the Balinese follows a rhythmic pattern, their main purpose in life being to appease ancestors and gods by prayers and offerings. In turn, the Balinese will be rewarded with abundant harvests and be assured of a safe passage to heaven. Consequently, it is the ambition of each Balinese to have a shrine of his own or for his family. If this is not possible, he will make use of the village shrine. Referring to their own lunar calendar, the Balinese always remember the birthdays of their temples and shrines, on which occasions they invite the spirits of their ancestors and gods to descend from heaven and enter the places of worship. Those who are lucky are chosen by the gods to go into a trance. There are prayers and offerings and even dancing and feasting. Since each Balinese belongs to so many temples, these frequent festivals take up much of his time. In fact, the Balinese live for their gods and look forward to the day when their bodies will be cremated and their souls will ascend to heaven or be reincarnated.

Bali is perhaps best known for its cremation ceremonies. Few tourists, however, have the opportunity of seeing one, for it is expensive to organize. It involves the construction of a large, wooden cow, which holds the body of the deceased, and a multi-tiered pagoda, which is the cremation tower. A *gamelan* orchestra has to be engaged and a feast prepared big enough for relatives, friends and helpers. This type of funeral is beyond the means of the average Balinese farmer. Most Balinese must, therefore, temporarily bury the corpse while they save up for a cremation, or await the mass cremation held once in a hundred years. However, cremation is essential, because only in that way can the soul be released to go to *nirwana* (heaven) or be reincarnated. It is the wish and ambition of every Hindu or Buddhist that his soul will reach the stage of *nirwana* which means that he need not be reborn again. Only when the soul is still imperfect must it be reincarnated, sometimes in the form of animals or into a genius, depending on one's past life. Balinese believe that only after the body is cremated can the soul be released for reincarnation or to attain the stage of *nirwana*.

According to Balinese metaphysics, human beings are made of three essential elements: fire, representing Lord Brahma; water, representing Lord Vishnu; and wind, representing Lord Siva. When one dies, one has to return to nature and this happens through cremation. When the body is cremated, it is fire. The ashes of the human body and bones are crushed into powder and thrown into the sea where it dissolves in water. When the water evaporates, it turns into wind in the form of vapour and ascends as the soul.

For the living to contact the soul, it is necessary to erect an altar in the temple complex. Some of the altars are just ordinary boxes supported by wooden pillars, resembling cages for pigeons. Others, which are more elaborate, are in the shape of pagodas. These are called *meru*, derived from the word Mahameru or Semeru, the name of the highest mountain in East Java, where all souls will ultimately rest, according to Javanese Hinduism. The altars, whether in the form of boxes or *meru*, are 'contact points' for dialogue with the souls of ancestors. Before contact can be made, a purification ceremony has to be performed. This involves calling in both a Hindu priest and a Buddhist priest to make offerings and chant *mantra*, and to sprinkle holy water on all relatives and friends. The holy water is brought from eleven sources including the Besakih, which is the supreme temple where the souls of the earliest Balinese ancestors are housed. Once the temple is purified, one can invite the souls of the deceased to enter the *meru*. A medium can be employed to go into a trance to have a dialogue with the dead, if desired.

The Balinese have adopted certain aspects of the feudal and caste systems of Hinduism from India. In the past, the cremation of a king involved the construction of a wooden dragon, called *Naga banda*, which had a long tail. The corpse of the king was placed inside the dragon for burning. In the case of heroes, the coffin takes the form of a flying lion called *Singa-Kaang*. A prominent person such as a priest, a rich trader or a community leader is cremated in a coffin shaped like a cow. The cows are again divided into three colours — black, white and yellow. The black cow is meant for deceased who were married, the yellow, for bachelors and the white, for holy men. The towers built for cremations are also differentiated according to the social status of the deceased. Only the tower of a king can have eleven tiers, a priest's can have nine, and that of other classes of people, seven. During the cremation ceremony, bearers of the cremation tower zig-zag their way along so that the soul of the deceased cannot trace its way back. Everyone rejoices for the dead, as a cremation means ambition fulfilled.

In order that all Balinese can fulfil their ambition of having a cremation, the Bali-Hindu religion provides an outlet for the less fortunate who cannot afford to pay for their own ceremonies. Once in every one hundred years, all the temporary graves in Bali, with the exception of those in Trungen and other Bali-Aga villages, are cleared and the corpses cremated in one grand ceremony. This communal cremation is held on a *gotong-royong* basis, with everyone lending a helping hand. This grand festival is called *Karia Taur Agung Ekadasa Rudra*, 'The Great Ceremonial Offering to the Eleven *Rudra*'. The eleven *rudra* are the guardian spirits of the eleven points of the Balinese compass. The last great offering was held in 1963, a few months before the beginning of the Balinese

Balinese Hindus carry a cremation tower across a river during a cremation procession. (Inset) The funeral pyre is lit and soon the flames will engulf the cow-shaped coffins which have been carved out of wood. Only the nobility are entitled to be cremated in coffins of this shape.

century — the ceremony should rightly have been held at the start of the new century. The Balinese were apparently too anxious to perform the great offering because for three centuries this festival had been neglected and this neglect, they believed, had brought many calamities to Bali. The great temple of Besakih, the central temple for all Balinese Hindu, was chosen as the rightful place to perform the purification ceremony for the whole island. The ceremony was sponsored by the Bali Provincial Government and took place during the Sukarno regime, less than two years before the September 30 Gestapu coup. It was an historic and very happy occasion for all Balinese as their ancestors, who could not afford the expense of cremation, were finally to have their souls released. The only expense that the poorer descendants had to pay towards the ceremony was the price of a small wood-carving of an elephant fish to contain the ashes of their ancestors. These little ash-containers were assembled at the Besakih Temple to join the cremation towers built by more affluent participants of the festival.

I mentioned the Gestapu incident because the Balinese mystics seem to link this second great national disaster with the wrong date of performing the Great Ceremonial Offering. The first disaster was the eruption of Gunung Agung, resulting in great damage to the Balinese countryside. When the volcano erupted, many Hindu and Buddhist priests went to Gunung Semeru, the highest mountain in Java, to pray. It is difficult to understand why they chose to pray to Gunung Semeru which is far away and not Gunung Agung in Bali which had erupted. Apparently, Gunung Semeru is regarded as the father of Gunung Agung and is therefore more powerful and sacred. The mystics explained that when Gunung Semeru was angry, its anger was expressed through its son in Bali. But why did Gunung Semeru get angry? Perhaps it was because it had been neglected for too long. Before the Hindus in Java escaped to Bali when the Muslims came, they must have prayed to Gunung Semeru, and since then their attention had shifted to Gunung Agung. However, the Balinese Hindus still believe that all souls ultimately return to Mahameru, the most sacred mountain.

When the coup of September 30 came to ravage Bali, some mystics said the gods were angry because they had been disturbed before the time was ripe for the Grand Cremation held earlier. The gods thus demanded human sacrifices as compensation. Other mystics believe that when Bali was cleared of its graves, the goddess of Durga felt lonely and needed company. These graves were soon filled up with new visitors — victims of the coup. This explains why the Balinese never resisted when the time came for them to die. The Balinese seem to have a mystical explanation for every worldly incident. When the Pan-American Airways aeroplane crashed in Bali recently, they believed that the plane had landed on an airstrip built by the underworld. Incidentally, the Dutch had plans to build an airport at the site of the air crash, but plans were shelved. The mystics say that the underworld helped to complete the airport and the pilot at the time of landing had, in fact, received clearance from airport officials to land at the 'devil's airstrip'.

I mentioned earlier that some Yama Raja *mantra* are recited at marriages, births, deaths and even to evoke spirits through black magic and sorcery. Balinese priests and mystics often make use of *mantra* as spells for good or evil purposes. Some *mantra* can cure the sick, others can place a curse on someone. The Balinese believe that such *mantra* and all the secrets of witchcraft were originally compiled in the *lontar* Book of Dirah, a kind of dictionary of black magic. Apparently, a large proportion of the Book of Dirah was burnt or destroyed during the battle between a famous priest named Mpu Bharadah, and an evil witch, Calon Arang, who had in her possession the Dirah. The image of Calon Arang, popularly known as Rangda, was the first thing that made an impression on my mind when I visited Bali. It was a wooden carving of an ugly witch with bulging eyes, Dracula-like teeth, tongue hanging out, untidy loose hair, and long sharp fingernails. It was so frightening a sight that I had to remove it from the wall of my bedroom. Only later did I dare to enquire about the story of the fearful Calon Arang.

One day, Calon Arang found a beautiful baby girl abandoned on the beach. The witch decided to rear the child as her own. When the girl, called Ratna Manggali, grew up, the powerful king Arlangga fell in love with her, and they married. At that time, Arlangga lived in a land of eternal life where nobody ever died. After the king married Ratna, however, the people died one after another and the king's subjects began to suspect that the new queen was a witch. The *patih*, military commander to the king, conspired with the people to separate the king from his beloved queen in order to save the people. One night, when Ratna was asleep, she was kidnapped by the *patih*. She was tortured and tortured, but she refused to admit that she was the daughter of a witch. Ratna's servant Lika, an ugly bald-headed woman, discovered the kidnap and turned herself into a *garuda* bird, fought the *patih* and blinded him in both eyes. The news soon reached the ears of the king who then realized that his wife was a witch and was responsible for the many deaths of his subjects. So he called upon the help of a famous priest named Mpu Bharadah to defeat Calon Arang and destroy her book of witchcraft. In the ensuing battle, most of the *lontar* pages were destroyed by fire, but some were blown into the sea by wind. These drifted to the shores of Sanur, which is now a popular beach resort for tourists. Sanur is famous for witchcraft because, according to legend, the people there salvaged some of the secrets of witchcraft from the *lontar* pages which were left on the shores. Residents in Sanur, particularly, have many stories of *leyak* (witchcraft) to tell. They believe that people who possess the secret *mantra* of Dirah could turn themselves into animals such as tigers, monkeys, dogs or pigs, to frighten away people. In recent times, *leyak* seems to be keeping up with modern technology; the preference now is to transform into motor-cars, scooters, bicycles or even aeroplanes which can run in and out of temples without drivers. When the Balinese speak of *leyak*, they always remember Rangda (Calon Arang) and her magic. That may explain why even choreographers and dramatists, when staging the Calon Arang legend, do not dare to make the witch lose face. Invariably, the play will end before the tide turns against Rangda. The staging of the Calon Arang play is, in fact, a form of exorcism, because the Balinese hope that by dramatizing Rangda's triumphs they might gain her goodwill. They fear her, as she is the queen of *leyak*, the mistress of black magic. As a matter of fact, the Balinese believe in the motto of using a devil to fight a devil or using a thief to catch a thief. That explains why ugly and frightening images of wooden demons are seen all over the place; the most common ones are those of Rangda and Batara Kala, the fearful-looking man-devouring monster sent down to earth by Siva to punish uncivilized humans.

Besides using the forces of evil against evil, the Balinese concept of good and evil is a compromise of vagueness. Nothing to them is perfectly good or bad. They believe that even gods are human and are susceptible to temptation and human weaknesses. For instance, Siva in his angry mood may act like the monster, Kala. Similarly, Rangda, known for her wickedness and damaging powers, sometimes reveals the finer side of her nature by transmitting her magical powers to cure human sickness.

Rangda's biggest contender for supremacy in the mystical world is Barong, a mythical animal which has the features of a lion and yet rather resembles a dragon. In Bali, Barong is also popularly known as Barong Sai. To the Balinese, Barong represents good and righteousness. He is the sun, the male element in the cosmic world, referred to as *yang* in Chinese cosmology. He is the defender of everything good. Rangda is the female, the *ying*, representing evil. The Balinese say Barong and Rangda had an ancient feud which has not been settled even till today. The feud is still depicted in the various Balinese dances, the most popular to the tourists being the Barong and Kris dance where Barong and Rangda demonstrate their magical powers. Rangda makes krises stab their owners, whereas Barong uses his power to protect them from being hurt.

The introduction of Barong into Balinese culture and religion presents a most intriguing problem to the anthropologists. A great deal of speculation still revolves around the significance of the word 'Barong', for which there appears to be no satisfactory explanation. Some suggest that the word may have been derived from the Malay word *baruang*, which means 'bear'. But the Malay language is a comparatively modern language and there were never bears in Bali. Evidently 'Barong' is not a native word of the Balinese. So how and from where did the word come and how did the Barong Sai dance originate? The sight of the Barong invariably brings to my mind the various Chinese lion dances I have seen in Singapore and Hong Kong. It is worth noting that the word 'Sai' attached to the Balinese Barong is a Chinese word which means 'lion' in the Hokien dialect, one of the major Chinese dialects spoken in the Fukien province and the predominant dialect of the Chinese in South-East Asian ports. In Singapore, the lion dance is called Boo Sai, *boo* meaning 'dance' and *sai* meaning 'lion'. Considering the fact that large quantities of ancient Chinese coins are still found and used for ceremonial purposes in Bali, I am inclined to believe that the Barong was also introduced from China. Having been educated in Chinese, I also venture to suggest as a layman that the second syllable 'rong' in the word 'Barong' came from the Chinese word *long* which means 'dragon'. The first syllable 'ba' may be a short form of Bali or may be *pa* meaning 'crawling'; thus, the 'Bali dragon' or the 'crawling dragon'. But one might ask, why should a lion be called a dragon? To explain the possible confusion, we have to return to the mythical animal, Chi-ling, which appeared on the wooden door of the Jagat shrine of Trungen. The Chi-ling, which belongs to the family of the dragon, is also called a lion-dog. In appearance, the face of Barong does resemble the Chi-ling. In any case, the Balinese themselves have chosen the words 'Barong Sai' to describe the mythical animal, which could mean the 'Bali dragon-lion'.

According to an anthropologist, Walter Spies, who made a study of Trungen, in ancient days the boys of Trungen used to perform a dance semi-naked. They wore a sort of primitive mask and ran around the temple grounds whipping savagely anyone they came across. These fierce, little monsters were called *barong berutuk*, a term for which there was no interpretation. Could it be that *barong berutuk* was the name given for Chi-ling? Could this be the origin of the Balinese Barong? I have seen the Barong dance many times and could not help noticing the remarkable similarities between the Barong Sai of Bali and the Boo Sai of Singapore and Hong Kong. Both have large bulging eyes, big noses and wide mouths with snapping jaws. Both also have long beards and large ears. One difference is that the Balinese lion has a pair of Dracula-like teeth protruding from the sides of its mouth, whereas the Chinese lion seen in Singapore has a set of properly filed, even teeth, ironically befitting the traditional Balinese requirement for all who wish to gain entry to heaven. All Balinese are expected to file their teeth during childhood, otherwise the gate to heaven would be shut to them. Balinese images of evil, mythical gods or demons such as Barong, Rangda or Kala always appear with long, fearful, Dracula-like teeth, perhaps to remind the people of the consequences of not filing their teeth. The other difference between the Balinese Barong and the Chinese lion is that the former has a longer, clean-cut tail, whereas the latter has a bushy, short tail. The bright golden colour of the lions' fur and the clusters of little bells that jingle at every move of the feet add to the similarities of the two. The way the Barong is manipulated by two men, one holding the head and the other moving the buttocks to deflect the tail, is exactly the same as in the Chinese lion dance. My personal impression is that the Balinese Barong presents a more frightful sight than the Chinese lion. The Balinese Barong dance has succeeded in synchronizing the *gamelan* music into a dance which also has an interesting drama behind it. It is really fun to watch Barong in his good mood wiggling his hindlegs, snapping his jaws and clicking his teeth like castanets when the tempo of the *gamelan* music quickens.

I had often wished that the Balinese Barong would meet the Singapore lion and dance together. My wish came true in early November 1974 when a Singapore cultural and goodwill mission visited Bali. The Singapore lion and the Balinese Barong met significantly in a village called Singapadu, which, when translated literally, means 'the lions fight'. It was not a fight but a happy reunion of the two lions which, in my opinion, may have originated from the same source. Excitement gripped the Balinese and

Singaporean spectators when the Singapore lion tried to flirt with the more timid Balinese Barong against a background of Balinese *gamelan* music, accompanied by Chinese drums. It was great fun and the crowd roared with laughter. It was the first time that the Balinese had seen a Singapore 'Barong'. They were greatly amused by the acrobatic stunts of the Singapore 'Barong' which sometimes rolled and sometimes stood on its hindlegs. The Bali Barong, in comparison, appeared rather shy and would hardly venture to make such wild moves. As the first performance was so well received, the Singapore sponsors suggested that the same act be repeated on stage at the Bali Beach Hotel theatre where the Singaporeans were to perform again. However, the priest of the Singapadu temple politely declined the offer and explained that the Bali Barong was sacred and could not, therefore, perform in any place other than a holy temple.

In ancient times, the Chinese Buddhist lion dances were also performed in temple compounds. Nowadays in Singapore, Hong Kong and Malaysia, the Chinese lion dances are still popular, but merely as entertainment. Few remember the origin of the lion dance. Nevertheless, Buddhists believe that the lion is the lord of the animal kingdom; it is fierce and aggressive. In order to tame the lion, a pearl was once used to tempt it until unwittingly it was lured into the parlour of Lord Buddha. Under the influence of Buddha's supernatural powers, the lion was tamed and became a friend of the human race. The legend tries to convey the message that even the fierce lion can be tamed by the meditative powers of Buddha.

In ancient days, the Chinese lion dance was also performed to exorcize demons, as the animal is the protector of religion. The lion is also the Buddhist symbol of courage, nobility and good luck. In the past, during Chinese New Year, lion dancers, accompanied by drums and fire-crackers, roamed from house to house to collect *ang pow* (gifts of money in red packets). The hosts would hide Chinese coins on top of a tree, which was called the money-tree, and the lion would try to climb up and collect the coins. This custom known as *chai ch'ing* has died out, and today lion dancers perform to welcome guests or just for entertainment. However, it is significant if we try to connect it to the origin of the Barong and the Chinese coins in Bali. The early travellers from China to Bali might have brought with them their lion dances as well as their coins. With the passing of time, the lion dances could have been absorbed into the Hindu-Bali religion to become the Barong, and the coins used for worship in the temples.

In Bali, the Barong is not just a mythological lion or a dragon to entertain the crowd. Both Barong and Rangda serve as representatives of gods. The god that usually enters the mask of Barong is called Ratu Anom. In a cluster of villages in the district of Gianjar, which is famous for trance performances, Barong and Rangda have their own temples. The masks of Barong and Rangda are carved from sacred wood, decorated and imbued with godly powers by a series of rituals and ceremonies. They are then wrapped in white cloth and kept in sacred boxes when not in use. Offerings have to be given to the masks on their birthdays and other auspicious occasions lest their magical powers diminish. On the birthday of Barong, all the Barong masks in the district are taken to the temple for the ceremony. Before a Barong dance begins, the dancer will have to go through a ritual to seek permission from the spirit behind the mask. An intruder to the mask may find the spirit behind it so powerful that he is likely to faint or go insane. A Balinese priest claims that in one village, a dancer was trying to test a newly-made Rangda mask in a graveyard at midnight when he fainted. He died after a week's illness. Not every mask, which a tourist finds in the souvenir shops, has magical powers. To imbue a mask with a spirit or magical powers, one must take it to a graveyard or the temple of death in the Balinese temple complex. There prayers and *mantra* are uttered by the priest so that magical powers will enter the mask. Apparently, a greenish illumination glows from the mask once the spirit has entered it. The priest who tried to explain this to me said that it was even necessary to give offerings to the tree from which the wood was taken for making the mask. Most of the masks sold to tourists are harmless. To know whether or not a mask is imbued with a spirit, one need only test it out in a graveyard at midnight. If a green light radiates from it, then the mask has special powers and must be handled carefully.

As I have said before, the Balinese live in a world of their own. They are not very much bothered by the world outside. Nor are they interested in what the world outside thinks of them. To them, Bali is the centre of the world and Gunung Agung its navel. As revealed by old manuscripts, in the beginning there was nothing in the universe except a magnet. Then the world serpent, Antaboga, through meditation, created the earth in the form of a turtle which floated on the ocean with the island of Bali resting on it. The Balinese concept divides the universe into the underworld, the middle world, and the upper world. The upper world is divided into different levels again: the level of the clouds where the god of love dwells, the middle level of the atmosphere and the dark blue sky where the sun and moon are, and the upper perfumed sky where the bird, Tjak, and the serpent, Taksaka, dwell with the stars. Higher still is the *gringsing wayang*, the flaming heaven of the ancestors. Above all the skies live the great gods who watch over the heavenly nymphs.

The underworld is ruled by Batara Kala and his goddess, Setesuyara. Kala was an offspring from Siva's sperm which fell to the ground while Siva made love to his wife, Uma, when she was in an angry mood. Siva wanted to destroy the sperm and ordered the lesser gods to shoot at it with their magic arrows. However, Kala managed to grow into a mighty, fearful giant who demanded food to fill his insatiable stomach. Siva sent him down to the earth to teach the human creatures a lesson, for they went about naked and behaved like savages. But Kala came down to earth only to devour the human race. Alarmed, Siva recalled Kala and sent down gods to teach the human race how to behave, to grow food and to follow a religion. Today, Kala is seen in every corner of Bali and in most parts of Indonesia. In Bali, particularly, large stone images of Kala are common at the entrance of houses, temples, and also hotels. He is no more the man-eating demon but a guard and protector against evil. However, some Balinese still believe in the legend which says that once a year, three days before the Balinese New Year, Batara Kala, also known as Galunggan Kala, would come down to earth in the form of Sanghiang Tiga Wisesa to eat people. It is therefore dangerous and sinful not to make special offerings to him.

The Balinese live in a world of gods and demons. They spend their whole life trying to contact their gods, seeking the blessing of the souls of their ancestors, and at the same time pacifying the anger of the demons. Thus, at the corner of every street, stone images of Vishnu, Siva, Brahma and other gods make their presence felt. And there are temples and small shrines everywhere. In the modern world of rationality, the Balinese may appear to be living in a world of myths. To them, however, the myths are realities. It will take some time for the Balinese to change their way of life. But then, is there any reason why it cannot withstand modernization? They are obviously much more contented than the tourists that flock to see them. Is not the increasing flow of Western hippies an indication that the Balinese have something to offer those who appear to have lost their way in the intricate cobweb of modern civilization?

6

The Myth of
Sampo
and His Aides

A thousand sages have but one mind,
and through ten thousand ages only a truth
holds good.

a Chinese proverb

About ten minutes' drive from the city of Semarang, on the northern coast of Central Java, is a famous Chinese temple called Sampo Beo, but more popularly known to the Javanese as Klenteng Sampo. Everyone knows that it was built to commemorate Admiral Cheng Ho, Muslim eunuch of the Ming dynasty, who led a Chinese fleet of treasure ships on seven expeditions to Java and other parts of South-East Asia and West Asia in the early fifteenth century. I came across the name of Cheng Ho, the Sampo eunuch, in Chinese textbooks during my younger days in a Chinese school. As far as I can remember, history textbooks described Cheng Ho as a prominent and successful explorer, a Chinese envoy who brought about goodwill and trade between China and the countries of the 'Western Seas'. In those days the 'Western Seas' meant the whole of South-East Asia as well as the Indian Ocean up to the Arab states of West Asia. A historical figure who found a place in the Ming chronicles, Cheng Ho has become a saint worshipped by peoples throughout South-East Asia and West Asia.

I have visited several Sampo shrines such as the Sampo caves in Ipoh, a town in northern Peninsular Malaysia, the 'footprints' of Sampo in Penang, and other shrines in Thailand. When I heard that there was a Sampo temple in Semarang, I naturally took an interest in it. I visited the temple several times, and each time it fascinated me more and more. It is not so much the shape and beauty of the temple itself, but the structure and paraphernalia of the temple, as well as its history.

The Klenteng Sampo resembles any other Chinese Buddhist or Taoist temple with oriental, pagoda-type, curved eaves and tall red pillars surrounding an open porch where incense holders made of brass are placed on a wooden altar. In front of the temple is a smaller pavilion for visitors to congregate and discuss their fortune-notes given them by the temple's attendant. When I last visited the temple, it was terribly crowded, and the air was heavily polluted by thick smoke from the profuse burning of joss-sticks. There was a long queue waiting to kneel before the altar of Sampo Kong (the spiritual name of Admiral Cheng Ho) in the inner chamber. The dark chamber was cramped with worshippers, each clutching smoking joss-sticks; I almost choked on the irritating, smelly smoke. Strange as it may seem, nobody uttered a word. Each worshipper diligently jolted a container of bamboo sticks, causing the harsh, hollow sounds to break the silence of the temple. Eventually, one bamboo stick would pop out of the container and fall to the floor. This would then be brought to a counter in exchange for a yellow piece of paper called the *chiam-si*, or fortune script. The *chiam-si* contains folk-tales of romance or war in Chinese history which are interpreted as either good or bad omens in relation to one's wishes. This scene of praying and seeking advice on one's fortunes is common in all Buddhist temples in Singapore, Malaysia and Thailand. The thing that struck me was the person who was looking after the *chiam-si* counter in the Klenteng Sampo. He was not a Buddhist priest with shaven head and yellow robes. He wore a *songkok* (a black velvet cap worn mainly by Muslims) and claimed to be a Muslim. Another interesting aspect was that the *chiam-si* was written in the Indonesian language with detailed interpretation of the Chinese stories. The majority of those who now visit the Klenteng Sampo are descendants of the early Chinese migrants in Indonesia who do not speak any Chinese dialects. They are known as *peranakan*, which means literally 'born locally'. Even the *tokoh* or *sin kheh* (terms given to describe the Chinese who are comparatively recent arrivals from China) can read and write Bahasa Indonesia, the national language.

When I was inside the dark inner chamber, I noticed a young girl holding three joss-sticks addressing the spirit of Sampo Kong in the Indonesian language. With tears in her eyes, she murmured softly into the ear of the statue of Sampo as she poured out her grievances and finally pleaded repeatedly, *"Tolonglah saya!*

The Klenteng Sampo at Semarang, where Admiral Cheng Ho, the Chinese Muslim eunuch, is worshipped as a saint known as Sampo Kong.

Tolonglah saya!" (Please help me!). She was so absorbed in her own thoughts and worries that she did not seem to notice anyone else around her. Outside the temple, in the pavilion, womenfolk chatted among themselves in their own peculiar dialect, a mixture of Indonesian and Hokien, some laughing with joy while others pensively mooning, apparently having been informed of impending ill-fortune.

Next to the main temple is another smaller temple under a giant fig-tree. It has three compartments: the one on the left displays a huge, ancient anchor, the remains of one of the ships of Admiral Cheng Ho's fleet; the compartment in the centre contains a picture of the famous Chinese sage, Confucius; and the one on the right has a plaque to commemorate the hundreds of unknown sailors who lost their lives during the long sea voyages to Java. The rusty anchor has become a *pusaka*, and people pray to it because they believe it holds magical powers. A root from the giant fig-tree near by has shot up from the ground behind where the anchor is placed. The snake-like root meanders up through the branches of the tree like a rope linking the anchor to the main tree-trunk. How this happened is anybody's guess, but it makes the magical powers of the anchor more convincing to those who believe in such things. The place where the anchor stands, I was told, was where a ship had anchored. Apparently, hundreds of years ago the whole vicinity was covered by sea.

The altar of Confucius in the Sampo temple has only helped to complicate matters further. How did the founders of the temple get Confucius mixed up in the whole affair? I asked the old Javanese Muslim caretaker, who replied, "I know Confucius. His spirit has been here since the temple was built." Never mind how Confucius came to be involved was his attitude, and nobody else could really throw any light on the question. This is typical of the spirit of tolerance of the Javanese people and shows the remarkable capacity for syncretism so prominent in Java. If Sivaism and Buddhism could find common ground in the fertile, spiritual soil of Java and merge to form Siva-Buddhism, there is no reason why Buddhism, Confucianism and Taoism should not merge into a consorted religion called Sam Kow, the religion of three teachings. The Sampo temple has the characteristics of these three religions combined into one. The Buddhist feature is the form of the temple, the Taoist is mysticism in making the anchor a *pusaka*, and the Confucianist features are the portrait of Confucius as well as the plaque honouring the souls of the hundreds of sailors, representing Confucius' teaching of ancestor-worship. I met a 90-year-old

Chinese in Bali who claimed to be a leading member of the Sam Kow religion. He is a Balinese of Chinese origin by the name of Ketut Jaya. His Chinese name was Tan Siong. Ketut Jaya claimed to possess Chinese documents and books on Admiral Cheng Ho's expeditions and explained to me how Buddhism, Confucianism and Taoism came to merge into the Sam Kow religion of Java. I am not sure whether the people who go to pray in the Klenteng Sampo really know what religion they belong to or whether they have even heard of the Sam Kow religion, not to mention knowing the origin of their god, the Sampo eunuch.

Sampo Kong was, in history, an unusual man — a Muslim eunuch and admiral who spent the best part of his life travelling in the South Pacific and countries of the Indian Ocean from 1405 to 1430. For more than 20 years, Admiral Cheng Ho led a fleet of 62 treasure ships with a total crew of 27,000 men, visiting 36 countries on seven expeditions. According to the Ming chronicles, the ships were called 'treasure ships' because of the tremendous amount of treasures such as gold, ivory and spices which they brought home to China. They also carried valuable Ming porcelain, tea and Chinese coins to be presented to the various kings and sultans of the countries who had paid tribute to the Ming court in Peking. One of Cheng Ho's gifts to the Prince of Aceh was a hugh bronze bell, which is now exhibited beside the museum in Bandar Raya Aceh, in northern Sumatra. Unfortunately, the inscription has been covered by a new coating of bronze and cannot be deciphered. In the past, the bell was used only in the event of imminent disaster when it was struck to warn the people of the town.

Cheng Ho's ability as an explorer, navigator and administrator was unquestionable, judging from the size of the crew he had to manage and the number of countries he visited. His gift as a diplomat was also beyond doubt as he had to deal with so many Heads of States of different races, religions, beliefs and temperaments. Historically, Cheng Ho's expeditions were glorious successes which brought about better understanding between the Ming dynasty of China and her southern and western neighbours which she then regarded as vassal states. Prior to Cheng Ho's expedition, China's image had been marred by the barbaric invasions of Kublai Khan's Mongolian troops. This was particularly so in the case of Java.

In 1292, Kublai Khan had issued an order to the Governor of Fukien, directing him to send Shih-pi, Ike Mese and Kau Hsing to command an army of 20,000 to subdue Java. He wanted to punish King Kertanegara of Java who had humiliated the Yuan throne by having the nose and ears of the Mongol envoy, who had been sent to inform him of Kublai Khan's accession, cut off and sent back to China. When the Mongol invaders arrived in Java, Kertanegara had died. The Mongols found themselves involved in a civil war between the son-in-law of Kertanegara, Raden Vijaya, and his rival, Jayakatwang, who had killed Kertanegara. The shrewd Raden Vijaya made use of the Mongol troops to defeat Jayakatwang by first pretending to submit to Kublai Khan's troops. When Jayakatwang was killed, Vijaya turned against the exhausted Mongols who then withdrew with whatever prisoners and loot they could gather. Some of the Mongol troops remained behind and refused to return. On his return to China, the Mongol Commander, Shih-pi, was punished by Kublai Khan with seventeen lashes and had a third of his property confiscated. By that time, the situation in China had changed, and the Mongols did not send any more military expeditions to Java.

For nearly a hundred years after that unpleasant incident, relations between China and Java and other South-East Asian states came to a standstill. The sending of Admiral Cheng Ho's expeditions to South-East Asia and West Asia could, therefore, be considered an attempt by the Ming Emperor, Yung Lo, to regain the confidence of the kings and peoples of China's southern and western neighbours. Cheng Ho's expeditions were recorded in the *Ming Dynasty Histories*, a voluminous work of about 900 large volumes. Cheng Ho also had biographies written, but more detailed descriptions of the voyages were recorded by two officers who accompanied him to South-East Asia. Both of them were also Chinese Muslims who could read and write Arabic. One of them, Ma Huan, published his book entitled *Ying Yai Sheng Lan* (A General Account of the Shores of the Ocean) in 1415, and the other, Fei Shin, published his work *Hsing Chia Sheng Lan* (General Observations of the Seas) in 1436. These writings were observations of the ways of life of the different peoples of the 36 countries, particularly Java and Sumatra. Another book by the title of *Hsi Yang Chi* (An Account of the Western Voyage), a novel written by a Ming author, Loh Feng-teng, describes the expedition to Java in 1293 and Admiral Cheng Ho's expeditions. It abounds with fantasies of saints, devils and mystical powers of the heroes.

According to these books, the deity, whom so many people still seek for spiritual guidance and advice, was born a Muslim in Yunnan at a time when Genghis Khan's troops were losing their grip over that province. Cheng Ho's real surname was Mah and his father, a prominent *haji* (a Muslim who has been to Mecca), was Haji Mah.

When the soldiers of the Ming Emperor, Chu Yuan-chang, entered the province of Yunnan, little Mah was among the thousands taken prisoner to Nanking to serve in the Imperial Palace. The Ming dynasty was noted for the practice of castrating male prisoners and then using them as eunuch servants at the Imperial Palace. Thus together with other boys, little Mah lost his manhood and became a eunuch. He was sent to serve the fourth son of Chu Ti, an ambitious prince who later overthrew his own brother and usurped the throne.

Little Mah was soon discovered to be intelligent and talented and was given the name Cheng Ho, although his nickname was Sampo. As he was a eunuch, he was called Sampo Thai Chien (meaning 'Sampo Eunuch') in the Imperial Palace. How did the word 'Sampo' come about? Historians have argued over this name by which he came to be known after his successful expeditions. Some said he got the name because he was the third child in the Mah family (in the Chinese language, *sam* means 'three' or 'third', and *po*, 'to protect'). Others argued that 'Sampo' was meant to describe the three admirals who were sent out on the expeditions. The three were Cheng Ho, Wang Ching Hung and How Sian. Somehow, the other two admirals were less known, and Cheng Ho became known as Sampo. There were also others who thought that the word 'Sampo' was used to describe a eunuch. According to another Chinese source, Cheng Ho was given the name Sampo when he started to take lessons on Buddhism as a young boy. The words *sam* and *po* meant the three pillars of wisdom in Buddhist teachings, known as *Tri Ratna* in the Sanskrit language. Whatever it may be, the word 'Sampo' is now identified with all temples or historical relics associated with Admiral Cheng Ho.

When Chu Ti became emperor, he assumed the name Yung Lo and promoted Cheng Ho to be one of his principal eunuchs because the latter had helped him with advice on how to gain power. Since the Ming dynasty, eunuchs in the Imperial Palace had begun to wield considerable power because they were masters in the game of intrigue and because of their proximity to the emperor. The dethroned king, Hui Ti, disappeared in a boat with the Imperial seal when the palace coup took place. The Imperial seal was regarded as an indispensable royal symbol of authority for those who wanted to claim the throne. It was sacred and whoever took possession of it had the blessing from the Almighty Heaven (God) to rule. According to a legend, the seal was carved out of a very precious stone found inside a huge rock during the Warring States period. Emperor Yung Lo and his advisers suspected that Hui Ti had escaped with the seal to the South Seas. Thus, according to some historians, Cheng Ho, being the most trusted eunuch, was chosen to lead a fleet to the Pacific to look for the seal and to dispose of Hui Ti.

The expeditions were sent at a time when the Yung Lo reign had gathered strength and wanted to show the world its power by making smaller countries pay tribute—something they had not done for a century. Emperor Yung Lo wanted to make China's presence felt not by conquest but by friendly gestures. During his reign, China was aware that the countries of the 'Western Seas' (it may have meant the countries of West Asia), such as the Arab states, were Muslim countries and the rest of the coastal states in South-East Asia were under Muslim influence. In 1297, there were already several Muslim states in Sumatra, the most famous being Samudra-Pasai, headed by Sultan Malk-us-Saleh. And by 1400, Malacca had already felt the impact of Muslim traders who made good use of the Straits of Malacca. That might have been the reason Admiral Cheng Ho, the Muslim eunuch, was chosen to lead the expedition. In addition, Cheng Ho's immediate advisers and interpreters, such as Mah Huan and Fei Shin, were not only Muslims who knew Arabic but were also believed to be *imam* (Muslim preachers).

Cheng Ho's expeditions to Java, Sumatra and other parts of Indonesia could not but leave an impact on the people who came into contact with him and his Muslim advisers. When Cheng Ho arrived in Java in 1405, King Hayam Wuruk of the Majapahit Empire had just passed away, and the Hindu influence was on the decline. Although Islam had established itself in Sumatra and Pasai, its influence was still not yet felt in Java. It is difficult to say what impact Admiral Cheng Ho and his Muslim advisers made on the Javanese population, not so much as Ming envoys but as Muslims. Ming chronicles and other Chinese historical writings have recorded many of Cheng Ho's exploits and adventures. There was the famous story of Cheng Ho's encounter with a Chinese pirate by the name of Tan Chor Ghee in 1407 in Kukang (now Palembang), who had terrorized the entire population. Cheng Ho's troops captured him, killed seven hundred of his followers, and sent him back to China for execution. In 1415 he also helped a Sumatran prince to dispose of a usurper who ruled a kingdom of people with tattooed faces. There were also stories of how sultans of the various kingdoms had paid tribute to the Ming court and how trade had flourished. But Chinese history seems to have overlooked the fact that Cheng Ho was, after all, a Muslim and that his immediate advisers were also Muslims. Chinese history was unaware of the impact Cheng Ho and his advisers' Islamic way of life must have made on the peoples they came across. The only reference to this aspect of Cheng Ho's adventure in Java was in the form of a light-hearted story in one of Cheng Ho's biographies. The story says that when Cheng Ho was in Java, he advised the people not to take food for one month nearing the end of each Islamic year for it would be good for their health and soul. They tried to follow his way of fasting but found it extremely difficult. One night, one of the local residents discovered that Cheng Ho was eating quietly at home and confronted him, "You asked us not to eat for a month and yet you are eating in the dark. You have broken your promise." Cheng Ho replied, "You can eat every night when the sun has gone down." The author of the book apparently had no knowledge of the Islamic rules of fasting and misinterpreted Cheng Ho's eating at night as being caught red-handed for deceiving the people. Obviously, the people misunderstood Cheng Ho's advice and thought that they were not allowed to eat for the whole month.

Could it have been that on one or more occasions Cheng Ho arrived in Java during the Ramadan fasting month? When the people heard that Cheng Ho was fasting for a month, they naturally asked for the reason, so he had to explain by expounding the origin, value and significance of fasting. This would naturally entail further exhortation of the goodness and advantage of becoming a Muslim. Since many people admired Cheng Ho's character, they started to listen to and then follow his teachings. This could have been the first time the seed of Islam was planted into the minds of the people, particularly among the Chinese residents who had come into contact with Cheng Ho and his Muslim aides. At that time, Islam had only penetrated the coastal states of Sumatra and Malacca, but Java was still predominated by Hinduism and Buddhism. According to Indonesian sources, the grave of Malik Ibrahim, a prominent Islamic teacher, was found in Gresik, East Java, dated 1419. Cheng Ho's first expedition to Java arrived in 1405, and it is my guess that subsequent expeditions must have caused a stir among the natives in the Javanese ports. It appears to me that Admiral Cheng Ho could have been the earliest Muslim of some prominence and status to have visited Java.

According to an Indonesian book *Tuanku Rao*, written by an Indonesian author, Mangaraja Onggang Parlindungan, as a result of Cheng Ho's expedition in 1405, Chinese Muslim communities were set up in Palembang in 1407 and later, in 1411, Muslim mosques were built in Ancol (Jakarta), Cirebon, Tuban, Gresik, Mojokerto and other parts of Java. The book also says that in 1413, when Cheng Ho and his ships called at Semarang, the Admiral and his two aides, Mah Huan and Fei Shin, went to the mosque in Semarang to pray. Fei Shin also visited the *kraton* of Majapahit three times. *Tuanku Rao* contains a great deal of information about the expedition and its influence on the growth of the Chinese Muslim community in Java. It even suggested that the Sultan of Denak, Raden Patah, who defeated the Majapahit Empire, was of Chinese origin who was named Jin Bun (meaning literally 'man of letters').

Mangaraja Onggang Parlindungan claimed that he got his materials from a Dutch colonial officer who was once the Resident of Tanpanuli (North Sumatra). The Dutch officer, Poortman, was instructed by his Amsterdam superiors to find out whether it was true that Raden Patah, the Muslim hero responsible for the defeat of the Majapahit Empire, was really a Chinese. Poortman, then adviser to the Dutch governor, visited the Sampo temple in Semarang some time in 1925 when the communists were starting a revolt. With the help of the police, Poortman searched the temple and discovered a large pile of Chinese documents purporting to have contained valuable information about the Chinese Muslim communities in Indonesia. The book *Tuanku Rao* was based on information from Poortman's secret report to the Dutch colonial administration. Poortman, it was said, took away three bags of Chinese documents from Klenteng Sampo of Semarang and studied them. His secret report confirmed that Raden Patah was Jin Bun and also revealed a great deal of information about the Chinese Muslim communities in those days.

Because of the sensitive nature of the Poortman Report, it was put on restricted circulation among the Dutch administrators. These documents were then kept in the archives of the Governor-General's office which later became the Istana Merdeka occupied by former President Sukarno. The Japanese took over the building, but it was re-occupied by the Dutch Governor-General. During these changes, the documents disappeared. According to the author Mangaraja, when he was studying in Delft, Holland, he had access to the preamble to these documents, a copy of which was in Poortman's home.

By 1430, the Sampo eunuch had already successfully laid the foundation for the spread of Islam in Java and had established several Chinese Muslim communities in Tuban, Cirebon, Palembang and Gresik. When he died in 1434, Haji Gan Eng Tju became one of the driving forces of the Chinese Muslim community. He appointed some locally-born Chinese to be its leaders, such as Swan Liong, a businessman in Semarang, and Bong Swee Hoo, the grandson of Haji Bong Tak Keng.

Bong Swee Hoo and Swan Liong took the initiative to Javanize the Chinese community. They encouraged the younger generation Chinese to assimilate with the Javanese community, to adopt Javanese names and the Javanese way of life. Jin Bun, the adopted son of Swan Liong who was also the son of the King of Majapahit and his Chinese wife, became known as Raden Patah. This, in brief, was the thesis purported to have been expounded by Poortman upon which the *Tuanku Rao* was based.

It is not the purpose of this chapter to discuss the truth or otherwise of the origin of Raden Patah. Even if Raden Patah were of Chinese descent, he was a locally-born Javanese Chinese who owed allegiance to his country of birth. So were some of his supporters who were of Chinese descent. What seems strange to me is that this aspect of Cheng Ho's impact on the people of South-East Asia, particularly Java, was overlooked by the chronicles of Chinese history or the Sinologist who apparently had no knowledge of Islam. Similarly, it was also left out by Islamic writers, probably because of the lack of knowledge of Chinese and Sinology. It is difficult to believe that the Sampo eunuch and his Muslim interpreters did not do anything to propagate their religion on their expeditions to South-East Asia.

This brings me back to the Klenteng Sampo in Semarang. It is now easier to understand the presence of songkok-wearing Muslim caretakers in the temple. According to the *Tuanku Rao*, after the death of Sampo and the subsequent decision to abandon the maritime enterprises, the Chinese Muslim communities in Java disintegrated, and the mosques which Sampo and his aides had built were turned into *klenteng* (temples) to worship Sampo and his aides. The Klenteng Sampo in Semarang could then have been built originally as a mosque. The shape of the Klenteng Sampo, like several others in Cirebon and Java, is similar to those in the southern part of China — they have oriental, pagoda-type architecture, with tall pillars, flat horizontal roofs, curved eaves, lofty arches, spacious halls and winding corridors.

When I visited Canton in March 1975, I heard from Chinese officials that there are five important mosques in Canton. Two are famous: the Hsiang-fen (Tomb of the Echo) where the Chinese apostle of Islam was said to be buried; and the Mosque of Holy Remembrance. The latter, the largest and oldest in Canton, is situated in the older part of the city beside a street called Smooth

Pagoda Street, a name derived from the mosque because it has a 48-metre high pagoda-type minaret with a very smooth surface. The Mosque of Holy Remembrance was destroyed by fire in 1343, but was rebuilt between 1349 and 1351. The maternal uncle of Prophet Mohammed, Su-ha-pa-sai (Sahib), is believed to have been the founder of the mosque. He died before it was completed and was buried near by.

Islam was introduced to China by Arab traders who came by sea to Canton as early as the T'ang dynasty. By the early fourteenth century, there were already pockets of Muslim population in South China, and mosques began to be built. When I was in Canton, I saw several Muslim restaurants. By the time the Sampo eunuch led the famous expeditions to the South Seas, there must have been a sizable Muslim population in Canton. When Sampo went about recruiting crews for his expeditions, many Muslims might have responded to his call because he was a prominent Muslim. Although Chinese chronicles made no mention of this, it is my contention that not only were his immediate advisers Muslim *imam* but a certain percentage of his crews might also have been Muslims from Canton and Fukien.

I have digressed a little because of the apparent connection between the Muslims in southern China and their brothers in Java. Of significance is the similarity between the architecture and design of the mosques in southern China and that of the mosque believed to have been built by the Sampo eunuch, unlike most of the domed mosques in Sumatra and Malaysia.

Let me return to the riddle of mixed worship, including Confucianism, in the Klenteng Sampo in Semarang. The *Great Geography of the Ming Dynasty* makes reference to Confucius in connection with the teaching of Islam in China. This helps to throw some light on the appearance of a Confucius altar at Klenteng Sampo. Confucius' name was mentioned in an inscription written in Chinese in an old mosque in Sianfu of the Shensi province, west of China, where Islam was once popular. The inscription dated A.D. 724 says, among other things, that:

> ... In all parts of the world, Sages arise who possess this uniformity of mind and truth. Mohammed, the great Sage of the West, lived in Arabia long after Confucius, the Sage of China. Though separated by ages and countries, their doctrines coincide one with another. Why? Because they had the same mind and truth. The proverb says: A thousand sages have but one mind, and through ten thousand ages only a truth holds good.

To my mind, the early Muslim preachers must have made use of the popularity of Confucius to spread the teachings of Islam, just as the Muslims in Java later used the popular image of Semar to propagate Islam.

The Sampo eunuch, though a Muslim by birth, was under the influence of Buddhism and the teachings of Confucius as he was brought up in the Imperial Palace of the Forbidden City. Was it the Sampo eunuch who had brought in the image of Confucius to help spread the teachings of Islam? Or was it erected after the death of Sampo when the mosque was turned into a temple? One thing is certain, however: the altar of Sampo Kong was installed after his death in 1434. In that year, Sampo's most trusted deputy, Admiral Ong Keng Hung, who was also a eunuch, led the eighth expedition to South-East Asian countries. Admiral Ong Keng Hung, a non-Muslim, might have been the person who converted the Semarang mosque into a temple to commemorate Sampo. It must have been the last expedition, for Ming chronicles made no mention of Admiral Ong's return to China. It is said that somewhere near the Semarang Sampo temple, there is a tombstone supposed to be the burial place of Admiral Ong Keng Hung. Worshippers in Semarang prefer to believe that the grave is that of Sampo, for it is a known fact that Ong died in China.

From the point of view of an orthodox Muslim, the act of turning the mosque built by Sampo into a *klenteng* to worship the idol of Sampo was contrary to the principles of Islam. According to the *Tuanku Rao*, in 1474 when Jin Bun arrived in Semarang for the first time, he rushed to the mosque built by the Sampo eunuch. He burst into tears when he found that the mosque had been turned into a *klenteng*, and prayed to Allah (God) for strength and blessing so that he could build a proper mosque near by. In 1477, when he led a 1,000-strong Islamic army to revolt against the Hindu Majapahit Kingdom, he also passed through Semarang. He was wise in leaving the non-Muslim Chinese unmolested and also left the Sampo temple undamaged. But he vowed that, if his revolt against the Hindu Kingdom was successful, he would make the non-Muslim Chinese conform to an Islamic rule in Demak. When he succeeded in 1478, Jin Bun kept his promise and built a mosque in Demak in order to spread Islam in its unadulterated form.

According to Professor Slamat Muljana, a prominent Indonesian historian, Jin Bun was the son of King Kertelehumi of Majapahit and his Chinese wife (*Putri Cina*). As a boy, the prince was sent to Palembang and was brought up by Swan Liong alias Arya Damar, son of another Majapahit King Wikramawadhana who also had a Chinese wife. Both Swan Liong and Jin Bun, who had become Javanized Chinese Muslims, contributed towards the eventual downfall of the Majapahit Empire. Professor Slamat Muljana wrote a controversial book entitled *The Fall of a Hindu-Java Kingdom and the Rise of Islamic States in Nusantara*. It is not the intention of this chapter to meddle with this most delicate controversy concerning the mystery of Jin Bun and other Chinese Muslim preachers in relation to the spread of Islam into Java. What appears significant to me is that as early as the fifteenth century, the process of Javanization of the Chinese had already begun through inter-marriage. Sampo's treasure ships brought not only material wealth to the rulers of Java but also Chinese maidens, as well as bridal gifts. This explains the existence of Chinese cultural products such as the *tandu*, or sedan chair, still used in royal weddings to carry the bride; Ming porcelain in the gardens of Javanese *kraton*; and spittoons inside the *kraton*. It also explains the origin of the Teochew *wayang* (Chinese opera) hair-do of Javanese brides at Javanese weddings, and the Chinese wedding-gown and head-gear of the bride in a Palembang wedding, all still part of today's custom.

The move to Javanize the Chinese became so intense that even the Sampo eunuch was given a Javanese name. To many Javanese, Sampo was known as Mbah Sedakar Jurangan Dampu Awang Sam Poh Kong, or the Guardian Angel, Sampo Kong. A legend says that when Sampo wandered in Java, he caught the romantic eye of a beautiful princess, daughter of King Browijoyo of Trowulan in the Majapahit Empire. Her name was Devi Kilisuci, Princess of Kediri, near Surabaya. Struck by her beauty, Sampo did everything he could to win her heart, but he had to contend with many competitors including kings. Devi Kilisuci took no interest in the others. Instead, she was delighted with the personality of Sampo. According to a Chinese source, Cheng Ho was an imposing figure. He was nearly three metres tall, had a fifty-inch waistline, a prominent forehead, cheeks and chin and a small charming nose. He had high eyebrows, long hanging ear-lobes and wholesome shiny teeth. His voice was commanding and he walked with firmness, like a tiger. All these features might have appealed to her. She promised to marry him if he could fill her *kukusan* (rice-boiler) with gold. Sampo ordered loads of the metal to be transported from the northern coast, where his treasure ships were anchored, to fill the *kukusan*. It was a hopeless attempt, for holes had been cut in all the bags containing the gold. Consequently, the gold flowed down the slopes of the mighty and mysterious Gunung Emas

Kemambang which became a mountain of gold; hence its name.

When Sampo discovered that he could not fill the *kukusan* because of the leaks, he bowed gracefully to the princess and apologized for not being able to fulfil his promise, admitting that he had nothing more to offer her. Smilingly, the Princess of Kediri replied that Sampo had done enough to prove his sincerity and she agreed to marry him. According to the Laws of Eternity and Immortality, they lived together in the Selomangleng Grotto of Gunung Emas Kemambang, the Mountain of Floating Gold. The understanding was that they would never touch each other as ordinary mortal humans, but would meditate together for spiritual happiness and pure wisdom.

This legend of platonic love befits the circumstances in which Sampo found himself when he arrived in Java. Although he was a eunuch, he was, after all, also a human in need of love and companionship. This legend is, however, far-fetched historically for Devi Kilisuci lived in the eleventh century and was a daughter of King Erlangga.

Cheng Ho was not the only one who left behind a temple in his name. Two of his aides, one Admiral Wu Ping, also a eunuch, and the other, his favourite cook, also had temples consecrated to them. The origin of both temples has a touch of romance. One of them in Jakarta near Bina Ria is called Sampo Swie Soe. The words *Swie Soe* mean 'aide'. The temple was unknown for many years until it survived a disastrous flood which overwhelmed the area, Ancol, where the temple is situated. People then began to believe in the spirit of Swie Soe.

Who was Swie Soe, the aide of Cheng Ho? The following legend was told to me by the caretaker, Ong Siang Ing, an old man who has since passed away and who claimed to be a fifth generation descendant of the aide. It is said that the aide deserted Cheng Ho's treasure ship because he fell in love with a Javanese *ronggeng* (dancing) girl, Sitiwati. It was love at first sight, leading to a lightning marriage. Years later, when they died, a temple was built to commemorate them. Today, the Sampo Swie Soe is also known as the *ronggeng* temple. Twice a year, during the fourth and eighth months of the lunar calendar, *ronggeng* parties are held in the compound of the temple by the light of the full moon to commemorate Swie Soe and Sitiwati. It is believed that the spirits of Swie Soe and his wife join in the temple festivities. However, this story of Ong, the old caretaker, can only be treated as a legend. It is more likely that the temple was built by Cheng Ho and his right-hand man, Admiral Wu Ping. According to the *Tuanku*

Rao, a mosque was built by Cheng Ho and his aides in Ancol. When Admiral Wu Ping died, the mosque could have been turned into a *klenteng* to commemorate him, just as the Klenteng Sampo was converted to commemorate the Sampo eunuch. All such temples bear the first name of Sampo in order to take cognizance of Sampo's leadership and to indicate the period in which it was built.

Another aide of Cheng Ho — a cook — also left behind a legend and a temple in his honour in the village of Batur, some 40 kilometres from the shores of Bangli, one of the districts in Bali. The temple, called Sampo Chong Poh Kong (meaning literally 'God of the Cook' in the Hokien dialect) is situated in the third chamber of the Balinese Batur temple beside the shrine for Lord Vishnu. Constructed on the top of a hill in Kintamani, the huge Batur temple commands a panoramic view of the volcanic Batur mountain and the Batur lake.

It is a simple temple resembling any other Balinese temple in architecture. The spirit of the temple is now referred to as Ratu Subandar, or 'God of the Harbour'. Two statues — one, an old, bearded Chinese dressed in the costume of the Ming dynasty on the left and the other, a woman holding a basket on the right — give away its Chinese origin. Inside the temple are all sorts of paraphernalia to indicate the origin of the saint. Ratu Subandar is prayed to by many people, particularly Balinese traders, for spiritual guidance in the field of trade and commerce. At the altar is a Ming brass incense-burner which is embossed with faded figures of Chinese Mandarin officials. On the walls are triangular red flags made of silk, with a yellow dragon and two Ming dynasty Chinese coins on each of them. Framed up on the wall is a Chinese poem written with Chinese brush which tells of the origin of the saint.

However, the most sacred items are the belongings of the cook: a meat-chopper, a pair of slippers and a bamboo smoke-pipe. These are now regarded as sacred *pusaka* and are carefully stored away inside a nine-storey *meru* which is situated next to the temple. Beside it stands the eleven-storey *meru* of Lord Vishnu. I asked the *pamengku* (caretaker of the temple) for permission to see the sacred remains of the saint. With a polite smile he said "I am sorry. These things are sacred and can be seen only once a year during the fourth month of the Balinese calendar, when a big ceremony is performed to commemorate the birthday of Ratu Subandar." No amount of persuasion could make the *pamengku* change his mind, for he feared that evil consequences might befall him if he did not obey the cosmic rules.

How did Admiral Cheng Ho's cook leave behind the temple which is now known as Chong Poh Kong? It was by a stroke of luck that I met a Balinese hotel owner, Kumpiang, and the Director of the Bali Academy of Dances, Dr Mertha Sutedja, who introduced me to the 90-year-old Balinese, Ketut Jaya alias Tan Siong. He lived in a humble shed in Denpasar. Tan, well-known in Bali as a *kuntow* (art of fist-fighting) expert, medicine-man, astrologer and geomancer, was taken by surprise when I visited his humble home one afternoon. Clad in the white costume of a Balinese priest, Tan came out from his dark, dingy room and smiled whilst stroking his long, white beard. His tiny eyes still sparkled despite his age. The remarkable thing was that his mind was so alert that he could still remember minute details of past events in Balinese history. He remembered how the Chinese had come to settle in Bali. It was he who told me about the Chong Poh Kong temple in the Balinese Batur temple and a brief history of Admiral Cheng Ho's visit to Bali. He is a third generation descendant of one Tan Hoon San, a Hainanese captain who had fought a civil war in Taiwan and then migrated to Bali. Tan Hoon San later became the military adviser to the Raja of Denpasar.

Stories about Admiral Cheng Ho's voyage to Bali have been passed from generation to generation in writing or by word of mouth. Tan Siong learnt a lot about the Sampo eunuch during his childhood and youth and can still remember the details. Some of the stories have become legends.

One legend says that when Admiral Cheng Ho's treasure ships arrived at Bali and anchored off the shores of the district of Bangli, one of the ships flew over to Lake Batur. On this ship was a Hokien cook by the surname of Kang. The beautiful scenery of Kintamani and Lake Batur captivated him and it was not long before he fell in love with a Balinese dancer and decided to desert his ship. He brought with him some clothing, a pair of slippers, a bamboo smoke-pipe, a meat-chopper, and some ground-nuts, lichees and white onions. That, according to Tan, was the origin of the *kachang cina* (Chinese groundnuts), lichees and *kesuna* (white onions) in Bali. (Bali happens to be the only place in Indonesia where lichees grow.)

Kang, the cook, married the Balinese girl and settled in Batur. They had a daughter named Kang Kim Hoi (Golden Flower). She grew into such an attractive maiden that the Raja of Batur made her his queen and named his kingdom, Balinkang, a combination of the words 'Bali' and 'Kang', the surname of his queen. Kang Kim Hoi became better known as Putri Cina (Chinese princess).

When her father, the old cook Kang, died, a small temple was erected outside the Balinese temple complex to commemorate him. Later, when an epidemic swept the village, causing many deaths, the village folk believed that the ravages were caused by old Kang because he was unhappy that his grave was outside the temple complex. Kang's temple was then rebuilt inside the temple complex where it now stands.

It is not known what happened after the Raja of Balinkang took Putri Cina as his consort. It has become a common superstition among the Balinese living in the Batur village that misfortune would befall them if they married girls of Chinese descent. They also believe that the descendants of the Kang family have an extra tiny toe protruding from their feet. A popular Balinese batik design today is called *patra cina* (Chinese pattern) which resembles a golden flower. Could it be that the design was inspired by Kim Hoi, the 'golden flower', the Putri Cina of Balinkang?

Sampo's voyage to Bali left behind not only Chinese coins which have become an indispensable spiritual currency, but also *guci* (*gu* means 'old' and *ci*, 'porcelain') which were used as water or ash containers, and *wangkang* (*wang* sounds like *wan* meaning 'bowl' and *kang*, the surname of the cook, Kang) which is a Balinese name for porcelain plates.

Guci and other types of Ming porcelain came to Indonesia in large numbers during the Ming dynasty, especially after Admiral Cheng Ho's expeditions to the South Seas. However, items made during the dynasty of Yung Lo are most popular. The porcelains were brought in exchange for spices and other treasures in the countries then known as *Nanyang* or South Seas. Till today, antique sellers in Jakarta, who are mostly Minangkabaus or Sundanese, can tell the names of the various Chinese dynasties and identify the porcelains easily. Outside Bali, the words *guci* and *wangkang* are not used to describe porcelains. It is interesting to see Indonesian antique traders, who know not a word of Chinese, speak with a certain degree of expertise about the quality of Yung Lo or Wan Li porcelains of the Ming dynasty or about the products of the reigns of Kang Hsi, Chien Lung, or Yung Cheng in the Ch'ing dynasty. Some of the *guci* which were brought into Indonesia were later used by Buddhist priests or prominent Buddhist believers to contain their ashes after their death. Many of these porcelain articles, which are known as 'export wares', were also buried beneath the earth to accompany their owners according to ancient Chinese custom. These were later dug out and became rare treasures much sought after by antique collectors.

Sampo has also left behind the habit of clapping the hands to call for the wind. According to another legend, one day when Sampo was taking a rest on the deck of one of the treasure ships, the weather was hot and stuffy. When he clapped his hands, a refreshing breeze came by. Soon it was the talk of the town, and everyone started to clap his hands whenever he wanted breeze. Till today, the Balinese clap their hands to invite the breeze when the weather is hot.

7

Isolationists: the Baduis and the Tenggerese

Touch not the dirty hands of civilization
Be pure and loyal to Nature's salvation.

a Badui saying

"Can I give you a lift?" I asked an old man who was walking alone on the outskirts of the town of Banten one evening on my way to Sukabumi just a couple of hours' drive from Jakarta. The sun had set and the road was quiet and isolated. With a polite smile, he answered, "No, thank you." He was wearing a peculiar black costume rarely seen in Jakarta. He had a white turban on his head, quite similar to that of the Sikhs, and was barefooted. As he walked along, he held on firmly to a parcel wrapped in black cloth.

"Why did he refuse to take a lift from me? Don't you think it is rather late for an old man to be walking alone on this deserted road?" I asked my Indonesian friend who was travelling with me. He smiled and said, "He is a Badui and it is taboo for a Badui to ride in a car, on a bicycle or use any other means of transportation invented by modern civilization. He is on his way to the mountain range of Kendeng, where the Baduis live." All Baduis have to travel on foot and barefooted as well.

My friend told me that the Baduis are also prohibited by their tribal laws from touching anything that is associated with modern civilization. Consequently, they have no furniture in their homes —no chairs, no tables, not even a toothbrush, comb or mirror. The Baduis are also against the 'civilized' methods of irrigation for farming. As they believe that the process of irrigation would harm the soil, they depend entirely on God-sent rain. Most surprising, however, is that education itself is taboo to the Baduis.

Yet the Baduis are by no means uncivilized. They have inherited from their ancestors very austere laws of behaviour and moral standards. For instance, a Badui does not normally remarry after his wife dies and will always cherish the memory of her. The Baduis must adhere to a rigid code of ethics somewhat similar to the Ten Commandments. They are one of the most puritanical peoples still living in this world and try truly to make peace with nature. They believe that their God is the only true God.

It was the first time that I came to know about the Baduis, and I began to take an interest in this minority group which had lived in isolation since the advent of Islam to Indonesia. Some time in the year 1523, when the Muslim religion swept into West Java, a group of people, who are believed to be the descendants of the old Kingdom of Pajajaran, refused to be converted to Islam. Now commonly referred to as the Baduis, these people escaped to the mountains, taking with them their own well-preserved religion and way of life. The Baduis, then numbering about 800, were pursued by Sultan Yusof, who became the successful leader of the Religious War, and later by his son, Pangeran Yusuf. The Muslim victors would pardon no one who refused to embrace Islam. So the Baduis retreated to the hills and finally settled down in an area on a mountain called Gunung Badui. Perhaps the name 'Badui' came from the name of the mountain or the near-by river. The Baduis, however, do not like that name, and prefer to be called Orang Kanekes or Orang Rawajan after the names of the villages where they now live.

From the time the Baduis settled down in Rawajan Village, they have isolated themselves from civilization as we know it. As far as they are concerned, life is the same as it was in 1523. The Islamization of Java, followed by the three hundred years of Dutch colonization, and then the fervent Indonesian Revolution did not affect the Baduis. They seemed to show little concern over matters of the outside world. To them, the most important thing was to be left alone to live their own way of life and to ensure that their sacred boundary was not infringed upon. Their zone was officially recognized through treaties with the Sultan of Banten and was later acknowledged by the Dutch Government for more than one hundred years.

Since 1822 Dutch scholars, colonial officials, missionaries and later Indonesian Government officials have from time to time tried to do research on the Baduis. Various reports have been submitted together with recommendations to improve the lot of the Baduis or persuade them to accept certain benefits offered by modern civilization. But the Baduis prefer to remain where they are and what they are. So far, only a very few people from outside have had the privilege of being allowed into Badui Dalam, the inner zone of Badui territory, which is still sacredly guarded. And only a handful of outsiders, including President Suharto, has come face to face with any of the three top chieftains of the Baduis, known as *pu'un*, who have not left the soil of Badui Dalam since they were born. The ardent desire of the Baduis to live in isolation and the strict rules guarding entry into their sacred land, therefore, make the task of research workers immensely difficult.

Most researchers have managed to get only to the outer area of Badui land. Badui Dalam is strictly guarded — not so much by armed guards or vigilante corps, but by natural obstacles. The inner zone, or zone forbidden to outsiders, is surrounded by such dense jungle that it is almost impossible to get even near it. It is commonly believed that the Baduis, particularly the *pu'un* and their *dukun*, have magical powers as well as such keen instincts that they would know immediately whenever a stranger sets foot on the soil of their sacred land. Without first seeking their permission and blessing, it would be dangerous to venture into this zone. The shyness and reticent nature of the Baduis concerning contact with the outside world also contribute to the obstacles encountered by researchers. I myself tried to arrange a visit with the help of several contacts, who had blood ties with the Baduis and even held high positions in the government. But I was not given the green light. I managed, however, to gather some useful information regarding the Baduis by visiting near-by places and interviewing Baduis who had grown up in the inner zone and who had been allowed to go to the outside world as couriers. I have also spoken to Reverend Geise, a Dutch priest, who spent two years living on the border of Badui Dalam and who has lived the best part of his life in Indonesia.

One Badui I met was brought to my Jakarta residence by some friends who were distantly related to the Badui people. I felt honoured to meet Yakmin, an aged Badui who had lived most of his life in Badui Dalam and who claimed to be 170 years of age. If appearances are true indicators of age, I was inclined to believe that Yakmin was 170 years old because I had never seen such a wrinkled face before! He had a white turban round his forehead, leaving his long, curly hair visible from the top. His tiny, oriental eyes were always cast downwards but his occasional glances were sharp and piercing, but friendly. Yakmin spoke freely in a soft voice, now and then smiling shyly as he sipped a glass of cold beer. He told me of his younger days, of the living conditions of Badui Dalam, and of how he had decided to leave the "sacred place meant only for pure souls". When it came to sensitive issues relating to the Badui religion and supernatural practices, Yakmin would say with a polite smile, "I am sorry, we are not allowed to disclose such matters." He spoke in old Sundanese, the language still used in Badui land. My friends, who made the meeting possible, acted as interpreters.

Yakmin was born in the inner Badui zone. He did not attend school for there was no school. The Baduis believe in developing their intuition and acquiring knowledge through natural instincts. Thus no education was considered necessary. In Badui Dalam, there are no shops, no market-places, no cinemas, no clinics, nor anything that is related to modern civilization. There are no churches, mosques or temples, or any building for worship, for they do not need any. The Baduis only worship their ancestors in a sacred place called Arca Domas where, they believe, their ancestors were buried. Through constant meditation, they communicate with the souls of their ancestors to seek inspiration, guidance and advice.

The forbidden land of Badui Dalam consists of three kampongs: Cikeusik, the most sacred in terms of hierarchy, then Cibeo and Cikartawan. There must be only 40 families in the three kampongs at any one time. Whenever the number of families exceeds 40, one of them will have to leave the inner Badui zone. It is the *pu'un* who decides which family should leave. No arbitration or argument is allowed, for the *pu'un's* decision is final.

When someone in the inner zone commits a crime, such as murder, theft or adultery, or violates serious *buyut* (taboos or prohibitions), he is exiled to a place just within or just outside the Badui territory. Each *pu'un* has his own place to keep his exiles: the *pu'un* of Cibeo exiles his undesirables to Ciyulu; the *pu'un* of Cikeusik's place of exile is Cibengkung; and the *pu'un* of Cikartawan's place of exile is Cilenggor. In other words, the exiles are entirely excommunicated from the inner community, but are normally allowed to go through some form of purification to redeem them from their sins.

During purification rituals, the sinner seeks the forgiveness of the everlasting Sun God. A tub containing *sirih* (betel leaves) is offered when asking for pardon; it is also a symbol of purification.

This tub is transported through the three sacred villages, finally reaching the most sacred village of Cikeusik. The sinner therefore receives pardon just before he is exiled to the outer zones.

As one would expect, the *pu'un* of Cikeusik is considered the highest ranking of the three chieftains. However, each *pu'un* is regarded as a descendant of the Badui ancestors who can be traced ultimately to their God Almighty called Batara Tunggal. The *pu'un*, being the descendants of the most sacred God, must not be seen by non-Baduis. As a sign of humility, even ordinary Baduis should not look at the *pu'un* when speaking to him. Whenever a *pu'un* dies, he is succeeded by his own son or, if this is not possible, by a member of the closest family such as a younger brother or a nephew. When a *pu'un* becomes a widower, he has to resign; when he is too old to perform his duties, he can retire but has to abide by certain strict rules, one of which is that he cannot leave the village. On retirement, the *pu'un* acquires the privilege of enjoying his rice ration from the *huma serang*. This is a sacred plot, the rice from which is normally only consumed during harvest festivals.

All Baduis believe that their *pu'un* possess supernatural powers. There are many strange stories about the mystical powers of the *pu'un* and the *dukun* who work under them. One source says the Badui *dukun* and *pu'un* can make themselves disappear like evaporating gas and go to any part of the world. Thus the invention of modern jet planes means nothing to them. This sounds rather ridiculous, but the Baduis firmly believe that their leaders possess such miraculous powers and, therefore, have a fearful respect for the *pu'un* and their decisions. They believe that their chieftains know what is happening throughout the world without even leaving the village. The *pu'un* know when it will rain and can even cause rain when a drought threatens their rice harvest. That is why they do not need modern irrigation.

Yakmin, the 170-year-old Badui, still believed in the mystical powers of his *pu'un*. He believed that when a visitor arrived at the border of the forbidden land, he need only tie a knot in the grass of the sacred soil, and the *pu'un* would get the message of the visitor's arrival.

Yakmin thought that to live a puritanical life was indeed noble. He confessed very humbly that it was too difficult a task for him. There were just too many *buyut* which Yakmin found impossible to observe. For him these included not being allowed to touch money, to smoke a cigarette, to drink wine or to look at a woman with covetous intentions. And above all, there is no entertainment in the modern sense. Thus, some years back Yakmin decided to quit the forbidden land. How did he manage to do it? It was a difficult decision especially as Yakmin was married to the *pu'un's* daughter. Being a law-abiding citizen by Badui standards, he discussed the matter with the *pu'un*, and they finally came to a compromise. Yakmin would accept the job of a courier despite his old age. He would be sent out from time to time to get rations and to act as a liaison officer between the outside world and Badui land. It was an honourable job of trust. As Yakmin described his job, I could not help wondering how he managed to keep up at his age. As a courier, he walked barefooted and at a lively pace by any standard. When I asked him the secret of his strength, he replied with a smile, "There is no secret. It is God's wish. I lead a very simple life." Yakmin has two sons and now lives on the outskirts of Badui land.

Many Baduis today live outside the forbidden zone in 24 villages mostly on the western and northern sides of the inner zone. The small villages are under the administrative control of three heads or *jaro* appointed by the Indonesian Government to preside over the areas of Cisemeut, Cibungar, and Karangcombong.

Speaking more on entertainment, Yakmin said that it is not entirely true to say that there is no form of relaxation in Badui Dalam. He told me about his friend who is deputy *pu'un* in the forbidden land and who plays a kind of string instrument called the *kecapi* of Sundanese origin. It is like the Chinese *ch'in* which is plucked with one's fingers. Whenever his friend played this instrument, the villagers would gather round and entertain themselves with *pantun* (short verses) accompanied by the melodious tone of the *kecapi*. Before the deputy *pu'un* played the instrument, he meditated for a short while. *Kemenyan* was often burnt to invoke the Goddess of Music to enter his soul and he would go into a trance. With his eyes closed, and in a trance, he would relate the history of the 25 Badui kingdoms for two or sometimes three hours in the old Sundanese language whilst playing the *kecapi*. According to Yakmin, there were originally 25 kingdoms but as time went on they were gradually reduced to three. The stories of these kingdoms, normally referred to as *Selawi Negara*, explain the origin of the Orang Rawayan, the Baduis. I asked Yakmin whether the Orang Rawayan had a written record of the *Selawi Negara*. The answer was negative, for the Baduis prohibit the use of writing materials, especially paper which is a product of modern civilization.

To me it seemed a pity that the Badui version of the origin of Orang Rawayan was still unrecorded. So I asked whether it was possible for me to have the music and *pantun* tape-recorded. Yakmin promised to invite me to his house on the outskirts of the forbidden land where he would ask the deputy *pu'un* to play for me. He also promised to try to seek permission to get the whole thing recorded. I waited for several months in vain, as it seems that the *pu'un* would not allow outside visitors even to the outer areas of the forbidden land during the months of April to August.

So far there is still no record of any kind about the history of the Baduis, their origin, religion or customs and traditions. In my conversations with Yakmin and others, I learnt that the Baduis are neither followers of Buddha, nor are they Hindus. Like animists, the Baduis believe in the spirits of their ancestors whom they can contact through meditation. Their supreme God is Batara Tunggal, their original ancestor. *Batara* means 'God' and *Tunggal* means 'the Only'. They believe that when a Badui from Badui Dalam dies, his soul leaves the body and goes straight to Arca Domas, the holy place where their ancestors were buried and where all souls reunite with Batara Tunggal. In the case of Baduis from the outer zone of Badui land, their souls must obtain purification before they can be reunited with Batara Tunggal. To be united with Batara Tunggal in the next world is the ultimate aim of every Badui, for it means eternal peace and happiness. Unlike the Balinese, the Torajans, or the Egyptians, who believe that, as the soul of a person may return to his body, it should be well preserved, the Baduis do not care for the actual corpse. The burial customs of the Baduis are therefore very simple. The bodies are buried without coffins or tombstones and are forgotten after seven days. In fact, the Baduis purposely bury the dead in obscure places without landmarks so that they cannot be easily identified later. Anyway, it would be difficult to find the graves later because they are soon overgrown by thick forest.

To the Baduis, Arca Domas, the sacred home of all souls, lies near the source of the Ciudung River. It consists of thirteen terraces arranged like rocky beds facing south. It is interesting to note that the Torajans also regard the south as the place where the spirits of the dead are found. The first terrace resembles a grave which is considered the spiritual home of Batara Tunggal. It is about two and a half metres high and three-quarters of a metre square. The second terrace is the Lemah Bodas, so named because of the white sand which covers it. (*Lemah* means 'sand' and *bodas*, 'white'). This is the resting place for the spirits of the Baduis from the inner zone. Another terrace is for the Baduis from the outer zone whose souls have undergone purification. Thus, each terrace is classified according to the different categories of spirits.

The name 'Arca Domas' can also be interpreted as having some historical significance. The translation of the two words *Artja* and *Domas* means 'eight hundred', perhaps referring to the 800 staunch Badui ancestors who fled from Islamization and eventually chose Arca Domas as their burial ground. The Baduis today consider it an act of courage to preserve their own religion, culture and way of life as well as a means of purifying their souls.

In order to lead a noble life and die with a pure soul, the Baduis have a strict code of behaviour to maintain moral standards that are high and stringent by any comparison. As I mentioned earlier, the Baduis have a list of *buyut* or taboos somewhat similar to the Ten Commandments. It is taboo to kill one's fellow-man, to steal, to lie, to commit adultery or to be violent. It is also sinful to receive presents or touch money or ride on vehicles. A Badui may not smoke or get drunk. He should never have dinner before dark. He should not wear clothing with colours other than white, blue or black. It is also a sin to sleep on anything except a mat on top of Mother Earth. A Badui should resist the temptation to sing or dance to the accompaniment of music which is considered 'vulgar'.

The number of things which are considered *buyut* runs into many pages. Apart from the *buyut* commandments, which are fundamental, any temptation to enjoy the fruits of modern civilization is also classified as *buyut*. For instance, it is *buyut* to use an iron plough, to cut a tree with a steel saw, or to tend the ground with a *cangkul* (hoe). Strange as it may seem, Badui laws prohibit the rearing of cows, pigs, horses, goats, ducks or even fish in a pond. The breeding of chickens, dogs, and cats is, however, permissible. In the inner forbidden land one can find hardly any of the domestic animals which are so common in the outer Badui zones. They probably have their own reasons for not allowing domestic animals to be reared in the sacred zone.

Of all the *buyut*, the ones that are most disturbing to those who want to help raise the standard of living of the Baduis are the *buyut* against reading and writing and the *buyut* against the use of irrigation for farming. The Baduis would rather develop their instincts and intuitive power through meditation. Education to them means corrupting the mind and contaminating the soul. Reading and writing are unnecessary as folklore, songs and *buyut* are passed down from generation to generation by word of mouth.

Despite the lack of medicine as we know it, the Baduis have great faith in the healing powers of the *pu'un* or *dukun*. A Badui friend of mine told me about the time he went back to Badui land to visit his relatives and took with him a first-aid kit in case of mishap during the long and tedious trek through dense jungle. Fortunately he did not have cause to use it, but when he was staying with his relatives, one of his neighbours accidentally cut his leg whilst chopping wood. My friend rushed to the rescue with his first-aid kit, but was prevented from helping. Instead, a *dukun* was summoned. The *dukun* stood by the patient, mumbled a few words and then applied herbs to the gaping wound. According to my friend, the injured man was back at work as usual the next day. The Baduis have, however, suffered a lot from contagious diseases such as smallpox and tuberculosis. In every family at least half the children die of one of these diseases. The Baduis, nevertheless, continue to fight the diseases with prayers and local medication. They believe that Batara Tunggal decides on life and death and, therefore, decides on the fate of each man. Smallpox is, in fact, considered a favour of Batara Tunggal because the Lord himself has a pock-marked face!

The *buyut* on irrigation is a major problem facing the *bupati* who controls the land adjoining the territories of the inner Badui zone. He is naturally eager to see an improvement in the yield of rice at harvest time. But engineers find it difficult to implement any irrigation scheme where the water supply must cut across the inner zone of Badui land. Until today, the jurisdiction over the territories of the inner zone of Badui land is entirely in the hands of the *pu'un*. And the Indonesian authorities have chosen to leave the Baduis alone to lead their own way of life in Badui Dalam. This, once again, is characteristic of the Indonesian spirit of cultural and religious tolerance.

Because of the *buyut* against irrigation, the Badui rice fields are dry, yielding a type of 'dry climate' rice. The staple diet of the Baduis consists mainly of natural foods—rice, vegetables, eggs, wild honey and coconuts. The rice-planting and harvesting times, therefore, call for special rituals to express thanksgiving for their continued food supply and their survival.

Rice is always planted first in the *huma serang* of the *pu'un*, as ordinary Baduis are not allowed to plant their rice before the *pu'un*. Preparations start around the nineteenth day of the seventh moon when the field is cleared. The actual planting begins when the constellation *kidang* (Orion) appears in the late evening sky. All members of the village sit cross-legged in the field while the *tukang melak* (master of ceremonies) chants, "Nyi Pohatji Sang Hiang Sri Laksmi" (May the young seeds survive and thrive, Goddess of Fertility). At day-break, *angklung* (West Javanese bamboo musical instrument) players accompany the *tukang melak* to the *huma* (field for dry rice cultivation). When they reach the plot, the music stops as the group solemnly approaches the *pungpuhanam*, a small bamboo cottage where the goddess Dewi Sari dwells. The *tukang melak* then takes some betel nut to chew and spits the juice at the sticks to be used for rice-planting. To mark the start of the planting season, the *tukang melak* finally takes a stained stick, digs a hole and plants two seeds of rice. After this ceremony, called *mitembej melak*, a representative from each Badui family assists in sowing the field.

The harvest festival is celebrated during the so-called *kawalu* month, but before the festival, the Baduis fast. The *pu'un* retires to Ci Simut, a cave near the source of the Ciudung River and meditates for three days and three nights, waiting for a message from Batara Tunggal, the Supreme God. When he has received the message, he will go hunting, taking along just one arrow. Invariably he comes across a deer. When the *pu'un* aims his arrow, the deer will remain spell-bound so that the arrow is shot straight through its heart. The deer is slaughtered and the feast begins. The festive food includes varieties of *ketan* (glutinous rice), such as *ketan siang, ketan putri, ketan buis* and *ketan lideung*. The festive *ketan* is served with venison, carp, squirrel meat, scorpion and cricket. During the feast, the Baduis rejoice and shout gaily as a sign that Batara Tunggal has given his blessing for them to enjoy the fruits of their labour. In the evening, they relax and sing to the accompaniment of the *kecapi*.

Following the *kawalu* festival is another festival named *laksa*, after a kind of compressed rice-flour. The *laksa* is distributed to everyone who has helped with the crop. The festival is started off by women who stamp on the rice contained in big *dangka* (square wooden containers) and make it into flour. Seven women are specially selected to knead and compress the flour in the *laksa* cottage.

To a certain extent, the Badui philosophy of life with regard to distribution of wealth in relation to each individual's contribution rather resembles that of a socialist system. In Badui Dalam, no one is allowed to own land or accumulate wealth. The urge to accumulate wealth and money is taboo. Everyone's reward is measured by his or her labour or contribution. In a society which has to depend on dry rice cultivation, idleness cannot be tolerated. This is another aspect of Badui society and its economy which is worthy of proper research.

Researchers are still working on the mystery of the origin of the Baduis just as they are trying to predict the future of these people.

The Baduis themselves, however, are quite content with the following legend explaining their origin and the founding of the three villages of Badui Dalam.

During the coming of Islam, the King of Pajajaran and his followers, who refused to be converted, fled to the hills. The king was looking for a safe place to resettle his people. In order to search further, he turned himself into a bird called *beo* and flew into the sky. When the bird flew across the Kendeng Mountain Range, he looked down and found the water in the Ciudung River sparkling and clear. The sand was white and the area rather fertile. The bird went down to the river's edge, took off his wings, and started to drink from the stream. As soon as the bird's beak touched the water, the King of Pajajaran was transformed back to his original self, so he decided to settle down there, naming the place Cibeo. Later he looked for another favourable site for his followers. He chose a site with white sand and called it Cikeusik. Then he found a site fertile enough for farming and called it Cikartawan which means 'a forest which is rich and fertile'.

I had an interesting talk with Romo Budi, a prominent mystic in Central Java, who had been to Badui Dalam. He thought the Baduis were the original Javanese before the arrival of any religion from outside Java. I found the comments made by Reverend Geise rather convincing. In his opinion the Baduis were the original Sundanese before the arrival of Islam. One sound argument is that the Baduis still use the old Sundanese language. He felt that a study of the Badui way of life, their religious beliefs, and so on would enable one to have a deeper understanding of the old ways of life and beliefs of the ancient Sundanese.

Whatever research unfolds in connection with the origin of the Baduis, it is equally interesting to keep track of their future. One naturally wonders how long the Baduis of Badui Dalam can resist the influence of modern civilization or even how long this small group of people will survive in isolation. According to a census conducted by Pennings, a Dutchman, there were 184 Baduis in the inner zone in 1888. This number was reduced to 156 in 1908 and to 140 by 1928. As tradition dictates, the number of families in Badui Dalam must not exceed 40. As more Baduis are slowly lured by modern civilization to the outer zone, it is inevitable that they will gradually mix freely with people of other races, cultures and religions just as Yakmin has.

I asked Yakmin what he treasured most in his long life of 170 years. Surprisingly, his reply was "money"! But he went on to explain, "I need money to provide education, proper sanitation and welfare facilities for my people." Despite Yakmin's noble intentions, it seems unlikely that the Baduis of the inner zone would appreciate his efforts at this stage. This is because President Suharto himself made an offer, as a sincere gesture, to upgrade their standard of living and to provide educational facilities. For the first time in history, the *pu'un* ventured out to meet the President when he visited the outer zone. The visit was well received by both sides, but the Baduis have still not taken up the offer of assistance. As the authorities have no intention of interfering with the traditional way of life of the Baduis, the *pu'un* are still permitted to rule their sacred territory as they wish.

Unlike the Baduis who had to flee for their lives in order to preserve their religion when Islam came, the Tenggerese in East Java were left alone to preach their Hindu-Brahma religion unaffected by the advent of Islam. They are called Tenggerese because they live in the Tengger mountains. In Tengger today there are some 40 villages scattered along the valleys between the famous volcano Gunung Bromo, which rises 2,000 metres above sea-level, and Gunung Semeru, which reaches a height of 3,680 metres. During the rule of the Hindu Majapahit Empire, believers of Lord Brahma worshipped on the famous volcanic mountain of Bromo and went there to meditate. They believed that it was a sacred place where Lord Brahma dwelt and where he could be contacted through meditation. The word 'Bromo' sounds like 'Brahma' and it could therefore be a corrupted version of 'Brahma'. The worship of Mount Bromo is recorded in the inscription of King Hayam Wuruk of the Majapahit Empire. The Hindu kings encouraged their supporters to settle down on Gunung Bromo and gave them special privileges such as exemption from taxes. The idea was to make Gunung Bromo the centre of worship of God Brahma. It was perhaps due to their harmless, self-imposed isolation and the dangerous distance that discouraged the Muslim invaders, who decided to leave the Tenggerese alone.

For centuries the Tenggerese went about their own way of life, worshipping their own gods, and showing little interest in what was going on in the outside world. However, unlike the Baduis, the Tenggerese do not isolate themselves completely from civilization. Instead, they welcome outsiders to visit their villages and share the wonderful experiences provided by breath-taking mountain scenery, especially when one views the surroundings from the top of Gunung Bromo.

The word 'Tengger' is a combination of two words, *teng* taken from Roro Anteng, a girl's name, and *ger* from Joko Seger, a man's

name. According to local legend, Roro Anteng and Joko Seger
were a happily married young couple living near a vast expanse of
sand which led down to the sea. The couple produced no offspring
and as years went by, their happiness turned to sorrow. So they
prayed to the God of the Sea that they be blessed with twenty-five
children and promised to sacrifice one of them as a token of their
gratitude. Time passed by quickly, and one child after another
was born, giving the couple untold happiness. When the twenty-
fifth child was born they were so thrilled that they forgot their
pledge to the God of the Sea. Consequently, the whole village was
plagued by an epidemic, and people began to die. One night, as
Joko Seger sat worrying about the fate of his village, a vision came
to him and reminded him of his oath. He immediately gathered
his twenty-five children and asked each of them, from the eldest
downwards, whether anyone of them would be prepared to sacrifice
his life to save the village. None was prepared to be the victim
except the youngest boy by the name of Kusuma. Joko Seger
embraced and caressed his son, and with tears in his eyes carried
him towards the sea to offer the boy to the God of the Sea. Before
he had quite reached the sea, Joko Seger left the boy, Kusuma, on
the sandy beach and returned home. Almost immediately a volcano
erupted, giving rise to Gunung Bromo, the crater of which now
resembles the surface of a sea.

Till this day, in order to commemorate the brave sacrifice made
by Kusuma and to pacify the god of the volcano, the Tenggerese
climb Gunung Bromo and throw offerings into the crater. On the
fourteenth day of the tenth moon each year, thousands trek in an
ant-like stream, some on foot and others on horseback, to Bromo,
bringing with them offerings of rice, sweets, chickens and goats.
They also bring with them thick blankets to pass the night which
is as cold as a European winter. Some of them go via Tosari to
Wonotoro and then on foot up the mountain. Others go through
Ngadisari and then continue on horseback. Either way, the journey
to the crater's edge covers about 12 kilometres. The ceremony
begins in the early hours of the morning. Led by the priest, the
devotees encircle the crater on foot. As they walk, prayers are
chanted, sometimes accompanied by *gamelan* music. This ceremony,
called the *Kasada* festival, is an important event and a sacred day
for all Tenggerese, young or old. Everyone, unless seriously ill,
makes an effort to climb to the top and gives offerings to gain
peace of mind as well as blessings from their God. It is also an
occasion to test new *dukun*. At dawn, the new recruits go through
a test and, if they succeed, earn their new social status.

There is every reason for the Tenggerese to pay homage to their powerful god whom they believe once dwelt in the sea and now inside the volcano. Whenever sulphurous clouds rise and Bromo rumbles, the Tenggerese murmur, "The God of Fire is hungry", or "The God of Fire is angry". Indeed, the wrath of the god was witnessed in 1930 when Gunung Bromo last erupted.

The Tenggerese seem to have forgotten the origin of their ancestors. Myth has proved to have a stronger influence than historical reality. Like the Baduis, the Tenggerese are proud of their own religion which is a mixture of both Hinduism and Buddhism plus elements peculiar to their culture alone. Like the Baduis, the Tenggerese do not have a specific name for their religion. They call their god Bumi Truka Sanghiang Dewata Batur and their bible, Panglawu. They prefer to be referred to as Kejavans, that is, followers of the original religion of Java. Unlike the Balinese, who also originally fled from the Islamization of Java, the Tenggerese do not practise cremation of their dead. Their wedding customs are also more similar to those of the Javanese. Generally, the Tenggerese way of life is similar to that of the Samins, who are advocates of *Kebatinan*.

The Tenggerese live in peculiarly built, double-storey wooden huts quite unlike houses elsewhere in Java. The houses, mostly green and white, are not shaded by trees but are built on spacious open terraces. The door of each house is situated at the end of the building opposite the fire-place. The Tenggerese regard their brick fire-places as sacred, and strangers are warned not to touch them.

The head of the village is called *petinggi* (the word *tinggi* means 'high') and he is assisted by a *kabayan*. Both of them are elected by the villagers. A village has four priests, or *dukun*, who look after the archives and sacred tribal writings inscribed on *lontar*. They tell of the Tenggerese concept of the world, the attributes of their deity, and prescribe the forms of worship to be observed on religious occasions. The *petinggi* and the *dukun* have lost track of the origin of the Tenggerese, but consider it their duty to pass on to their children and grandchildren the sacred books in order to perpetuate the traditions and culture of their ancestors.

The customs and rituals of the Tenggerese relating to events of life such as birth, marriage and death are different from those of the Balinese, the Baduis or the Trungenese, all of whom shared a common fate when Islam came to Java. When a wedding takes place, the bride and bridegroom are brought before the *dukun*. They first bow to the south, then to the fire-place, then to the earth, and lastly upwards to the first floor of the building where the tools for farming are kept. After bowing to the *dukun* and the elders, the bride washes the feet of the bridegroom. An exchange of gifts takes place when the ceremony ends. The gifts can include krises, buffaloes, farm tools, or betel leaves. The marriage is not consummated till the fifth day after the ceremony. This interval is called *undang mantu* (inviting a son-in-law), a custom which is still observed in many parts of Java. It is interesting to note that in present-day Javanese weddings, the bride also washes the feet of the bridegroom, but he first breaks an egg with his right foot.

The burial ceremony of the Tenggerese has special features of its own. The corpse is lowered into the grave with the head facing south; this is contrary to the direction observed by Muslims. The corpse is covered with bamboo and planks and does not come into contact with earth at all. When the grave is finally covered with sand, two posts are placed upright over the body. Resting horizontally on the posts is a length of hollow bamboo. For seven successive days this bamboo is watered with clean water which is considered to be holy. Offerings of two dishes are made to the deceased. At the end of the seventh day, a feast is held for relatives and friends and a fully-clothed dummy of the deceased, adorned with a garland, is erected in a prominent place. The *dukun* chants *mantra* and sprinkles water over the feast. After the ceremony, the clothes of the deceased are distributed to the relatives and friends who then gather round to eat. No more solemnities are observed until a thousand days later.

There is no stipulation of punishment against crimes such as adultery, theft or cheating, for such sins do not exist in the peaceful land of Tengger. When a man commits a sin, a subtle reproach by the *petinggi*, the village chief, is sufficient embarassment and punishment. The Tenggerese are an honest, industrious and happy people with high moral standards. It is known that one can leave one's doors open day and night without fear. Theft, gambling or drug abuse is unheard of.

An impression of Lake Toba, the largest mountain-lake in Asia.

A bird's eye impression of Tangkuban Prahu, the volcano that looks like a capsized boat, in West Java.

A Dhani village in Wamena, West Irian.

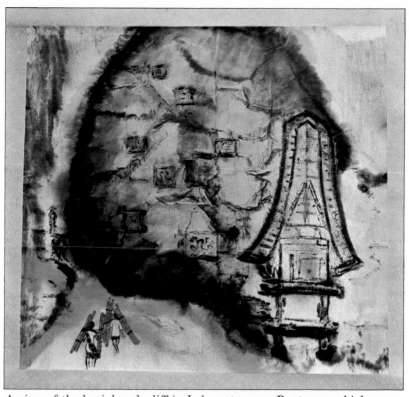

A view of the burial rock-cliff in Lokomata, near Rantepao, which seems to have 'eyes'.

The poor Torajan's burial ground is a huge cave at Londa. ▶

A village scene near Tampak Siring, Bali.

An impression of the Klenteng Sampo at Semarang.

The fury of a cockfight in Bali.

8

The Kris
and
the Gem

Java is a land of mysticism. It is common belief that after a person has passed away, his spirit, whether good or evil, will *numpang* (take a ride or seek temporary accommodation) in worldly objects such as the banyan tree, the kris, the gem or other heirlooms. Such materials inhabited by spirits are called *pusaka*.

Of all the *pusaka*, the most popular is the kris, or dagger. He is a rare Javanese who does not possess a kris. On ceremonial occasions, a Javanese always wears a kris tucked in his belt. A person who has studied the kris would know at a glance the status of the person wearing it, for there are krises symbolizing higher status which can be worn only by people of high standing. It is believed that the kris knows where to look for its master. A sacred kris, for instance, will never fall into the hands of a common man. If a person gets a kris which is not *cocok* (befitting) to him, he will feel uneasy, and sometimes misfortune may befall him.

The Javanese kris is a slender dagger with a fine blade. It is mounted preferably in a handle made of gold, ivory and precious stones and encased in a sheath of beautifully carved and polished wood. The blade is either straight or wavy and is sharp along both edges. When the blades are being forged, the steel is first made white hot before being hammered and shaped. It is then tempered in rice-water to blacken the metal so that delicate and fine engravings can be seen effectively.

The finest krises are made in Central Java on the outskirts of Jogjakarta. The master craftsmen, who flourished during the days of the Majapahit Empire, were not only expert metal workers but also *kyai* (mystics). On completion of a kris, the mystic crafts-man would mumble magical words into the kris to give it mystical powers. In the past, some *dukun* even resorted to sacrificing a beautiful maiden so that her soul could enter the kris. The kris is said to have added mystical powers if it has tasted the blood of an enemy. When I visited a Javanese friend, he took his kris down from the wall and showed it to me. When I attempted to pull the kris out of the sheath, he stopped me. "Please don't do that," he said, "for if the blade leaves the sheath, it looks for blood and I have to cut my own hand or anything that produces blood to satisfy its need." The kris he possessed had been in many battles during the Indonesian Revolution. Now he has to tend it every week by burning *kemenyan*, otherwise the kris will lose its power and may even bring bad luck.

The kris is designed to inflict maximum injury on an enemy. The wavy blade opens a wound that is wider than the blade itself, and can even pierce through bones of the body. In fact, mystics believe that the kris need not even touch an enemy to cause harm. They believe that a powerful kris need only be pointed at the enemy from a distance and the man would die of an incurable illness. They also believe that a mystical kris can move, speak, swim in deep seas or fly over mountains to attack the enemy. Sometimes a kris would vanish, later to return to the owner after performing its job.

I personally witnessed a 'flying kris' demonstration one evening when I visited Wonogiri, a village in Central Java. Through the introduction of Mr Anada Surjono, we met a police officer, Pak Musnadi, who claimed that he could invoke the spirit of his dead father to make a kris fly. Out of curiosity, we requested a demonstration.

The demonstration took place at night in a Muslim cemetery about 30 kilometres from Wonogiri. When we arrived, we had to use a torchlight to find the way to the grave where Pak Musnadi's father was buried. As I sat down with the others on a mat in front of the grave, watching as the necessary offerings were made to the spirit, my eyes wandered, but there was nothing to see except the stars twinkling in the dark sky. As usual, *kemenyan* was burnt and everyone had to sprinkle flowers over the grave. Musnadi

On ceremonial occasions, the Javanese always wear their krises tucked in their belts.

Pak Musnadi performing the 'miracle' of the flying kris at his father's grave.

meditated and prayed, then mumbled some words in Javanese to invoke the soul of his dead father. Then there was a long wait. As mosquitoes hummed about our ears and our feet grew numb, Musnadi explained to us how his deceased father had given him the power of making a kris fly. Before his father died several years ago, he willed that his most precious *pusaka* be buried beside him in the grave. He also instructed that someone in the family should watch over the grave for at least forty days and forty nights. Musnadi was the only son who took the trouble to carry out his father's will.

As he was watching over the grave one night, he begged his deceased father to bestow on him some magical powers. It was then that he was inspired to make a kris fly and, indeed, found that he was able to cause his kris to fly. However, he explained that it was not actually his power that would make the kris fly but the power of the soul of his father.

A sudden spark of green light from the darkness of the woods interrupted Musnadi's story and he asked everyone to be silent for the spirit had arrived. He proceeded to perform the ceremony of encircling a sacred spot to the accompaniment of tape-recorded Javanese music. Musnadi explained that the sacred spot was a demarcated cosmic sphere where the spirits hovered, although not visible to the human eye.

After the ceremony, a kris was placed within the cosmic sphere and Musnadi asked everyone to examine it. He explained that the invoked soul of his father would make the kris fly to his garden some 30 kilometres away. To ensure that it would be the same kris that would land in his garden, I suggested that a piece of paper with my signature on it be stuck to the tip of the kris. Musnadi agreed to my suggestion. Everyone waited with excitement when suddenly white and greenish lights began to flicker from the dark spot where the kris was placed. Suddenly Musnadi announced that the kris had flown away and asked us to examine the dark spot where the kris had been. We scrutinized the spot and found the kris missing. I asked Musnadi why we were not allowed to see the kris flying. He replied that the glare of the beam of light radiating from the kris would be so strong that it might blind us. He claimed that once, when he was experimenting with the art, a chicken walked past and was instantly killed by the rays.

Some time was wasted chatting at the graveyard about the kris that had disappeared. Then Musnadi decided to repeat the feat with another kris before going back to his house. When we finally got to Musnadi's house, we saw the two krises stuck in a banana tree. I examined the one which I had marked with paper and found the paper missing. It was later found inside a cupboard in Musnadi's bedroom. I asked Musnadi how the paper got into his cupboard and he explained apologetically that the kris was confused by the piece of paper and went into his bedroom first and then went out through the window to the banana tree.

It had indeed been a most interesting experience for me. My friend, Hartadji, who accompanied me, is convinced that the kris actually flew, for he later took the trouble to have the piece of paper examined by a medium in Solo who said the piece of paper contained radiation.

There are many legendary tales about the kris. The most popular one is that of the Pasopati Kris, the most powerful kris in Java's history. The story tells of King Kajamojoyo who was kind and brave. He possessed a kris that had extraordinary powers of conquest. During wars, he always led his people to the front-line and his kris never let him down. News about the magic kris soon reached an evil monster. One day, when the King was taking a nap under a tree, the monster arrested him, locked him up and took away his magic kris. As the King had lost his kris, his whole kingdom fell. One night in the prison cell, the King had a dream. A voice from above told him that he would one day obtain a kris more powerful than the one he had lost. Soon after, he heard another voice and it was the voice of a lady giving him the same message. The King recalled his dream so often that he became ill. Seeing that the King was about to die, the evil monster took pity on him and agreed to release him on the condition that the people in his kingdom surrendered all their weapons. The people agreed and their King was released and soon recovered from his illness.

One day, when the King was conducting a Cabinet meeting with his Ministers, an old man by the name of Pasopati came along and sought audience with the King. He looked like the person whom the King saw in his dream. Pasopati told the King and his Cabinet members not to worry, for the King would soon get a more powerful kris to defeat the enemy. The Cabinet Ministers laughed at him and, in fact, put him in jail for spreading false information.

Not long afterwards, the Queen gave birth to a son who had a golden kris tied to his left hand. The King realized that the old man had spoken the truth and ordered that he be brought before him. When Pasopati was brought to the King, he was about to die. His last words were that the King should believe in Islam and that the kris should only be used for protection. The King felt very sorry and named the kris, Pasopati. He eventually used the kris, which was almighty, to defeat the evil monster.

Pasopati happened to be the first man who embraced Islam in the country. The Pasopati Kris has therefore helped to spread the teaching of Islam.

Another mystical tale by Junan Giri was about the kris belonging to a Muslim king whose kingdom was surrounded by the powerful forces of Majapahit. The king was writing when the news came and he became so angry that he threw the pen to the floor. The pen turned into a kris, went flying to the battle-field, killed the enemies, and returned to the king. Stories of magic krises are numerous and are passed down from generation to generation. They may seem incomprehensible to some, but are not taken lightly by the Indonesians.

My friend Mr R.T. Hardjonegoro, alias Goh Teck Suan, the *bupati* of the *kraton* of Surakarta, showed me several precious and historical krises when I visited his home in Solo. Hardjonegoro is of Chinese descent but does not speak any Chinese dialects. He has been completely absorbed into the Javanese way of life and culture so much so that he has become related to the royal family. One of his krises, which belonged to Pakubuwono VII, is carved like a dragon with seven curves along its blade. The carving is etched in gold, and the seven curves signify that Pakubuwono was the seventh descendant of the throne. It took the craftsman twenty-eight years to finish this magnificent kris. The king was so impressed that he ordered seven more of the same design. According to Hardjonegoro, there are only three left in Indonesia. The other four were presented to foreign dignitaries: one is now in the hands of Emperor Hirohito of Japan, one with a descendant of Mussolini, the dictator of Italy during World War II, one with the King of Sweden and the other in the collection of the Queen of Holland. It was a tradition in the past for kings and noblemen to order a number of krises to be made with specific designs to commemorate their reign and to derive magical powers. There are many shops all over Indonesia selling krises, but it is believed that a kris bought from a shop loses its magical significance. To be *pusaka*, a kris must be given by someone and not bought.

Apart from the kris, the other *pusaka* popular among the Javanese are precious stones. In any market-place in Jakarta or Central Java, there are stall-keepers and itinerant pedlars displaying an assortment of polished and unpolished stones of little or no intrinsic value. They are mounted on the spot into rings which may cost the buyer only a few hundred rupiahs. It is not the value of the stone that matters but its mystical and spiritual connotation which the Javanese believe in. Most Javanese wear rings with stones of a variety of shapes and colours. It is not uncommon to see *becak* (trishaw) drivers, waiters and ordinary workmen wearing rings displaying their favourite stones.

Gemstones are generally appreciated for their beauty and value, but rarely are they treated with such reverence as they are in Indonesia. Like the kris, the gemstone is preferably acquired as a gift. Elderly people warn that if the spirit that dwells in a stone does not befit you, it may bring bad luck, bad health, and even harm. Some people consult the mystics for advice before wearing a certain stone. They believe that each stone has its own *dzin* or spirit dwelling in it and therefore must be examined for its suitability to its new owner.

Modern science confirms that each mineral has its specific radiation which can affect one's skin or even endanger one's health. Some stones have become famous or infamous in the course of history. The jewels from the Russian Imperial Crown, scattered throughout the world, each seemed to bring disaster. The Black Prince's ruby in the British Imperial State Crown is second to none for its romantic history. Other stones have gained the reputation of having peculiar or mystical properties. The amethyst is said to prevent nervous tension and drunkenness; the black opal is said to cause tragedy to certain wearers; jade is said to darken its colour if worn continuously.

In Indonesia, belief in the mystical properties of gems and stones is still very strong. There are so many beliefs related to specific stones that it is impossible to list them all. So I shall confine myself to the more popular ones.

The *tapak jalak* is a stone with the design of a bird's footprint which looks like a cross. (*Tapak* means 'footprint' and *jalak* is a kind of bird.) This stone is much sought after by policemen and soldiers who believe that wearing the *tapak jalak* will make one strong and powerful and will help attain one's goals.

The *kendit*, a stone with one or more circles, helps to protect the wearer against danger especially attack by enemies.

The *suleiman* has an eye-like design which is supposed to be King Solomon's eye. Wearing this stone on your finger helps you to think clearly and justly. It is believed that the stone will bring the wearer better prospects of promotion.

The *benteng* has a square-like design resembling a fort. It is supposed to give protection against almost anything.

The *cempaka* is a stone with the colour of the *cempaka*

flower, the *michelia champaca* in Latin. The Javanese believe that the wearer of *cempaka* will lead a happy, romantic life.

The *jahman* is a brownish, black stone. It is an extraordinary stone which is always in great demand, for it is believed to contain special magical powers to protect the wearer from danger. It also brings good luck.

The *krong buntut* looks like an unopened clam and is said to bring success in business.

The *musika* is pink and resembles the seed of the pomegranate fruit. It is said to provide eternal youth and protection from evil spirits. The Trungenese of Bali consider it a sacred stone which they insert into the mouth of a deceased person to help preserve the body and ensure the soul's smooth passage to heaven.

The *krishna dana* is a family of colourful stones of shades of blue, black, grey and violet. They help to fulfil one's wishes.

The *ngagah satru* is a rare stone and therefore more expensive. It keeps away enemies.

The *mirah pingaseh* is another expensive stone, keenly sought after by the Don Juans who wish to attract young ladies. This stone is also known as the Ruby of Love.

In the higher circles of society, one often hears stories about expensive stones. The most talked about and sought after stone is the *buntut mustika*, a big, black magic stone obtained from the anus of a special breed of insect in Banjarmasin, Kalimantan. It is found in one out of a million of such insects. The *buntut mustika* provides the wearer with protection from evil spirits, brings him good luck, fortune and position. It is also used for its medicinal properties by dipping the stone in a glass of water for the sick to drink.

I also learnt of the huge, 'sacred' black stone found in a village called Cibinong close to Bogor in West Java. The stone is consulted on matters of mythology, astrology and the weather, such as, will there be rain or sunshine tomorrow. One gets the answer by lifting the stone. If it is light there will be sunshine, but if it is heavy there will be rain. Many people still go to Cibinong to consult the stone on various mystical matters.

9

The Wayang

A good leader has to be like the
Earth, bearing the burden of the planet;
Sun,   giving warmth without expecting
        anything in return;
Moon,   giving joy and comfort to all;
Stars, maintaining high ideals to serve
        mankind;
Ocean, great and therefore broad-minded;
Fire,   fierce but just;
Wind,   knowing the aspirations of the
        people;
Water, giving knowledge to all who thirst
        for it.

verse by a *dalang*

The first time I saw a Javanese shadow-play, known as *wayang kulit*, was in Jogjakarta in 1955 during my holidays after a hectic week in Bandung covering the Afro-Asian Conference. It was my first experience with the *wayang*, and I must confess my impression was that of a jumble of leather puppets casting mysterious shadows on a white screen. The performance was in a dimly-lit village near an old *kraton*. The reverberating sound of the *gamelan*, accompanied by dreamy sounds of the Javanese violin and a pot-pourri of other unfamiliar sounds, attracted me to the place. A single oil-lamp flickered overhead, casting a hemisphere of pale yellowish light. It drew darting reflections from the gongs and the lacquered stands of the *gamelan* orchestra. The soothing and harmonious rhythm of the *gamelan* music was interrupted by harsh and soft voices of the spectators who milled round. Vendors of sweets, balloons, pin-wheels, cigarettes, ice-cream, and vile-coloured soft-drinks circulated among the spectators, screeching their wares. Beyond the *gamelan*, at the base of the white screen, the *dalang* — puppeteer, story-teller, and philosopher all in one, whose magic touch brings shadows to life — sat cross-legged on the stone floor of the pavilion. To the left and right of him was an array of lacy, coloured buffalo-skin puppets, some taller and others shorter, some handsome with slim and refined bodies whilst others were ugly and gigantic. There were also some funny-looking clowns with distorted features. The *dalang*, who was an old man dressed in sarong and wearing a headgear, started to chant his recital in Javanese, first wishing the people a prosperous and peaceful state. He turned on the oil-lamp, the symbol of eternal life, and raised a large, triangular leather puppet to the middle of the screen to indicate that the performance was about to begin. This figure, which is called the *gunungan*, is an intricately cut, beautiful sheet of leather. Its upper half shows the branches of the tree of life. At the centre is a red-faced demon with a protruding tongue. Monkeys climb about the branches and cat-like creatures sharpen their claws. Snakes crawl about and fight with other animals. Surrounding the branches are blossoms, birds spreading their wings, peacocks displaying their tails, and insects flying. My Javanese friend explained to me that the tree of life represented the world of nature created by God. He then went on to point out the lower parts of the *gunungan* and their significance. Below the red-faced demon is a house with a pyramid-shaped roof and curved eaves. The elaborately decorated doors are locked and are guarded on both sides by two ferocious-looking dwarfed giants holding huge clubs. On the roof-tops are two cannons guarding the house which represents the personal life of man. The two weapon-carrying dwarfed giants symbolize punishment for wrong-doings and evil thoughts. As a whole, the theme of the *gunungan* depicts man having to master his longing for food and his carnal desires before he is able to attain perfection of the soul. The distractions and obstacles to perfection are symbolized by monkeys and other animals which obstruct the way in the search for inner peace of mind, which is hidden away behind the closed doors. It is not easy to get there because of the many distractions, obstacles and temptations. The *gunungan* as a whole is somewhat of a tapestry of life, interweaving the real and mythical, with God Almighty determining all activities in the Universe.

As I sat enthralled, listening to the explanation of the significance of the *gunungan*, the flame of the oil-lamp flickered in the breeze and the punched leather puppets cast their shadows in a quivering manner across the screen. The voice of the *dalang* floated through the thin muslin screen, narrating the introduction to the *Maha-bharata*, the great Hindu epic which for centuries has championed the victory of good over evil in India and then in Indonesia. Adapted to a Javanese setting with Javanese characters, the Hindu *Mahabharata* relates the story of the endless war and intrigues that went on between the Pandawas and the Kurawas over the power of the throne.

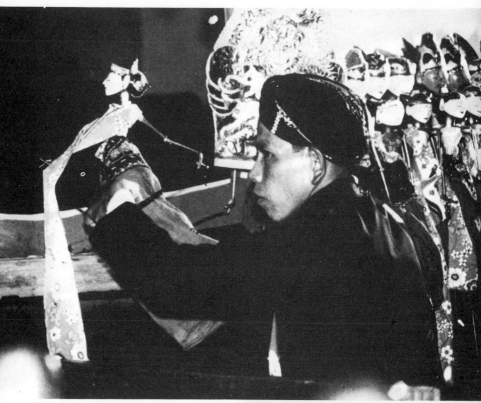

The *dalang* manipulating the *wayang kulit* puppets behind the screen.

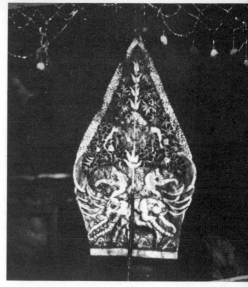

The elaborately designed *gunungan* is used to indicate the beginning and end of a *wayang* show.

Once upon a time, Prabu Abjasa ruled the great kingdom of Ngastina with justice, peace and prosperity. Yet the King had a secret sorrow. His three sons were invalids. The eldest, Drestarata, was blind; the second, Pandu, was an albino; and the third, Widura, was incurably lame. When the King abdicated due to old age, he named Pandu his successor because it would be difficult for Drestarata, the blind elder brother, to rule. The throne was handed over, however, on the condition that it would later revert to Drestarata's line. However, Pandu, once crowned sovereign King, was entitled to nominate his own successor and it was feared that he would not abide by the condition. This was the origin of the bitter feud between the sons of Drestarata who were referred to as the Kurawas and the sons of Pandu, called the Pandawas. The Kurawas consisted of 99 boys and one girl and the Pandawas, only five in number, all boys. Most of the theme centres around the five Pandawas and their feuds with their Kurawa cousins. The eldest of the five Pandawas was Prabu Judistira, who was a humble aristocrat, who never raised his voice in anger and never said no to anyone, a passionless inward-looking intellectual who spent most of his time in meditation. The second Pandawa, Wrekudara, more popularly known as Bima, was a most feared warrior, hot-headed and impulsively brave, who created havoc with his terrible club and atrocious fingernails (the *pancanaka*). But he was honest, loyal and truthful. The third was handsome, romantic Arjuna, who was tender-hearted, yet iron-willed, a hero whose romantic episodes with his wives and mistresses filled the many pages of the *Mahabharata*. And yet he was capable of extreme discipline and self-denial and had a deep feeling of loyalty for his family. The other two younger brothers, who were the twins Nangkula and Sadewa, born to Pandu's second wife, were less popular and less known.

On the death of their father, the Pandawas were still small children and were left to the care of their blind uncle, Drestarata, who became regent till their maturity. Both the Kurawas and Pandawas were brought up together at Ngastina, and from the very beginning the cousins were in constant bitter rivalry. Through trickery, the Kurawas usurped their position and forced the Pandawas to flee. For many years they roamed the forests, befriending all creatures and in the meantime acquiring strength and spiritual power through meditation and privation. In the cultivation of their land, the Pandawas were helped by the monkey Hanuman, the elephant Lakubanda, the griffin Waneya, the serpent Basuki and the giant Jayah Wreka. They built a magnificent palace and crowned Judistira king and called their kingdom, Ngamarta. The Pandawas attracted many people to settle down there because of their wise and humane rule. The popularity of the kingdom of Ngamarta brought about the jealousy of the Kurawas who tricked Judistira into gambling away his kingdom. Once again the Pandawas were forced to roam in lonely poverty through the woods and mountains, attended as always by their faithful servant-clowns called *panakawan*, such as Semar, Gareng, and Petruk. Whenever the Pandawas were in trouble, Semar and the others were around to give them comfort and assistance. When the Pandawas became strong again with the help of one of their cousins, Kresna, who was the reincarnation of the mighty Vishnu, they negotiated for a partition of the kingdom of Ngamarta into two on the basis of peaceful co-existence. The Kurawas not only turned down the request but also tried to assassinate Kresna who was sent as the envoy of the Pandawas. That led to frequent confrontation leading ultimately to a settlement by the last war known as the Bharatajudha Jayabinangun, the Bharatajudha War.

The war ended in pure slaughter. The Kurawas fled from Arjuna's magic arrows, and Bima's club destroyed the eldest and most powerful of the Kurawas, Suyudana, together with his 98 brothers. In the last episode, Bima tore to pieces the slanderous mouth of Sakuni, the cunning Chief Minister of the Kurawa regime, with his thumbnail. The war was over. The Pandawas got back their kingdom of Ngastina and Ngamarta, but their splendour had gone. The Pandawas were tired of war as their sons had been killed in the battles. After a long and beneficent reign, the Pandawas abdicated and wandered about in search of truth.

It was a long story which went on until the early hours of the morning. The *dalang* imparted so much life into the puppets that we forgot that we were watching only shadows. The Javanese spectators were quite acquainted with the stories of the *Maha-bharata*. They liked to hear the jokes of Semar, to see the mighty warrior Bima using his *kuku pancanaka* (thumbnail) tearing the cunning Sakuni into pieces, and they were always fascinated by the romantic adventures of the refined Arjuna. Apart from the excitement, the people went to the *wayang* to gain wisdom and insight, and peace of mind. When Arjuna was being groomed to be a good leader, the *dalang*, imitating the low voice of a *guru* (teacher) said, "To be a knight or a good leader, one must have a strong mind and character to bear troubles and sorrows, just as the earth has to bear everything which exists on the surface of the planet. A good leader must be like a sun, giving warmth and life to all creatures without expecting anything in return; like the moon, giving peace and joy to all; and like the stars twinkling in the sky, maintaining high ideals to serve mankind. He must also be like the ocean, vast and broad-minded; like fire, fierce but just; like the wind, intelligently knowing the aspirations of the people; and like water, giving knowledge to all those who thirst for it."

The *dalang* placed the *gunungan* back at the centre of the screen to indicate that the show was over. Some of the spectators, apparently thirst still unquenched, stared blankly at the screen on which the shadows had faded out as the rays of the morning sun seeped in. Some were fast asleep. Many stretched their arms and legs and dragged their feet homeward.

After the show, I talked to the *dalang* who did not show any signs of tiredness. Against the morning sun his face looked more wrinkled. He wore a moustache. I wanted to know what it was like to be a *dalang*. His answer was a quotation from a poem called 'Serat Centini' which says, "The dalang has to be proficient in four ways. Firstly, he has to be able to tell the story. Secondly, he must know the music and the art of chanting. Thirdly, he must have a sense of humour and lastly, he must be able to handle the *wayang* puppets skilfully throughout the performance." A *dalang* is an expert only after long years of practice and experience. He said the younger generation nowadays was luckier, for courses in this art were now conducted in both Solo and Jogjakarta. Some of the students of Gaja Mada University attend such courses because it is compulsory for those in the Faculty of Letters to know the art of the *wayang*.

The *dalang* told me that there were altogether some six hundred puppet figures, half of them kept on his right and the other half on his left. To me, however, they all looked alike, and I was curious to know how he could remember the faces, names and characters of each one of them. With usual Javanese politeness, the *dalang* said the puppets on his right were the Pandawa family and those on the left, the Kurawas. Roughly speaking, the puppets are divided into various groups. The giants, called Rakhasa or Buta, are easily recognized by their huge size and the fangs protruding from the corners of their mouths. The servants like Semar, Gareng and Petruk have extraordinary, ugly faces and distorted figures and are painted black and white. The deities, like Sanghiang Batara or Dewa, and priests wear cloaks and shoes. There remains the larger group made up of kings called Prabu, princes called Raden and ministers called Patih. The upper part of their bodies is unclothed, but they wear the *dodot*, a long piece of cloth wrapped round the hips. The headgear worn by the figures also indicates the rank and social status of the characters.

I asked the *dalang* which characters he liked best in the *Mahabharata* epic. With a soft voice he said, "As a *dalang*, I should not favour either the Pandawas or the Kurawas. Every character has a role to play just as every man has a place under the sun. It would be a mistake for me to make a king dance like a clown or a clown behave like a king."

During the performance, I noticed the *dalang* tapping a stick against a box from time to time. This puzzled me, so I asked the *dalang* what it meant. He explained that each tap was a signal that he was about to start talking so that the audience would listen carefully. He would also punctuate his speech with a gentle tap.

"What about the clinking sound which I heard from time to time?" I asked. He said it was a signal for the *gamelan* orchestra to start playing or was simply done to add colour and to create the mood of excitement during a violent battle. Although the *gamelan* orchestra has its own conductor who normally plays the *kandang* or *rebab* (the Javanese violin), he takes his cue from the *dalang*.

Every *dalang* has a handbook, called the *pakem*, which contains certain rules on what he should do and say. The *pakem* varies from place to place, but the *pakem* of Solo and Jogjakarta are regarded as the most outstanding and refined, and *dalang* from most regions usually adhere to one of them. Basically, there are two kinds of *pakem*, one with detailed rules stipulating exactly what a *dalang* should do and say. This is meant for the beginners in order that they may acquire a good foundation. The other, the incomplete one which contains only the outline of a story, gives the more experienced *dalang* room for improvisations which often appeal more to the audience.

The mysterious shadows of the *wayang* which I saw in Jogjakarta in 1955 left a mixed impression on my mind. I was reintroduced to the shadow-play when I returned to Indonesia as a diplomat in 1970. The four and a half years gave me time to see more *wayang kulit* performances and I decided to make a closer study of the subject. I have enjoyed watching many stories of the *wayang kulit* and have talked to people who have a similar interest. There are so many *lakon* (stories) in the *Mahabharata* and the *Ramayana* epics that it is impossible for most people to view all of them. On the rise and fall of the Pandawas and Kurawas alone there are more than two hundred *lakon*. But of all the *lakon* that I have seen, a few have left a striking impression on my mind. One of them is the 'Lakon Dewaruci' which relates the adventures of Bima through dangerous mountains and unpredictable oceans in search of the holy spring, Tirtapawitra, which could give him eternal youth and wisdom. This *lakon* happens also to be one of the most popular among the ordinary Javanese folk.

Bima one day heard about a holy spring from his old teacher, Durna, in the Ngastina Palace. Durna was under the influence of the Kurawas who wanted to eliminate Bima, the strongest and most daring of the Pandawas. He told Bima that the holy spring was hidden in the Candramuka Grotto, at the foot of Mount ·Gadamadana. Little did Bima know that it was a trap to kill him. When he reached the place after much difficulty, the giants, Rakmaka and Rukmakala, were waiting to devour him. Bima caught them by their hippie hair and whirled them one by one against the rocks till they died. He uprooted trees and looked high and low but found no holy spring. In desperation, he gave up and returned to the palace, only to be told by Durna that it was meant as a test of his bravery, determination and patience. Durna then told him that he had to go into the ocean where the holy spring was really hidden. Bima left immediately for the ocean and again encountered many obstacles. He met a gigantic sea-serpent with darting flames from its protruding eyes and poisonous venom pouring from its huge mouth. It was exciting to watch the fight between Bima and the sea-serpent. Bima nearly gave up when he suddenly remembered the strength of his *kuku pancanaka*. He struck it into the monster's jaw and blood spurted in all directions, turning the ocean red. Having disposed of the most dangerous demon of the ocean, he went on searching for the holy spring Tirtapawitra, but in vain. Finally he met Dewaruci, a tiny unknown creature the size of a small child who appeared from nowhere. Bima was surprised that Dewaruci knew all about him, including his ancestors, where he came from and what he was looking for. The tiny creature asked him to enter into his body. At first it appeared to Bima that it was impossible for he was huge and the creature tiny. He was finally persuaded and found no difficulty entering Dewaruci's body through his little ear. Through Dewaruci's eyes he saw the whole universe in its real perspective. As all sorts of symbols, colours and patterns appeared before him, Dewaruci explained their significance. Through the soft-spoken voice of Dewaruci, Bima discovered himself and the meaning of life. The giant-sized hero, Bima, found himself bowing humbly to Dewaruci who, though so minute, knew the secrets of life, wisdom, strength, peace of mind and everlasting happiness. After imparting to Bima truth and wisdom, Dewaruci disappeared and the enlightened Bima returned to the palace. The Pandawas rejoiced over the safe return of the wiser Bima.

It was through the conversation between Bima and Dewaruci that the *dalang* imparted to the audience the Javanese philosophy of life. Bima's search for the holy spring, Tirtapawitra, represents man's search for eternal life, immortality and happiness. Man looks for them high and low without realizing that they are all hidden in the holy *pramana* (inner soul) within him. Once he is able to reach his soul, he will be able to communicate with God. To do so, he has to learn how to subdue smell, hearing, sight, feeling and taste. He must suppress these feelings of the senses so that the physical world ceases to exist. Only then can the physical body conform to the spiritual, a union of which enables him to receive impulses from God and attain peace of mind. This is the purpose of meditation which helps to subdue human sensual desires and leads him to better self-control, so that he may be the master of his own destiny.

The necessity of exercising self-control over one's sensual gratifications and carnal desires was stressed over and over again in all the themes of the stories of the *Mahabharata*. Arjuna was known for his romantic episodes. His biggest weakness was the opposite sex. Yet he was capable of extreme self-control and self-denial after long moments of meditation. On another occasion in Solo, I saw a *wayang kulit* performance called the 'Lakon Arjuna Mintaraga' which showed how Arjuna's self-control was tested. When he was doing penance one day, seven beautiful nymphs were sent to tempt him, one of whom was the wife of Suyudana (the eldest of the Kurawas) with whom he was secretly in love. But he was unmoved. A priest was also sent to arouse his temper by passing sarcastic and insulting remarks. Arjuna was so absorbed in his meditation that he did not even notice the presence of the priest nor did he hear the remarks.

Other Javanese values in moral and social matters, such as loyalty and dedication, were subtly imparted to the audience by the *dalang* through conversations between one personality and another in the many *lakon* of the *Mahabharata* and *Ramayana*. The most touching story about loyalty and dedication to duty which I saw was a *lakon* called 'Semar Papa'. Semar, the powerful but loyal servant of the Pandawas, was always associated with hilarious jokes and laughter. But there were moments when his selfless loyalty to his masters made him so pitiful that the audience burst into tears. The Pandawa kingdom of Ngamarta was struck by an inexplicable plague and a seer warned that the disaster could only be dispelled by the death of Semar. Despite the fact that Semar was the one who waited on them from birth and rescued them from innumerable troubles and crises, the Pandawas, being Satrya (warriors), did not shy from their duties to society. They decided to do away with Semar. Judistira, the eldest of the Pandawas, ordered his nephew Abimanju, the eldest son of Arjuna, to do the unpleasant task. So Abimanju took Semar to the forest. The audience was tense and one could hear sobbing from the crowd when Semar blew his nose and cried like a child. He did not resist Abimanju, but was prepared for his fate. The tender-hearted Abimanju could not bring himself to carry out his uncle's orders. He released Semar, who hurried away with profound gratitude and started again to crack jokes. The audience, with a sigh of relief, broke into laughter again.

In the Javanese sense of moral code, the Pandawas did the right thing in ordering the execution of Semar for the sake of the community. Abimanju's behaviour was considered an act of cowardice for he acted like a woman and not like a warrior. Semar's willingness to die was interpreted as moral courage and a great sense of loyalty.

Besides the *Mahabharata*, the *Ramayana*, another world-renowned Hindu epic which originated in India, is also exceedingly popular among the Javanese and Balinese *wayang* fans. I have enjoyed the *Ramayana* stories on many occasions in Jogjakarta, Surabaya and Bali. The story tells of King Dasarata in the state of Ngayoja in the northern part of India who wanted to abdicate his throne in favour of Crown Prince Rama. This was interrupted by his second wife, Dewi Kekayi, who reminded the king that he had once promised to make her son, Barata, his successor. So she plotted to get Rama banished from the country. The noble Barata, however, did not approve of the ambitious plan of his mother and offered Rama the throne. Rama insisted on fulfilling his father's promise to Dewi Kekayi and went into exile for fourteen years with his faithful wife, Dewi Sita, and his brother, Lesmono.

Rama went to the Dandaka forest and fought with *raksasas* (giants) who created havoc there and gave no peace to the surrounding hermits. Dasamuka, the king of *raksasas* who resided in Ngalengka (Sri Lanka) scared off Rama but did not dare fight him. Instead, he abducted Rama's beloved wife, Dewi Sita. In order to free her, Rama sought the help of the white monkeys in the jungle, whose king was Sugriwa, and their general, Hanuman. After defeating Dasamuka and rescuing his wife, Rama returned to the palace of Ngayoja and assisted his brother Barata to rule the country.

The Ramayana stories are depicted on the walls of the Siva temple at Prambanan in Central Java. The history of the old Javanese *Ramayana kakawin* was already popular during the peak periods of power of such kingdoms as Kediri, Singhasari and Majapahit (eleventh to sixteenth centuries). In the court of Jogjakarta, the Javanese developed a new choreography for the *Ramayana*, using huge crowds of people imitating monkeys. This perhaps was the origin of the now famous Kecak monkey-dance of Bali, which is one of the main attractions for tourists to Bali.

The *Ramayana* epic, though originally from India, has always made a tremendous impact on the Indonesians. The Government of Indonesia, inspired by the *Ramayana* stories, chose the image of Rama in a pose — bending the bow of Sita — as the emblem for the 1962 Asian Games. The pose was taken from one of the reliefs at the Siva temple at Prambanan. In 1972 the Indonesian Government also organized an Asian *Ramayana* festival in Pandaan, East Java. Nearly all the Asian countries including India, Burma, Sri Lanka, Thailand and Malaysia participated in the great festival.

Telling the story of Rama and Sita is not the only aim of the *Ramayana* epic. Many of the stories contain important lessons on morality and good conduct, especially on how to be a good and wise leader.

I became more and more interested in the *wayang kulit* because I found that nothing has influenced the Javanese mind more than the *wayang*. To understand the *wayang* is a first step towards understanding the Javanese. There is at least one *wayang* group which performs regularly for viewers of all ages in every village throughout Java. It has become a way of life — not so much a form of entertainment as part of social education. From a tender age, the Javanese mind is moulded not only by the strict Javanese home discipline, but also by direct exposure to the *wayang* performances. Through the screen and the mythical characters of the *Mahabharata* and *Ramayana*, the *dalang* conveys to the viewers and listeners the Javanese concept of the universe. As he relates and captivates the crowd with interesting stories, he also expounds poetically the existential position of the Javanese personality, his relationship to the natural and supernatural order, and the importance of maintaining harmony and stability in a world of conflicts. By frequenting the shadow-play, a boy soon becomes familiar with characters like Arjuna, the frail-looking, tender-hearted romantic but well-disciplined hero; or Bima, the ill-tempered, courageous dare-devil fighter; or Semar, the clown with supernatural powers, and so on and so forth. The young Javanese audiences have so many characters to choose from as an ideal for them to mimic. These diversified characters also provide mental guidelines for them to interpret personalities they happen to come across.

During my stay in Indonesia, I often heard my friends commenting that so and so was like Arjuna just because he had many lady friends. Someone told me that the former President Sukarno liked to compare himself to Bima as he was not afraid of the Dutch colonialists. There were others who were even proud to be referred to as Semar. This habit of associating some real personalities with mythical beings, because of the similarity in characters, is very much like that of the Chinese-educated Chinese who are fond of nicknaming a leader who is loyal and cool-headed as Liu Pei; or an upright and just leader as Kuan Kong; or a daring but impulsive type as Chang Fei; or the cunning and treacherous warrior-strategist as Tsao Tsao. These characters and many others were real personalities of the Three Kingdoms, one of the most intriguing periods in Chinese history. Almost every Chinese who is familiar with Chinese literature has read the *Romance of the Three Kingdoms*, a classical novel which is a must for those who wish to understand the Chinese mind. The special characteristics of personalities of each of the heroes of the *Mahabharata* were spread far and wide to the Javanese audiences through the *wayang*, just as the characters of the *Three Kingdoms* were done through Chinese *wayang* on the streets of traditional China and South-East Asia.

Perhaps nowhere in the world has mythology and mysticism made such an impact on the minds of its people than in Java through *wayang*. Mythological stories of war between the Pandawas and Kurawas, between right and wrong, and stories of the supernatural powers the warriors derived from their *alat*, as well as stories of reincarnation, cannot but influence the Javanese minds, particularly the younger ones. Apart from conveying mythical tales and mysticism, the *wayang* has also more serious philosophical connotations. The *wayang*, in fact, represents the whole Javanese philosophy of vagueness and their idea of man and God. The use of the shadow to project one's philosophy is typical of Javanese genius. The shadow itself is a vague thing. It is perhaps the only thing in the world that one can see but cannot touch and feel. It is real and yet unreal. It has two dimensions. The Javanese have chosen the shadow to illustrate their concept of the invisible world. Through the shadow, they project the spirits of their ancestors which they believe, exist but are not visible to the eye. Through the shadow, the *dalang* tries to convey the meaning of life and the destiny of man. He tries to teach man his place in the universal order, the cosmos as well as his relationship to the Divine. The *wayang* implants in the Javanese mind the philosophy that everyone has a different role to play in society, and everyone must know his own role. In other words, a king must behave like a king and a clown, like a clown. A king should never behave like a clown, nor a clown, a king.

In philosophical terms, the illuminated screen is the visible world and the puppets represent varieties of God's creations. The *gedebok*, the banana trunk, used to support puppets by sticking them in, represents the surface of the world; the *blencong*, the lamp over the head of the *dalang*, is the light of life; and the *gamelan* orchestra is a symbol of harmony of all worldly activities. The *dalang*, who manipulates the puppets and gives them life, is the personification of God. Without the *dalang*, no puppet can come to life. Thus, the Javanese feel that it is wrong for humans to think that they can decide things by themselves or to act as they wish. The *dalang* and the *wayang* serve as an external expression of the various ways in which God acts and works in the world. He holds in his hands the fate of every single human being as He orders and guides all events. Fortune or misfortune, a short or long life, success or failure are all in the hands of the *dalang* of the Universe —God.

There is to my mind another philosophical aspect to the *wayang*. It concerns the two categories of audience present at each *wayang* performance—one group sits in front of the screen, and the other group behind the screen. Those in the front see only the shadows and are not aware of what goes on behind the screen. They represent the majority, the masses who only see things superficially. Those viewing from behind, the privileged few, see how the *dalang* operates and are aware of what is going on behind the screen. Perhaps the privileged few can be considered as having a deeper understanding of the feelings, behaviour and aspirations of decision-makers.

Wayang puppets are very colourful. Their faces are painted according to their characters and their different roles. They also wear colourful clothing to match their status. I sometimes wonder why colours are necessary at all for puppets, since colours are not visible through the screen. What is the idea of having the puppets painted when the audience can only see their shadows? But such colours are not meant to be seen by the common audience or, shall I say, the masses. Only the audience behind the stage, those who are closer to the *dalang*, have the privilege of seeing the true colours of the faces and clothing of the puppets. When a warrior like Arjuna or Bima goes to war, he wears a black mask, but when he is not at war, he puts on a golden mask. So, the audience close to the *dalang* behind the stage knows in advance that a war is about to begin before the front audience sees it over the screen. Moreover, the audience in the front has no means of knowing when the hero has changed masks. Perhaps it is meant to be that the dual personality of a puppet should be hidden from the ordinary eyes. After all, vagueness is the criterion of a *wayang* culture. The leather puppet is real, but its shadow, a myth. A *wayang* performance is, therefore, an interplay between myth and reality.

The term *wayang* has the same etymological root as the Javanese word for 'shadow'. However, the term may also have another origin connected with ancient traditions of remembering one's ancestors. A legend says that the Hindu King Joyoboyo in the year A.D. 861 ordered his artists to make drawings of the stone figures of his ancestors on palm leaves called *lontar*. He named the *lontar* images *wayang purwa*. It is said that the present word *wayang* was borrowed from the word, which originally referred to the images of Javanese ancestors.

The real origin of the *wayang*, however, is still a matter of argument among scholars concerned with the subject. Some of them believe that the *wayang* originated in Indonesia because as early as the seventh century A.D. there was already a *prasasti* (inscription) which contained the word *angringgit*, which means 'to perform the shadow-play'. Other scholars argue that India was the place of origin of the *wayang* because of a kind of shadow-play called *chayanataka* which was performed in India in ancient times but which is now extinct. Wherever it may be, nobody can deny the fact that in Indonesia the development of the *wayang* has reached a high standard of perfection and popularity unparalleled in any country in the world. And, indeed, the *wayang* has not lost its grip on the Indonesian audiences despite the introduction of modern types of entertainment such as the cinema. In the olden days when there were no schools in the rural areas in which general education could be given, the teaching of morality and standards of human behaviour could only be done through the *wayang*. It became so deeply rooted that even the *Wali* (Muslim saints) found it necessary to decree later that the *wayang* was, in fact, an invention of Sunan Kalijaga, one of the most celebrated and honoured saints of Islam in Indonesia. The powerful clown Semar in the *Mahabharata* was so popular that the *Wali* had to use wooden figures of Semar, patterned out of Arabic scripts, to preach Islam in the hinterland of Java. They have also introduced stories of Amir Hamzah, the heroic uncle of the Prophet Mohammed, into *wayang* performances. Such stories were later known as *wayang menak*.

Historically, the *wayang* was first mentioned in the inscription of Kedu dated A.D. 907. The first mention of the leather puppets of a *wayang* was made in the *Arjuna Wiwala* (which is about the marriage of Arjuna, one of the first heroes, to Dewi Suprabha) written by Mou Kanwe in the eleventh century. The Javanese kings were, since olden times, protectors and patrons of culture and thus took great pains in the development of the *wayang* until it reached the present standard. The Dutch rulers allowed the *wayang* to flourish and when the Indonesian people gained their independence, it received the support and encouragement of the government. This explains the uninterrupted development and continuity in the art of the *wayang*.

Besides the *wayang kulit*, there are also other kinds of *wayang*. The *wayang golek*, for instance, uses puppets made of wood, which are three dimensional and resemble human figures. For the *wayang golek* no screen is necessary, as it is not actually a shadow-play. Apparently it was created by Sunan Kudus, one of the Islamic priests in 1583. The *wayang golek* is very popular in Cirebon, a town on the border of Central Java and West Java, where both the Javanese and Sundanese languages are spoken. (It is a common mistake among foreigners to think that all the people who live in Java speak Javanese. The residents in West Java speak Sundanese and many of them do not understand Javanese. Neither can the average Javanese speak Sundanese.)

The *wayang golek* is divided into three types, differentiated by the stories they perform. The one that performs stories from the *Ramayana* and *Mahabharata* is called *wayang golek purwa*; the one that shows the Panji stories is called *wayang golek gedog*; and the third kind called *wayang golek menak* gets its stories from Persian and Arabic sources, mostly about Amir Hamzah who was considered to be the uncle of Prophet Mohammed and whose Javanese name is Wong Agung Menak Joyengrana.

Another type of *wayang* created in the beginning of the nineteenth century by Mangkunegara IV in Surakarta is called *wayang madya*. The repertoire was taken from the *Book of Hajipamasa*, a book of mythical stories, the main figure in it being Aji Saka. It tells of the coming of the Hindus to Indonesia.

The *wayang topeng* of Malang in East Java is also known throughout Java. It is a dance-drama based on the stories of the Panji cycle. The *wayang topeng* is performed by human actors wearing wooden masks. (The word *topeng* means 'mask'.) As the human actors dance with masks on, the *dalang*, who in this case does not manipulate them physically, tells the story. This type of mask-dancing is also popular throughout Asia, particularly in Japan and Thailand. In Indonesia, different regions have different types of *topeng*, costumes and styles of dancing. Malang is the centre of *topeng* culture.

The latest invention of the twentieth century is the *wayang suluh*. It is used by the Ministry of Information to relate the contemporary history of Indonesia and to disseminate propaganda. The *dalang* uses Bahasa Indonesia instead of Javanese. The puppets are also made of leather, but have human profiles. The figure Arjuna, for instance, wears a military cap and carries a modern pistol, symbolizing a revolutionary hero, and the theme is often a guerrilla fight against the Dutch colonialists. The modern figure of Arjuna has the new name of Nusantara Putra. The *wayang suluh*, which utilizes the shapes and figures of the *wayang purwa* heroes and characters but with variations, is used to convey new standards of social behaviour and modern concepts. For example, experiments are being made to use the *wayang suluh* to teach the people the importance of family-planning, with Semar cracking jokes about those having too many children. Modern social values are put across through the subtle mingling of old and new stories. It is also a useful weapon for political elections to publicize party platforms or to have a dig at opponents.

It seems to me that the *wayang* tradition is here to stay. In olden times, the *wayang* was only performed at night until the early hours of the morning, as it was the appropriate time for the ancestral spirits to attend. Nowadays, the shadow-play is intended mostly for entertainment. A great deal of religious significance has been lost in the course of history. The *wayang* is performed these days in Indonesia to celebrate the birth of a child, a wedding, an anniversary, or the so-called *tumbukan* — when someone reaches the age of 48, 56, or 64 years according to the Javanese eight-year cycle. The *wayang* performances which are still reminiscent of old-time religious festivals can still be seen in Java during the month of Ruwah (the eighth month of the Muslim calendar) or during the big harvest. The first is a kind of ancestor-worship festivity; the latter, a thanksgiving party.

The *wayang* culture is taken very seriously in Indonesia. It is treated not merely as a form of entertainment but as one important stream of Indonesian education. Children in primary and secondary schools are taught the stories on which the *wayang* is based and learn to recognize the various characters which appear on the screen. They also learn to appreciate and play *gamelan* music. As I mentioned earlier, at the Gaja Mada University there is a special course to train *dalang*, as well as a course of higher studies on Javanese literature, forms and music connected with the *wayang*. Thousands of business companies, public and private buildings and schools are named after the heroes of the *Ramayana* and *Mahabharata* epics. Even batik designs derive inspiration from the Pandawas, with such subjects as Arjuna, Bima, Semar, Rama, Sita, or the mythical bird, Garuda. Indeed, the *wayang* has become an important part of the Indonesian cultural heritage.

10 Semar, the Guardian Spirit of Java

Of all the characters in the Javanese *wayang*, none fascinated me more than Semar. It is not because he looks funny and ugly or because he is the most popular clown. I took an interest in Semar because I found the character most original. It is a character not found in the Hindu-inspired *Ramayana* or *Mahabharata* epics. It is a creation indigenous to Java.

The ugliest features that can be found on the human anatomy are ascribed to Semar. He has a peculiar forehead with a pear-like crown above his 'third eye'. His other two eyes are slanting, his nose is curled, and his ears look like butterflies. His large mouth displays uneven teeth and his chin droops down. Semar has a big, round stomach and huge buttocks. His arms are long and flexible, but his left hand usually points to the ground while his right hand rests on his buttock. His short legs and flat feet make him look like a duck. However, despite his ugly and ungainly features, Semar is the most popular clown on the *wayang kulit* screen. His appearance alone is amusing enough to provoke laughter from the audience—even more so when the old clown laughs like a baby or cries with a running nose! To make people laugh he sometimes takes off his golden ear studs and replaces them with red chillies. Semar is especially humble to children, but readily pokes fun at adults.

The ugly figure of Semar, formed with Arabic characters.

In *wayang* performances, Semar is the servant of the five Pandawas, especially Arjuna. Semar's instruction from the God, Sanghiang Tunggal, is to see that his masters keep a good balance of their senses and are not swayed by their emotions. Semar's role is also to expose the evil in the human character. He looks ugly but is kind-hearted, powerful but humble, brave but faithful. He appears stupid, but is often brilliant and wise. Endowed with supernatural powers, Semar never once misuses them, but always comes to the rescue of the helpless. Whenever a good kingdom is about to fall, he is there to save the day.

However, Semar is a controversial figure among the Indonesians. He has a many-sided character and means different things to different people. As a clown, he is known as Semar. As a *guru*, he is called Batara Manikmaya. And as a saint, he is known as Sanghiang Ismaya. It is commonly believed that Semar is the brother of Siva, a god of many attributes and various functions. Javanese Hindus, on the one hand, believe that Siva was sent as a guardian to the Indian continent, whereas Semar was sent to the South Pacific and is thus regarded as the guardian spirit of Java. Balinese Hindus, on the other hand, regard Semar as simply an old, clumsy clown, whom they call Twalan.

"Do you know why Twalan looks so ugly and disfigured?" a Balinese friend once asked me. He then went on to give me the Balinese version of how Twalan became so ugly. It is acknowledged that Twalan is the son of Tintiya, the original God, and is thus the brother of Siva. However, Twalan has another brother, Togog, known to the Balinese as Delam, who is as ugly as Twalan. Delam is bald-headed, has huge, round eyes and the mouth of a toothless crocodile. He, too, has as big a belly and buttocks as Twalan. At one time, however, both Twalan and Delam had handsome and attractive features. They were always quarrelling and fighting for supremacy, until one day both challenged each other over the superiority of their supernatural powers. Siva stood aloof and watched the two fight it out. The first challenge was to swallow the huge mountain facing them. Twalan transformed his mouth and belly as large as he could so that he could swallow the mountain. He failed and became disfigured because he could not regain his original appearance. Delam followed suit and also met with the same fate. This explains how the two brothers acquired such gross features.

As mentioned earlier, although the Balinese Hindus acknowledge Semar as the brother of Lord Siva, they do not regard him as their guardian spirit. To them, Semar and his brother, Togog, were both given to worldly pleasures and did not care to become gods. They preferred to remain as servants so that they could indulge in eating and drinking. However, the Balinese do concede that Semar has exorcising powers and can defend a good prince and his country from evil.

The Javanese Hindus, however, place Semar high in the hierarchy of the cosmic world, guiding the destiny of Nusantara (the Indonesian archipelago). Romo Hardjanta, a Javanese Hindu and founder of Majapahit Pancasila — now officially recognized as a branch of the Hindu-Dharma religion — is of the opinion that as Semar has the *Louna* or *Dohi*, the crown on his forehead, he is even more powerful than Siva, who does not have this. The image of Semar is also used as the emblem of one of the major schools of *Kebatinan* — Sapta Darma, a Javanese spiritual organization. Although Semar is venerated mainly by Javanese Hindus, you can ask any Javanese either in the streets of the big cities or in the villages in the countryside, and it would be a rare case if he has not heard of Semar. It was because of Semar's widespread popularity that I was spurred on to find out more about this interesting character and his religious significance.

To the Javanese, Semar is a deity and is real. Sanghiang Ismaya (the spiritual title of Semar) can even be consulted; some claim that they have heard his voice, and others that they have seen him. In order to communicate with him, one should visit either of the two holy caves of Semar — the Guwa Ratu cave on Gunung Srendang near the village of Adipolo and the Guwa Semar on the Dieng Plateau, both in Central Java.

The Dieng Plateau where the Guwa Semar is situated is surrounded by live volcanoes such as Mount Perahu to the north and Mount Sundoro to the south. One can even see the heat rise from the volcanic inferno and hear the lava bubbling. But the cave itself is set in idyllic, cool surroundings, quite unaffected by the volcanic heat. Guwa Semar is a natural cave, the entrance of which is identified by a huge rock resembling Semar himself. When I visited the cave, the small entrance gate was locked. The assistant caretaker, Padmadijoyo, told me that an important person was meditating inside the cave and did not want to be disturbed. He explained that from time to time very important persons would come incognito. The former Australian Prime Minister, Mr Gough Whitlam, was reported to have made a brief visit to the cave, accompanied by President Suharto, when he made an unofficial visit to Indonesia in August 1974. Some visitors would spend days fasting and meditating inside the cave in order to make contact with the spirit of Sanghiang Ismaya for spiritual guidance.

There is actually nothing inside the Semar cave. It is cool, quiet and serene. However, it is so dark that one cannot see even one's own hands. In this complete darkness, a meditator would sit cross-legged and wait for the spirit of Sanghiang Ismaya to descend and communicate with him. The meditator often fasts for days at a stretch. Sometimes, the fasting is observed so strictly that not even a drop of water is partaken. And day in, day out, only silence and darkness prevail. The voice of Semar is not heard by everyone who comes to meditate in the cave. Many have gone away disappointed. A few have even lost their lives. The care-taker told me that such persons had usually died of poisoning, perhaps from poisonous snakes, such as the cobra, that may lurk inside.

The Guwa Ratu, the other cave where Semar is supposed to dwell, is situated on the treacherous mountain, Gunung Srendang. This cave is bigger than the Guwa Semar, but is extremely difficult to reach. Nyoman, the caretaker of the cave, suggested we approach the mountain by boat, for he considered the journey by sea less difficult. The night was dark; the moon and stars were hidden. All I could see was a long, narrow boat without any sails. One could see hardly anything beyond the boat. The sea was in complete darkness. I thought it too dangerous to cross the sea in that small canoe, especially with a party of twelve people crammed into it. Should the canoe capsize, one might swim in the wrong direction due to lack of visibility. I decided that we should go by land instead of by sea. On reflection after our visit to the cave, I realized that it was a mistake to have gone by road for it turned out to be even more dangerous.

To reach the Guwa Ratu by land, one must first go to the foot of Gunung Srendang by car along a remote jungle track covered with *lalang* (tall wild grass). This track then climbs the mountain as it winds precariously along the tops of steep cliffs. A slight misjudgement of even a few inches may result in the car plunging into the deep valleys below. We were glad when we finally reached the top of the mountain safely. The sky was still pitch-black. Only the fire-flies gave some flicker of light. Frogs were croaking in the swamps, owls hooting in the forest, and crickets chorusing in a loud, monotonous dirge, which only helped to make the bleak, dark night more eerie.

"Where is the cave?" I asked Nyoman rather impatiently. "We're not there yet. This way please," he replied. Walking through *lalang* taller than ourselves, we groped down a slope in darkness. After about half an hour, we came to a halt. Nyoman called out, "Be careful! We have reached the end of the path and now have to climb down the rocky cliff face." Imagine my feeling of alarm as we stood in darkness on the edge of the cliff with valleys far below! But this was not the time to panic for we had already come so far. What was needed were calm nerves and courage. With the help of a torchlight, which we bought in a shop in Adipolo along the way, we started to move downwards, one foot carefully after another, step by step, our hands fumbling to cling for support. I can't remember how many steps there were, or how long we took. But we made it. There was a sigh of relief all round. Our clothes were wet and dirty. Nyoman asked us to bathe ourselves in the stream at the entrance to the cave. Bathing was symbolic of cleansing one's soul before entering a sacred place. We approached the entrance of Guwa Ratu by torchlight, passed through the big, iron gates, and soon found ourselves inside the cave. We lit a few candles which revealed a small guest-room partitioned off by carved wooden pillars. Walking barefooted on the blackish, volcanic sand, we entered the guest-room and found mats made of bamboo leaves scattered over the floor. We sat down on the mats to wait as it was nearing midnight.

It was my curiosity and a burning desire to know more about the spiritual significance of Sanghiang Ismaya that prompted me to make this risky trip. I was travelling incognito. The arrangements were made by a Javanese, Ananda Suyono, who plays an active role in the development of the spiritual life of the people of Solo. Nyoman, our guide and medium, had earlier outlined a little history of the cave. Leaders of the past had always gone to the cave to seek spiritual guidance from Semar; before the Indonesian Revolution, the young Sukarno often went there for inspiration and meditation. During the Dutch colonial days, Guwa Ratu was a prohibited area, for the Dutch rulers were afraid that the cave would be used by revolutionaries as a place for plotting against them. During the Japanese Occupation, the Indonesian people were again barred from visiting the cave. It was only during the last few years that the place was properly done up and made accessible for anyone wishing to go there.

At about one o'clock in the morning, Nyoman called for me. According to him, the spirit of the God had descended. Leaving our candles behind, we passed through a small wooden gate carved in the shape of an Islamic dome and reached the inner chamber of the cave. We then walked along a bleak, dark tunnel until we reached the end where Nyoman beckoned me to sit down and wait quietly.

It was there that we soon heard a low voice speaking in classical Javanese. The tone of soberness was occasionally interrupted by a jovial roar of laughter. It was somewhat similar to the voice of Semar which I had heard during a Javanese shadow-play. The *dalang* would speak in a low and sober tone when Semar was defending a good general against evil, then suddenly burst into laughter when poking fun at people. It was remarkable that the voice echoing within the cave so closely resembled that uttered by the *dalang*. Some Javanese *wayang* fans believe that when the *dalang* speaks for Semar, it is not the *dalang* expressing himself, but Semar who has entered the soul of the *dalang*.

The voice in the cave was accompanied by three other voices, one sounding like a lady's. I was later informed that she was Lara Kidul, Queen of the Indonesian (Indian) Ocean. The other two voices were those of Ki Bondoyudo, the spiritual knight, and Noyoginggong, his companion, both guardians of Sanghiang Ismaya. The four voices spoke for about twenty minutes, and all the time I was recording them on my tape-recorder.

When we returned to Cilacap, my friends tried to interpret the utterances, which seemed to concern mainly the world situation and warned of imminent changes. It was not so much the message that interested me, but the satisfaction of having visited the cave where few foreigners have been. It was indeed an unforgettable and rewarding experience, for it enabled me to have a deeper understanding of the spiritual life of the Javanese people.

During my stay in Indonesia, I was honoured to have met several *guru* who are highly respected as prominent spiritual leaders of Java. According to Romo Budi, a 76-year-old *guru* living in Jogjakarta, Semar is at least 4,000 years old and it was Sanghiang Ismaya who created the ancestors of the Javanese, long before the advent of Hinduism, Buddhism or Islam. Chatting together in his home one evening, Romo Budi told me how, from time to time, the spirit of Sanghiang Ismaya would enter his soul. He explained how the spirit even spoke through him in Chinese. At that moment in the conversation, Romo Budi suddenly went into a light trance and uttered words which sounded Chinese. When he came out of the trance, he claimed that he had just been visited by the spirit and asked me whether I understood the message. I regretted I was unable to catch the meaning, perhaps because of the unfamiliar Chinese dialect used.

Romo Budi then went on to tell me a fantastic but interesting story. About fifteen years ago, the spirit of Semar told Romo Budi that he would receive a photograph that he should treasure. Soon afterwards, a Dutch friend sent him a picture thinking that it belonged to him. The photograph was taken when a group of twenty-three junior high school students went to the Guwa Ratu area for a picnic. When one of them was about to take a picture of the group, he heard a voice call out, "Wait for me! Wait for me!" He looked about, but saw nothing amiss. So he took the picture. When the film was developed, none of his twenty-two school-mates was in the photograph. Instead, there appeared the image of Semar. Romo Budi paused, then went to his bedroom to fetch the photograph. The picture clearly showed Semar with his plump figure and a human face with a long nose curling upwards. Romo Budi was kind enough to let me borrow the photograph to have it reproduced. All this time, the same questions kept passing through my mind — was the photograph a true image of Semar? Did the incident actually happen? Although it sounds scientifically impossible, people believe that it may well be one of those rare phenomena that are not easily explained by modern science. My meeting with Romo Budi was a valuable one, as it gave me another glimpse of the spiritual significance of Semar which intrigued me.

Through an introduction by Ananda Suyono, a friend of mine, I met Pak Parno, who, like Romo Budi, claims to be able to communicate with Sanghiang Ismaya. Although Pak Parno is an executive in an Indonesian bank, he is also a *guru* capable of conducting group meditation. Besides communicating with Semar, he can also communicate with the spirit of Mangku-negara I, the deceased Sultan of Solo. Pak Parno related how he spent his childhood days in adventures in caves and on mountains, and later in meditation in these solitary places, thereby gaining much experience in being able to communicate with the spirits. It was Pak Parno who got the blessing of Sanghiang Ismaya for us to visit the cave Guwa Ratu.

I had often wondered what Javanese Muslims thought of Semar and whether belief in Semar would contradict belief in the Prophet Mohammed. So I sought the views of Javanese Muslim leaders. It was interesting to learn that in the early days of Islamization of Central Java, the *imam* had used the puppet Semar to help propagate the religion. When I visited the *kraton* of Mangkunegara, the host, Sultan Mangkunegara VIII, showed me several old wooden carvings of Semar, inscribed with Arabic characters. These were once used to help convince the commonfolk that even Semar had been converted to Islam.

I also met Pak Daryatmo, an 82-year-old Muslim leader of the community of Wonogiri, as he was receiving villagers who had come to him for advice. They considered him doctor, teacher, preacher and wise man who could cure many illnesses whether physical, mental, spiritual or emotional. Pak Daryatmo has already been mentioned in another book *The Smiling General* by the German author Roeder, who tells how President Suharto in his youth stayed with Pak Daryatmo for three years. When I asked Pak Daryatmo, a staunch Muslim, what he thought of Semar, his reply summed up the views of many Muslim leaders: "Semar is the spiritual guardian of Java." The answer was short but firm. He found it unnecessary to elaborate. The Javanese, like all other Indonesians, have an extraordinary capacity for syncretism and an unusual sense of tolerance for all religions.

The more scientifically-minded scholars and historians regard Semar as an imaginary figure introduced into the Javanese *wayang* performances. Historically, Semar first appeared on the relief of Sudamala at Candi Tigamangi, in 1358. Later, Semar was found on the relief of Candi Sukuh, completed in 1439. The story of Sudamala was copied from the original during the Majapahit period. Before that, there was no Semar in the *wayang* performances. In the Kediri period, the clownish servants of the Pandawas, known as *panakawan*, were Punta, Juru Deh and Prasanta. These were the first *panakawan* in Javanese literature created by Mpu Panuluh in the *Ghatotkacasraya* (a story). However, these *panakawan* had no appeal to the *wayang* audiences and were not popular. When *panakawan* like Semar and his family were invented, they immediately captured the imagination of the Javanese audiences, and the earlier *panakawan* faded away from the scene. Semar's popularity grew to such dimensions that he became more than just a legendary figure in *wayang* performances. The Javanese audiences found in Semar the personification of an ideal character —someone who is powerful and yet humble and generous, who always likes to joke but at the same time is clever, faithful and wise. The Semar personality has created in the minds of the Javanese a belief that whatever he says must be the truth. Both the preachers of Hinduism and Islam had exploited this belief in spreading their religions to Java. The philosophical connotation was that without the support of the native population, neither Hinduism from the Indian sub-continent, nor Islam from the Arab states could have flourished in Java. Another philosophical aspect of the Semar myth was that without the support of Semar the Pandawas would not have won in their feud with the Kurawas. The lesson to all in modern terms is that without the support of the masses, no ruler can succeed in staying in power.

11 Ancestral Spirits and Predictions

M *Besuk yen wusana jago wiring kuning*
Saka lor witan lekani
Iku bakal ilangi kebo bule
Siwer matand
"Tomorrow the yellow peacock from the
north-east will come to drive away white
buffalo with blue eyes" — meaning 'the
Japanese from the north-east will come to
drive away the Dutch colonialist'.

a Joyoboyo prediction

Like most Asians, Indonesians, too, worship their ancestors
and prominent leaders of the past. In Chinese history, sages like
Confucius, generals like Kuan Kong, or even Admiral Cheng Ho
were mortals. Today, long after their deaths, millions of people in
South-East Asia still pray to them either in temples or at private
family altars. Once a year, during the Cheng Beng season, the
Chinese go to the graveyards of their ancestors to pray. The Malays
do that on the first day of the Islamic new year. Similarly, the
Indonesians, especially the Javanese, pray to their ancestors for
blessings and guidance.

Ancestor-worship started in Java long before the advent of Islam.
The Candi Prambanan temple complex built around the eighth
and ninth centuries, the golden age of Central Java, could have
been the centre of ancestor-worship in those days. Ancient monuments such as the Prambanan were usually referred to as *candi*,
a name probably derived from the word *Candika*, one of the names
of Durga, the Goddess of Death. Thus Candi Prambanan could
have been a burial ground for kings and prominent leaders who
were in power in those days. When a king or a prominent leader
died, he was referred to as *ciandi*, which meant 'placed in a *candi*'.
Actually, the things that were placed in the *candi* could have been
ashes of the deceased and their valuables. These ashes might have

been placed in a stone casket and then deposited at the base of the *candi*. Above the casket, the statue of a god, of which the deceased king was the incarnation, was erected. This statue then became the object of worship for those who wished to remember their king.

Archaeologists have found a stone casket on top of a pile of charcoal and remains of burnt animal bones in the Siva temple of the Candi Lorojonggrang group, situated near Jogjakarta in Central Java. Amidst the burial mound were sheets of gold leaf inscribed with Varuna (God of the Sea) and Parvata (God of the Mountains). Inside the stone casket, sheets of copper mixed with charcoal, ashes and earth were discovered. There were also twenty coins, some jewels, pieces of gold and silver, seashells (five of which were shaped like turtles), a dragon, a *padma* (lotus) flower, an altar and an egg. The discoveries indicate that the Candi Lorojonggrang group was once an important burial complex of a kingdom. It was a place where the relatives and supporters of the king or his successor could contact the spirits by means of meditation or through a medium.

Candi Lorojonggrang is an exact replica of Mount Mahameru. In the centre rises the main temple, symbolizing the top of the mountain, home of Siva; the two other temples on its right and left are for Brahma and Vishnu. Though originally built with an essentially Hindu concept, many of the relics reveal a happy compromise between Sivaism (Hinduism) and Buddhism. For example, the statue of Siva, the mightiest god in Hinduism, stands on a lotus, symbol of Buddhism, inside the tallest temple erected in honour of him. But the underlying purpose of the temple was to practise ancestor-worship in the Javanese tradition, which had existed long before Islam, Hinduism or Buddhism had reached the shores of the country.

Each empire had its heroes who were worshipped religiously as a mystical source of guidance. These heroes were buried in sacred places, which became places of worship or meditation. The tomb of Diponegoro, the revolutionary hero who rose against the Dutch colonialists, in Makassar today serves as a source of spiritual mysticism. Mystics still frequent mountains, caves or landmarks known for their connection with past heroes and gods. To Muslims, the sacred graves of holy men of Islam in Cirebon, Demak, Tuban, Gresik, Surabaya and Denpasar are places for religious devotion. Among some groups of devotees, the merit of making a pilgrimage to such Javanese Muslim graves is considered equal to that of performing the obligatory pilgrimage to Mecca, which is one of the pillars of Islam.

The custom and tradition of paying respect to dead heroes has almost become institutionalized in present-day official functions. Once a year, on 1 October, the Armed Forces and the whole Cabinet, led by the President, pay homage to the seven *pahlawan* who were massacred in the Gestapu coup and buried in Lubang Buaya on the outskirts of Jakarta. There is also a touch of mysticism about the Lubang Buaya affair, for on the day the six generals and a soldier were massacred, an extraordinary *durian* fruit with seven seeds was found about a foot away from the hole. (During the Sukarno regime, Heroes' Day was officially celebrated on 10 October.) Even at the opening session of the Indonesian parliament, there is always a silent pause of three minutes to remember the dead heroes, "*mengheningkan cipta kepada para pahlawan*".

It is interesting to note that in the history of Java, whenever a new king emerged to succeed the old one, the poet of the court, known as the king's *pujangga*, would write about the new king's divine descent. The new king would therefore be justified to be the leader of his people, who would then regard him as being endowed with supernatural powers. Historical facts interwoven with popular beliefs and mystical phenomena, therefore, dominate the historical records of Java. The old Javanese writers perhaps had to strengthen the king's image and legitimacy by emphasizing his mystical powers, for this was the main pillar upon which his kingdom and the well-being of his people rested.

In later Javanese history, whenever a new leader emerged to lead the people to revolt against oppression or against foreign colonial domination, one would come across stories that the leader had heard a voice from above giving him inspiration or instruction. Most mystics believe that rulers and leaders are chosen by the Almighty God and that they are given *wahyu cakraningrat* (blessing for ruling the country), which ordinary people do not possess. This belief is also shared by the commonfolk.

Mystery surrounds the birth of Gaja Mada, the greatest Prime Minister of the Majapahit empire. The Balinese believe that he was born in Bali Agung and later moved to the Kingdom of Majapahit. The Balinese also believe that Gaja Mada had no father and no mother, but that he was found in a coconut — the reincarnation of Sanghiang Narajana, or Vishnu. Even Chinese chronicles added a touch of mystery to the birth of Gaja Mada. According to the Chinese source on Java entitled *Ying Yai Sheng Lan* written in 1415, the Chinese who visited Java heard a legend that went something like this: "It is told that in olden times, a King of Devils (Mararaja) with a green face, a red body and brown hair, who lived in this country, united himself with a bad spirit in the shape of an elephant and ate more than a hundred children, living on human flesh and blood. One day, a flash of thunder and lightning split open a rock, inside which was a man sitting cross-legged. The people were greatly astonished at this and at once took him for their leader. He then led the people against the ghostly elephant and drove it away. The scourge was thus done away with and the people multiplied again in peace." Gaja Mada's name strangely has some connection with the elephant for the word *gaja* means 'elephant'.

Gaja Mada was a Buddhist and often went to the mountains to meditate for inner strength and to contact Vishnu for spiritual guidance. In 1355, at the height of his victories, King Hayam Wuruk gave him a piece of land near Purbalingga, in East Java. This place, which was named Madakaripura by King Hayam Wuruk to honour his distinguished Prime Minister, became the spiritual retreat for Gaja Mada to meditate. According to a legend, sometime in 1364 when Gaja Mada was 60 years old, he took his wives and a group of beautiful maidens, all of them enchantingly dressed, to Madakaripura one evening. When they were there, they saw Gaja Mada vanish into thin air never to return again. He had done a *moksa*, a Javanese term to describe the mystical skill of making oneself disappear. King Hayam Wuruk went hunting high and low for him, but in vain. Since then, mystics have believed that Gaja Mada's soul and spirit can be contacted in Madakaripura. Some still go there to meditate.

It was Gaja Mada, the dynamic Prime Minister, who did most to glorify the Kingdom of Majapahit. He became an inspiring hero after his death, with historical writings and legends enhancing his image. Some things which he used during his lifetime such as his kris, his mask, and other *alat-alat* or *pusaka* were believed to contain magical powers. The most sought after *pusaka* of Gaja Mada were his wooden mask and magic kris.

The mask is now carefully preserved in an inconspicuous temple called Pura Penopengan in the village of Belah Batu in Bali. I had the rare honour of not only seeing, but also touching the mask which is now considered holy. It was through the kind courtesy of the Panglima (military commander) of Bali, Brigadier-General Pranoto. The keeper of the mask, a 60-year-old Balinese of royal descent, I Gusti Ngurah Mantra, is a collector of masks. Gusti's family has been keeper of Gaja Mada's mask for six hundred years. It was given to his great great grandfather Aria Rohaya, Commander of War of the Vassal State, by King Hayam Wuruk. Aria Rohaya had served under Gaja Mada when the latter conquered Bali. During a revolt in East Java, Commander Aria was sent to subdue the rebels. When he had accomplished his mission, King Hayam Wuruk asked him what he wanted as a reward. Aria knew about Gaja Mada's mask and took a liking for it, as he was a collector of masks. So he asked for the mask and a set of antique leather puppets used in the *wayang kulit*. He got them.

For six centuries, the mask and *wayang kulit* were kept in a small dilapidated temple and nobody except the keepers took much notice of them. Then one day, sometime in 1967, someone from Jakarta came to borrow the mask. Gusti said that when the mask was first opened for the visitor from Jakarta, a sudden thunderstorm shook the whole of Bali. It was a good omen, the keeper said. It was also a manifestation that the mask had tremendous supernatural power. The mask was kept in Jakarta for one thousand days and after that returned to the Balinese owner. The borrower wanted the mask in order to obtain Gaja Mada's spiritual blessing.

Word soon spread that Gaja Mada's mask had been removed from the Belah Batu Temple in Bali and sent on loan to Jakarta. The news disturbed certain mystics in Bali. One prominent Balinese was annoyed and upset that he himself had not yet had the privilege of seeing the mask, and now it was being displayed in Jakarta. His mental torment was so great that one night, Gaja Mada came to him in a dream, appearing in the form of a gigantic shadow image. The spirit had apparently come to console him and told him to look out for a gift. For three successive days, on his return from work, he would ask his wife whether anyone had brought a gift. The answer was negative. On the fourth day, when he had almost given up hope, a parcel in banana leaves was mysteriously delivered to his house. He opened it and found a stone image of Gaja Mada, similar to that kept in the Belah Batu Temple. (I would just like to add here that the person concerned is not an illiterate, but has a B.A. degree, holds an important job, and is highly respected in the Balinese community.)

Nowadays, to see the mask in the Belah Batu Temple, a special ritual has to be performed, as it was when I visited the shrine. A priest uttered *mantra* and sprinkled holy water to purify the temple. Barefooted and with a piece of cloth tied round our waists, my companions and I stepped into the temple which is the home of Gusti's masks. The priest again sprinkled holy water and *komkom* (fresh flowers in water) and spoke his prayers. The box containing the mask was put on the altar, and another ritual of seeking permission to open it was performed. I could feel the tense atmosphere and excitement as the box was opened, for it was indeed a rare moment. The mask was wrapped in the *merah putih* flag, a sign of official recognition. Gaja Mada's mask was handsome with its high forehead, dynamically piercing eyes, large nose, high cheekbones, broad mouth, long ears and well-formed chin. The most conspicuous part of the reddish-brown mask was the third eye between the brows which signifies his possession of mystical powers. But Gaja Mada was not so handsome after all when the large nose was detached from the mask. The removal of the nose uncovered the ugliness behind. His flat nose and huge, wide mouth with eight sporadically placed uneven teeth turned the mask into an ugly figure. The contrast between beauty and ugliness was exposed so suddenly that it came as a shock to everyone. Explaining to us the story of the detachable nose, Gusti said the maker of the mask obviously wanted to convey the story behind his creation.

Gaja Mada was not as handsome as the mask because of his flat nose and uneven teeth. When he conquered Bali, he fell in love with a Balinese girl, Gunti Ayu Bebet, and asked for her hand in marriage. She refused because Gaja Mada's face did not appeal to her. So Gaja Mada prayed to God for supernatural power to make himself more presentable. His prayer was answered. When Gunti Ayu saw him next, he appeared rather handsome with a high nose and a charming, broad smile. The mask apparently was made to commemorate the successful romance. The story of Gaja Mada's mask therefore hangs between myth and reality.

However, the disappearance of Gaja Mada's kris still remains as mysterious as the disappearance of its owner. Nobody knows the whereabouts of his kris, which is said to be the symbol of authority. Some people claimed that Sukarno was in possession of the kris but when he lost his political grip and *wahyu* (God-given spiritual power), the kris disappeared. A search is still on to locate the kris. Because it is priceless, many have claimed that they possess the kris, but few, in fact, have actually seen the great kris of Gaja Mada. Perhaps it is in keeping with tradition that the kris of a prominent leader be hidden so that his descendants continually search for it.

Today, the image of Gaja Mada, made of stone, is used by mystics in their reading-rooms for spiritual communication. Every morning and evening, the owners place flowers below the statue and hope that one day the soul of Gaja Mada can be invoked. In some homes, there are huge paintings of Gaja Mada standing triumphantly on an elephant at the height of his victorious battles. This is a common theme for artists, particularly those from East Java. I visited an artist's studio in Surabaya and on the wall were at least ten paintings of Gaja Mada riding on an elephant or holding his magic kris. There was also a scene where Gaja Mada bowed before King Hayam Wuruk to demonstrate his loyalty. The artist told me that these Gaja Mada paintings were in great demand. This trend clearly illustrates the respect and veneration that the Indonesian people still have for Gaja Mada today. It is not uncommon, therefore, to find streets named after him in many towns and cities of Java.

However, on one visit to Bandung in West Java, I was most surprised to discover that there is not one street named after Gaja Mada or even Hayam Wuruk. Bandung is the capital of Sunda, West Java. It seems there was an unfortunate incident between Gaja Mada and the Royal Sundanese family. The young King Hayam Wuruk of East Java wished to marry the daughter of the King of Sunda. After negotiations were conducted by the Prime Minister, an invitation was extended to the Sundanese King to visit the Majapahit capital with his daughter. The Sundanese were proud that the daughter of their King was to become the official queen of the mightiest empire of Indonesia. The wedding would have meant the inauguration of an alliance between two kingdoms whereby the poor state of Sunda might share some of the wealth of its eastern neighbour. But Prime Minister Gaja Mada wanted the King of Sunda to deliver his princess to the royal harem as a tribute from a vassal to his overlord. The Sundanese, being a proud people, refused and a battle ensued in which the Sundanese King was killed. According to the story, the princess killed herself on the battlefield beside her father's body. After that massacre, rancour and hostility existed between the Javanese and Sundanese, and the latter never submitted to Gaja Mada's authority.

Another leader that still inspires the Indonesian people is Prince Diponegoro. He was an anti-colonialist hero who fought against the Dutch. Today, there are many streets all over Indonesia named after him. One of them is in Jakarta where the Singapore Embassy is situated. In the Presidential Square, next to the National Monument, stands a bronze statue of Diponegoro on horseback. In the Presidential Palace hangs a beautiful oil painting of Diponegoro by Basuki Abdullah, one of Indonesia's more famous painters. The hero's name will invariably pass through the lips of all Indonesians when they relate the anti-colonial struggle of the past.

Diponegoro was born in November 1785, the eldest son of Sultan

Hamengkubuwono III, also known as Sultan Raja. He grew up during a turbulent period that witnessed the decline and fall of the Dutch East India Company, the subsequent occupation of Java by the British, and then the return of Dutch colonial administration. But in his youth, Diponegoro was more interested in spiritual matters and lived in Tegalrejo in Central Java where he was educated by his grandmother. He soon led a life of seclusion and meditation in the mountains, interrupted occasionally by distasteful news of the court and of his brother, Sultan Hamengkubuwono IV, who was indulging in a life of pleasure and ignoring his state duties. The Queen Mother was equally corrupted and was more interested in court intrigue than anything else. The situation in the court was described in a poem composed by a famous Javanese poet, R. Ng Ranggamarsita. It was a satire on Javanese society of that period which was marked by moral decline. A stanza in the *Kalatida* (The Age of Darkness) reads as follows:

> We have witnessed a time of madness
> In which everyone is confused in his mind.
> One cannot bear to join in the madness
> But if he does not do so, he will not share in the spoils
> And will starve as a result.
> Indeed, it is the will of Allah
> That those who are careful and vigilant
> Are much happier than those who are careless.

Diponegoro wanted to change the situation. So one day he sent his servant, Jaya Mustapa, to the tomb of Sultan Agung, the great ruler of the Mataram Empire in the seventeenth century, to wait for a mystical sign. Jaya Mustapa was admitted to the tomb and spent the night in meditation. The next morning after finishing his prayers, he saw on the curtain covering the entrance of the tomb a bloodstain as big as a plate. He asked the caretaker what it was and the latter replied that there was no bloodstain there the night before. The caretaker, Kyay Ballad, then remarked, "It is God's will that much blood must be shed in Java; it is a sign that war will come. The will of God is absolute, his decision cannot be changed."

When Diponegoro heard about this, he went further into meditation and contemplation, until one day, as he sat dreaming, he heard a voice from heaven asking him to change his name to Ngabdulkamid, Servant of God. The voice told him that he was destined to be the man of action who would bring Java back to its original splendour and prestige. In order to do that he would soon receive Sarutana, a magic arrow. When the Prince woke up, he saw a flash of lightning hit the ground before him. When he lifted his head, he was surprised to see an arrow-head, Sarutana, stuck in the rock. The voice that he heard was believed to have been that of Queen Lara Kidul.

The news of Diponegoro's mystical experience spread like wildfire. Soon after, Diponegoro led a rebellion against the Dutch, but failed as the time was not ripe for a revolution. However, his uprising sparked off a movement which inspired the Indonesian people to finally oust the Dutch in 1945. When Diponegoro's insurrection failed, he was arrested by the Dutch and exiled to Menado on the island of Celebes, where he wrote his autobiography. Later he was brought to more habitable quarters in Makassar. His last years were spent in ascetic practices, in meditation and writing. In 1855 he died in Makassar. His grave became a shrine and has attracted many visitors and worshippers from all over Indonesia.

In Jogjakarta, the authorities have made a Diponegoro Museum of the old residence of the hero. The museum has a big hall for theatrical performances and another smaller compound-house where all the belongings and *pusaka* of Diponegoro are kept. An old painting showing the scene of Diponegoro's narrow escape from capture by the Dutch attracted my attention. The scene was of the place where the museum is now situated. In that painting, the houses were ablaze, having been set on fire by the Dutch, and Diponegoro was directing his relatives and supporters to escape through a hole in a solid brick wall. My guide, who was the caretaker of the museum, took me to the broken wall. He told me that Diponegoro had shattered the thick wall with his bare fists. Of course, it is not so much his magical powers but his courage to fight the Dutch colonialists that has won him the respect of the Indonesian people.

The Diponegoro Museum is also the meeting-place for the Rumpun Diponegoro, the unit of all members of the Diponegoro Division headed by President Suharto. I was told that President Suharto himself grew up in a village very near the residence of Diponegoro.

Visiting the graves of heroes and kings is now common practice in Java. I once visited the graves of Mangkunegara I, II and III on the top of a mountain. One has to get special permission to visit such sacred places. There, I accidentally met a friend of mine who is related to Mangkunegara III. He told me that he and his family visited the grave once a month to pay their respects. From the top of the mountain one has a panoramic view of beautiful valleys below. I experienced a feeling of peace and serenity. Before entering the shrine where the graves were, we had to take off our shoes and wait for the spirits to be informed of our arrival. Two *imam* offered prayers as fragrant incense was burning. Flowers were sprinkled on the graves. The stone graves were simple but stately. The grave of Mangkunegara II was inscribed with old Javanese script, but that of Mangkunegara III had an inscription of Javanese mixed with Arabic.

On the following night, I visited the house of Pak Parno, the *guru* in Solo, who got his disciples to contact the soul of King Mangkunegara I. The disciples pressed their left hands to their necks and their right hands to their left armpits and meditated. After fifteen minutes, one of them reported that he had established contact with the spirit of the King. Through him, the King said that he was pleased with our visit and that when I was at the grave, the King had touched my forehead and had provided me with a yellow umbrella over my head as a sign of welcome.

Communicating with the souls is nothing new to me, for during my childhood, I used to visit Chinese temples where Taoist priests invoked the souls of desired ancestors. But I was keen to know the reason behind Javanese ancestor-worship, and so I asked Pak Parno for his opinion. The Javanese believe that spirits are like humans except for the physical body—they have thoughts, desires and feelings. Therefore, the ancestors continued to take an interest in their descendants so that the latter could gratify their desires through them. From the mystical point of view, the contact between the living and the dead was a matter of sending and receiving vibrations. Those who have been properly trained and have acquired mystical powers have stronger perception, or more powerful 'transmitters', to enable them to transmit and receive messages from the spiritual world. This was briefly the theory of mystics as explained to me by Pak Parno.

A similar theory applies to those who make predictions. According to legend, there was a king who had extraordinary powers of predicting the future—in fact, he is said to have accurately predicted the history of Indonesia up to the present day. This king, Prabu Joyoboyo, lived in Kediri around 1157, or 1079 according to the Javanese calendar. His full name was Sang Mapani Jayabaya Sri Dharmaishwara, Petera Makhota Sri Erlangger Raja. He was an unusual king in that he was not only a good warrior and administrator, but also a gifted poet and astrologer. He was responsible for the revised version of Bharatajudha, the popular theme of the *wayang* play depicting the bitter war between the Pandawa and Kurawa families. Like a prophet, he received inspiration from God and predicted the whole history of Java including the birth of the Indonesian nation, all beautifully written in Javanese *pantun*. His predictions were considered so accurate by his followers that both the Dutch and later the Japanese colonialists banned the Joyoboyo predictions for fear that they might inspire the people to revolt. It is claimed that Joyoboyo had predicted hundreds of years ago that a "yellow peacock" from the north-east would come to drive away the "white buffalo with blue eyes" from Indonesian soil. When events had transpired, believers of Joyoboyo's predictions interpreted "yellow peacock" to mean the Japanese and "white buffalo", the Dutch colonialists. The prediction later added that "the black ants will lay eggs on fine ashes" which was interpreted to mean that the Indonesian people would achieve their independence by revolution.

Another Joyoboyo prediction, *"Ana merak bandrek lawar haja"* meaning 'a peacock commits adultery with a crocodile', was interpreted to mean that the red men, the British, conspired with the crocodile, the Dutch (the enemy of the Indonesians), to regain their colonial possessions.

The Joyoboyo predictions also give advice, such as *"Kuching gering ingkang nunggonni"* meaning 'the sick cat is unable to guard against rats'. A cat is a symbol of the guardian or administrator. If it is sick or lazy, the rat, which represents the villains, will be free to run round it in circles.

"Si Percil ingkang and jaga" (a little frog guards the well) means that there is hope in the younger generation who will safeguard the nation.

Since Joyoboyo is believed to have predicted very accurately the past history of Indonesia, the people are waiting for the last phase of his prediction, the arrival of Ratu Adil, a just king who will bring peace, justice, stability and prosperity to the nation.

Sometime in 1972, through an Indonesian friend, I met a young mystic who claimed to have supernatural powers. He had five hundred needles stuck all over his body and asked me to touch a needle to see for myself that it was real. He said the needles helped him to communicate with the supernatural beings in the cosmos. He said some of these supernatural powers could be contacted through meditation. In order to convince me, he soon went into a trance with his eyes downcast. He sat cross-legged and spoke in Javanese for about ten minutes. When he awoke, I asked him with whom he had communicated, and his reply was "Joyoboyo".

"You mean you have contacted King Joyoboyo, the poet king and astrologer who was supposed to have existed some nine hundred years ago?" I asked him.

"Yes," he replied.

"And what did he tell you?" I asked.

He replied that King Joyoboyo predicted that there would be further trouble in the country and one had to be on guard. That was sometime in the middle of 1972. Incidentally, there were riots in Bandung in August 1973 and further riots in Jakarta in January 1974. The young mystic often went to the mountains with his *guru* to communicate with the supernatural. I asked him how he managed to get the five hundred needles into his body, thinking it had something to do with the methods used in Chinese acupuncture. He replied, "It was quite easy. My *guru* put the needles in his mouth, said some *mantra* and blew them into my body without my feeling any pain."

Having heard a lot about the coming of Ratu Adil, I was naturally curious to know more about him. According to the *Babad Diponegoro*, which described the most famous revolt against the Dutch (1825–1830), Diponegoro himself claimed to have seen Ratu Adil at the foot of a mountain situated south-east of Rasamuni in Central Java. Excerpts from the long chronicle said, "Ratu Adil was standing on the top of the mountain viewing the sun's splendour, so that he paled for a time. Because of this, the Prince (Diponegoro) was unable to behold Ratu Adil's face, but he clearly saw his apparel. His turban was green, his shirt, outer garment and trousers were white and his scarf was red .... Ratu Adil told Diponegoro, 'I have summoned you to tell you that you must lead my whole army into battle. Conquer Java with it'."

In the history of Java, several leaders had tried to claim that they were the Ratu Adil or were instructed by Ratu Adil to save the nation.

Since the Joyoboyo predictions, many more predictions have been made by mystics from generation to generation. They form part of the pattern of life in Javanese society. Those who are in close touch with mystical predictions sometimes have an advantage over others. Some of the predictions have, somehow or other, turned out to be true.

In 1965, just before the September 30 Gestapu coup, a young mystic made a prediction in a letter to General Yani. I read a photostat copy of the letter dated March 1965, written by the mystic who called himself Sjah. General Yani was then Chief of Staff of the Army under former President Sukarno. Sjah's letter predicted a big change in the Indonesian government, involving chaos and bloodshed. Sjah predicted that after the upheaval, a new leader would emerge to lead the Indonesian nation towards peace and stability. It would be for the better. But the letter warned General Yani, repeatedly using the word *berhati-hati* (be careful) in the months of August, September and October. General Yani received this warning six months before he was murdered. He died in the early hours of 1 October 1965. Therefore, a new mystical element has been added to the death of one of Indonesia's national heroes.

I was told that before the riots of 15 January 1974, a well-known mystic received messages of warning that dark clouds would loom over Jakarta and that the fate of the country would be decided on 16 January. That was the day when stern action was taken after General Mantik's radio warning to rioters who demonstrated their anger against the official visit of the former Japanese Prime Minister Tanaka.

My friend told me that it was also due to the advice of supernatural powers that the controversial Muslim Marriage Bill was pushed through in Parliament before the January affair. The Bill tried to impose some form of restriction on an Indonesian Muslim from marrying four wives indiscriminately. There would have been far-reaching consequences, it is said, if the riots had taken place when the controversy arising from the Bill had not yet been settled. The inspiration from supernatural forces to hurry the Bill through may appear like a myth to many, but I have no reason to doubt that the advice was taken seriously, and acted upon. The January riots could have been worse if the delicate and sensitive issue of the Muslim Marriage Bill had not been resolved.

Ancestral spirits and predictions are, therefore, not simply matters pertaining to the past or to mystics alone. A knowledge or an appreciation of such beliefs can help one to better understand the present-day Indonesian society.

12

When Indonesia gained her independence and declared herself a Republic in 1945, the people did away with feudalism. In Indonesia political power is no more decided by inheritance. Sultans lost their political grip as the system of feudalism and aristocracy was phased out. The *kraton* of Surakarta and Jogjakarta have now become symbols of ancient Javanese feudalism and aristocracy. The same applies to the *kraton* in Cirebon, Siak, Kota Waringin in Langkat and Goa in Sulawesi. Although the Indonesian Revolution stripped the sultans of their political powers, the influence of *kraton* culture still lingers in the minds of many people, particularly the Javanese commonfolk who had lived in the shadow of the *kraton* for centuries.

Was it not a fact that, in the past, Javanese aristocrats always regarded Central Java as the centre of the universe? The names of the Javanese kings throw light on this concept. Hamengkubuwono means literally 'the universe (*buwono*) is on the lap (*mengku*) of the king'. Thus, Sultan Hamengkubuwono, the present Vice-President of Indonesia, is supposed to be a descendant of the king who had the whole universe on his lap. Similarly, Mangkunegara means 'the whole country on the lap of the prince', and Paku Alam, the title held by another Sultan of Jogjakarta, means 'nailing (*paku*) the universe (*alam*)'. In other words,

Jogjakarta is the centre of the universe where the nail is pinned so that it is under control.

In the sixteenth century, there was only one *kraton* in the capital of the Mataram Empire — in Surakarta, also known as Solo. Later, a land dispute between the Susuhunan (Prince) of Surakarta, Pakubuwono II, and his younger brother, the Prince of Mangkubumi, brought about a partitioning of the realm into two self-governing principalities in 1755. The Sultanate of Jogjakarta thus came into being and Mangkubumi assumed the title of Sultan of Jogjakarta. A further dispute followed between the Susuhunan of Surakarta and one Raden Mas Sahid, a member of the Surakarta aristocracy, resulting in a further split of the Surakarta realm. This was the birth of the small self-governing principality called Mangkunegara in 1757, headed by Sahid, who took the title of Prince Mangkunegara.

In the realm of the Sultanate of Jogjakarta, a similar divide-and-rule tactic was adopted by the British when they took over control during the interregnum from 1811 to 1816. They created a small enclave within the Jogjakarta Sultanate and appointed Prince Notokusumo, a brother of Sultan Hamengkubuwono II, as the ruler. Sultan Hamengkubuwono II was then exiled by the British Government. The new principality, which was smaller in size, took the name of Paku Alam, and its ruler became known as Prince Paku Alam.

By 1816 the former Mataram Empire had been split into four self-governing principalities and each had its own *kraton*, which remains until today. Under the colonial period, the ruler of each of these realms was no longer a monarch with absolute political, military and religious powers. In theory, the rulers held sway over all lands within their borders, but, in practice, they were left only with the right to continue with their traditional ways of administration, culture and ceremonies. With considerable means at their disposal, they were able to devote themselves to the cultivation of courtly art forms and to the maintenance of the *kraton* culture. Many of the art forms in the traditional *kraton* dances, such as those we see today in the Jogjakarta and Surakarta *kraton*, were refined during this period. Despite the 350 years of Dutch rule, nothing much has changed in the field of cultural tradition and court ceremonies, for there was little interference in such activities.

It is not an exaggeration, therefore, to say that to understand the Javanese, who, after all, comprise approximately 60 per cent of the Indonesian population, it is necessary to visit Central Java more often, particularly the *kraton*. These *kraton* in Jogjakarta and

167

Surakarta were once the centres of political intrigues and cultural activities of old Java.

Whenever time permitted, I would visit the *kraton* which never failed to stimulate my imagination. I always tried to imagine what had transpired in those palaces during the days of the Sultanates. I never missed an opportunity to examine the array of *pusaka*, the former rulers' collections such as krises, spears, sacred musical instruments, carriages and other objects which formed an integral part of every *kraton*. It is not easy anymore to find such people as the albinos, clowns, dwarfs and soothsayers who once wandered about in the *kraton* compounds. It was believed that these extraordinary people provided an additional source of spiritual energy for the rulers who were able to absorb their powers. Their disappearance was considered a diminution of the king's power and a sign of impending collapse of a dynasty. The customs and traditions that originated from the *kraton* are most fascinating and still make an impact on the Javanese way of life.

The *kraton* of Surakarta has a mystical past. The Kingdom of Mataram was founded by Panembahen Senopati in 1582, with its capital at Kota Gede. Later, the capital was moved to Kartasura and finally to Surakarta where the present *kraton* is situated.

The transfer of this capital had something to do with voices from the cosmic world. The Tumenggung Tirtawiguna and Pangeran Wijil were sent by King Pakubuwono II of Kartasura to look for a suitable site for a new capital. It was just after a revolt, and the palace had suffered great damage as a result of the fierce fighting. While doing penance at the side of a river, Tirtawiguna and Wijil heard a voice which said, "You who do penance, if you want a site for a capital city, go to the village of Solo, because it is the place decreed by Allah, and it will become a great and prosperous city." They went to the village of Solo and found a site near a lake which was considered the most suitable place for the construction of a *kraton*. The problem was how to drain the water from the lake. At first, King Pakubuwono II ordered all the regents of the near-by regions to come with timber to fill the lake, but it was of no avail. The lake not only could not be filled, but seemed to get deeper and deeper and fishes were seen swimming in it. Then came again another voice saying, "If you wish to stop the water swelling in the lake, cover it with the *gong sekerdelima* and the head of a woman dancer together with rubber leaves." The King interpreted the revelation as follows: a *gong* is also called *gangsa*, and *gangsa* is also the name of an orchestral instrument which can sound like a voice; in other words, it refers to a story-teller. A woman dancer is a *ringgit*, and *ringgit* also means 'money'; the head refers to the amount of money — namely, 10,000 *ringgit* which was to be given to the story-teller. Thus Kyai Sala, the village chief and story-teller, was given 10,000 *ringgit* and ordered to stop the lake waters from swelling. He succeeded and the place came to be known as Kedung Lumbu, which means 'a swamp of water-plants'. The lake was, in fact, drained and filled with the soil taken from Talawangi, the present Kadipolo. The *kraton* was then built on the site together with other buildings.

According to the records 'Surat Nitik Kraton' from Pangaran Kusumoyudo and the book *Sri Radya Laksana* written by a committee of seven people headed by Mas Ngabehi Prajaduto, the grandest of all ceremonies took place when the King and his household moved from Kartasura to Surakarta. It was a complete transplantation of everything belonging to the King in the old *kraton*, including the court banyan trees. The King, dressed as a bridegroom, was seated in the royal wagon, Kyahi Garuda, accompanied by high-ranking officials, regalia-carriers and 200 soldiers of the *Tamtama* (Royal Bodyguard) on each side of him. Behind him came the ladies of the court, wives of Ministers and their respective attendants, followed by *pusaka*, the royal heirlooms, placed in wooden boxes, then by the *gamelan* orchestra and animals such as horses and birds, as well as the King's pet lion in a cage, and so on. The cooks with their kitchen utensils came in groups, carrying food and water for the King and the royal family, followed by officials and people carrying everything connected with the preparation of food. The banyan trees were carried by attendants from the coastal districts. The people from the coastal areas also helped to carry the cannons of the King, including the most prominent cannon called Nyai Setomi. It was fun and laughter all the way. The tunes played by the *gamelan* during the parade mingled with the tunes produced by *gamelan* orchestras along the road welcoming the King. The removal of the capital from Kartasura to Surakarta took one whole day, ending with a big feast after the King had proclaimed Surakarta the new capital.

There is a story behind the cannon, Nyai Setomi. It was said that the King of Pajajaran had a dream in which he saw a very powerful weapon which sounded like thunder. He ordered his *Patih* (Prime Minister) to look for the weapon and threatened him with death if he failed to find it. The *Patih*, whose name was Kyai Setomo, went home with a heavy heart and discussed the matter with his wife, Nyai Setomi. Both of them went into seclusion to meditate and to ask the help of the Almighty. After a long while, when the King received no news from his Prime Minister, he ordered a messenger to see what had happened to him. A big search was organized, and the messenger discovered two strange objects in the room of the *Patih*. The King, on hearing the news, rushed to see the strange objects and recognized them as the weapons he saw in his dream. A voice from the cosmic world then told the King that the two cannons were the transformations of Kyai Setomo and Nyai Setomi.

It was not long before Sultan Agung of the Mataram Empire heard about the two cannons and ordered them to be brought to him. Kyai Setomo, the male cannon, refused to go to Mataram, so one night, he fled on his own to Jakarta. On arrival, he stationed himself in front of the gate of the Kasteel in Jakarta. It was already dawn and he could not move any further. So he stayed there. Thus, the people came to regard him as a holy cannon and called him Kyai Jagur, offering a little paper umbrella to protect him from the sun's heat. Nyai Setomi was left behind in Mataram and remained there, unhappy and lonely. From time to time she wept, and her tears were caught in a bowl. (The cannons were, in fact, brought by the Portuguese for the artillery unit in Malacca in the fifteenth century. When the Dutch captured the city of Malacca, they took the cannons to Jakarta. One was perhaps later taken to Central Java.)

When I last visited the Surakarta *kraton*, it was a privileged occasion because I was to witness a royal wedding. The whole ceremony gave me a glimpse of the past grandeur of Javanese aristocracy. It was a traditional Javanese wedding, one of the most interesting and elaborate that I have ever seen. It was the wedding of the second daughter of the Susuhunan of Java and the Governor of Central Kalimantan, who happened to be a friend of mine. The hosts were General Sudjono Humardani, then Presidential Assistant for Economic Affairs, and General Surono, then Deputy Commander of the Indonesian Armed Forces. I was their guest. It was, indeed, a rare opportunity for me. The bridegroom was a Christian Dayak and the bride, a Muslim Javanese, a nominal one as many Javanese are. It was one of the grandest weddings ever performed in Solo in recent years and the first held inside the palace since independence.

The bridegroom arrived from Kalimantan three days before the wedding. He reported to the Susuhunan and was immediately confined by the guards to a small room inside the compound of the palace. For three days and three nights he was kept there with only one companion — a small chicken — and offerings, such as flowers and Javanese rice-cakes. Among the offerings was a pair of human figures — a bridal couple — made of rice-cake. The bridegroom had his meals brought to him as he was not supposed to leave the room until the third day when the grand wedding ceremony was to take place. On the third morning, he was escorted to the palace hall for the initiation ceremony. The official conducting the ceremony was an *imam*. Can an *imam* bless a marriage between a Christian and a Muslim? With the traditional Javanese spirit of compromise and tolerance, nothing is impossible. The *imam* had just to bless the marriage contract and everything was happily settled.

The real show began at twilight. The bridegroom, with bare chest and wearing a silvery *songkok* and a pair of loose trousers, arrived to fetch the bride from the inner chamber of the palace, called the *dalem*. He was ushered all the way by two older female court-dancers with painted faces, apparently meant to be clowns to attract attention. The beating of drums accompanied them all the way. At the *pringgitan* (outer chamber) of the palace, the Susuhunan gave away the bride. Together, the bridal couple emerged from the *pringgitan*, followed by relatives and friends. The bride had a hair-do similar to that of an actress in the traditional Teochew *wayang*. The undulating curls of the hair above the forehead were exactly the same. The bride was beautifully powdered and wore the sparkling, traditional off-shoulder Javanese dress. A pagoda-like carriage, called *tandu*, with wooden handles on both sides, was lowered for the bride to take her seat accompanied by a bridesmaid. Eight muscular men in *kraton* costume then lifted the *tandu* onto their strong shoulders. I noticed that a colourful dragon and phoenix decorated the pagoda-like carriage. It reminded me of the ancient Chinese wooden palanquin, known as *chiao tse*, which was used for similar occasions. I saw a similar *chiao tse* in one of the Imperial palaces of the Forbidden City in Peking during my visit there in March, 1975. It was used to convey the Empress Dowager of the Ch'ing dynasty around the Forbidden City. The Javanese wedding entourage was preceded by an army of spear-carrying soldiers in traditional military uniform. The bridegroom had to walk beside the carriage until he reached the entrance of the palace where a horse was waiting. He was assisted onto the horse and the journey to another ceremony began. All the way, the bridegroom was escorted by another army of soldiers carrying bows and arrows. The whole procession was a spectacle of colour and pomp. The crowd milled along to watch the fun.

The bride at a traditional Javanese wedding washes the foot of the bridegroom after he has stepped on an egg.

On arrival at the house where the bridegroom was staying, the bride alighted from the carriage and the bridegroom, from the horse to perform the most symbolic part of the wedding ceremony. An egg was placed in front of the bridegroom. He stepped on it, causing it to crack under his foot. It is a vow that he would be faithful to her for as long as the broken egg could not turn into a chick — that is, forever. With a smile on her sweet face, the bride washed his foot with water taken from a basin as a token of gratitude. The washing of the feet was also a symbol of willingness to obey.

The ceremony entered its third phase when he carried her in his arms to the chamber. When the two were seated at the *pringgitan*, the bridegroom fed the bride with some *klimah* (rice-balls). This gesture signified that she would take anything that might be offered to her by the bridegroom, symbolizing her willing-ness to go through life with him for better or for worse and through thick and thin. This traditional wedding ceremony is being revived throughout Java in what seems to be a conscious effort to uphold tradition.

The bride and bridegroom spent the rest of the evening seated at the *pringgitan* of the *kraton* facing the *pendopo* where a royal dance was performed to entertain the dignitaries. When the soft tones of the *paleton* and the melodious *suluk* were heard accompanied by the reverberating *gamelan*, nine dancers appeared from inside the palace to perform the Bedaya. Slowly and stately, they advanced in single file towards the stage surrounded by pillars. Two female attendants crouched on their heels all the way to see that their feet did not step on the wine-red *cinde* cloth which trailed at their ankles. The dancers wore dark blue, gold embossed *dodot*, heavy gold armlets and bracelets, and crescent-shaped gold medal-lions hanging from their slender necks. Again, their faces and hairlines reminded me of Teochew *wayang* actresses. However, it was the Surakarta court style of bridal make-up. The costumes were esoterically designed with patterns symbolizing animals of the forest, mountains and oceans. Their hair was coiled into buns with centrepieces of a *garuda* bird, surrounded by quivering gold butterflies, flowers and metal spirals. Moving slowly and languidly with eyes downcast, the dancers occasionally flicked their long sashes and gently kicked their swirling trains. The hypnotic bell-like sound of the *kamandak* (an archaic instrument played only on royal occasions) and the dreamy chanting gave added charm to the tranquil atmosphere. When the last heavy gong struck, the dancers stopped. The nine dancers rose slowly, and gracefully returned to the inner chambers followed by the two crouching attendants. It was a rare and unforgettable sight. This dance was originally ordered by Sultan Agung to commemorate the Queen of the Indonesian Ocean, Lara Kidul. It was really a dance befitting Queen Lara Kidul. Sultan Agung was the last of the great kings whose lives and miraculous exploits were the subject of tales connecting them with spirits and ancestors. He was also accredited with supernatural powers.

The *kraton* of Jogjakarta is one of the finest examples of Javanese palace architecture in existence. The greater *kraton* is enclosed on four sides by high brick walls within which some 26,000 people live. There is a market, some shops, cottage industries making batik and silverware, schools and mosques. A large section of the *kraton* also houses the medical college of the Gaja Mada University.

Outside the entrance is a rectangular cage with wire fencing above a wooden stage. It was used in ancient times to confine a convict who had been sentenced to death. This was to give everybody a chance to look at the convict before he was brought to the gallows.

The basic concept of most Javanese palace architecture is to provide open pavilions and spacious courtyards. The two large northern courtyards — Pagelaran and Sitihinggil — were used until very recently (1949–1973) by the Gaja Mada University as classrooms and administrative centre.

The gateway to the inner courtyard is guarded by two giant demons, Lindoroboro on the right representing the goodness of man, and Bolokukoto on the left symbolizing evil. The significance is that both good and evil spirits dwell in the heart of every man, and the fight goes on eternally to possess the soul.

I am always enchanted by the sweet, unpunctuated chirps of thousands of little sparrows from the *sawo* (a juicy fruit) trees which give the spacious inner compound of the *kraton* an atmosphere of mellowed calm. The blue and white Ming and Ch'ing porcelain here and there all round the edges of the compound adds to the beauty and aristocracy of the palace. I am always tempted to pause a little whenever I put my feet on the 'sacred square'. I feel silently guilty for having my shoes on, for I can visualize the sacredness of the place when large numbers of leafpickers were employed in the old days to pick leaves with their sharp-pointed spears to clean up the garden. In those days, the compound was considered sacred and no brooms were allowed. At least a hundred or more servants were employed to pick the leaves daily. Times have changed and the traditional way of keeping the place clean has now given way to brooms.

The subtle and indirect Javanese approach has been applied in hinting at the year of construction of the *kraton*, which was completed in 1853. The date is depicted by a *candrasang kala*, a chronogram of a crown (meaning one), a curled snake in the figure of 8, and giants which look like the numbers 5 and 3. The four figures are all interwoven into a harmonious design reading from right to left, the way Arabic characters are read.

In another section of the *kraton*, there are separate entrances for the opposite sexes. This is indicated, not by means of characters in terms of 'ladies' and 'gentlemen', but by two giant-sized dragons, one a 'he' dragon and the other a 'she' dragon. To me, the two dragons look alike. But perhaps it was meant to be that way. Unlike the Chinese dragon, a Javanese dragon has no horns and has the tail of a snake. It is not so fearful.

At another entrance, I saw an old Javanese in traditional dress, sitting cross-legged, reading an old Javanese script of the *Mahabharata* which contained *wayang* puppet figures. While killing time this way, he occasionally glanced at an antique grandfather clock to see that he did not neglect his duty of striking the drum every half hour to keep inmates of the *kraton* informed of the time of day. This century-old tradition goes on despite the invention of watches; perhaps the grandfather clock is more reliable. It is yet another example of Javanese conservatism. Perhaps the tradition is meant to bring home the Javanese philosophical approach to time and space. Time is important (shown by keeping everyone informed of the correct time) and yet unimportant (by wasting manpower just to strike the drum every half hour). At the corner leading to the rooms is a huge, bottle-shaped, wooden gong. This used to be struck as an alarm in case of fire, disasters or other acts of God.

The most interesting section of the *kraton* is the room where old photographs, showing the royal family tree, are kept. In this room are also the personal belongings of past Sultans, their wives and children, including precious dowries of past royal weddings. Among the photographs are some showing the grandest mass royal wedding of the century which took place about thirty years ago. There were seven couples involving the two brothers and five sisters of Sri Sultan Hamengkubuwono. Some of the pictures show the brides and bridegrooms walking together with their little fingers intertwined to indicate that the bride was a commoner. Other pictures show the bridegrooms carrying the brides in their arms—an indication that the brides were from royal families. The dowries of olden days consisted of gold in the shape of different types of animals. There were the dragon (*hardowaliko*), the cock (*sawung*), the duck (*banyak*), the deer (*dalang*), and the peacock (*galing*), each having its own mystical meaning. The rice bed, called *demisori*, which resembles a bed, is still being used at royal weddings for the bride and bridegroom to sit on. It is meant to bring fertility to the married couple to produce as many children as the harvests of rice produced on a fertile farm.

History repeated itself on a smaller scale in the Jogjakarta *kraton* sometime in May 1974 when Sultan Hamengkubuwono gave away four of his daughters in a mass royal wedding ceremony. It was less spectacular compared to that of thirty years ago, for the Sultan, who is also Vice-President of the Republic of Indonesia, wanted to show a good example of austerity which is being propagated throughout the country.

The Jogjakarta *kraton* also has a special room which houses the *wayang* puppets. They are kept like sacred humans. Every Thursday, they are brought out to the garden one by one to breathe some fresh air. Once a year, they are given a holy bath together with other royal articles when a special ceremony is held.

About two minutes' drive from the *kraton* is a large royal godown where all the royal carriages are kept. One made in England has a British crown embossed on it and the others were either specially ordered or locally made. When I visited the royal garage one Friday, I found fresh flowers sprinkled round it. Offerings of this nature are made by many Javanese every Friday. Some believers even sleep in the carriages overnight, hoping that the souls of past kings might descend on them to provide spiritual guidance.

In Solo, not very far from the Surakarta *kraton*, is the Mangku-negara *kraton*. Occupying an area of more than 900 square metres, the Mangkunegara *kraton* dates back to 1757, after a bitter struggle launched by Raden Mas Sahid, the founder of the House and of whom the present First Lady of Indonesia is a descendant. Like all *kraton*, it is divided into three sections consisting of the *pendopo*, the *pringgitan* and the *dalem*. In the Mangkunegara *kraton*, old Javanese traditions and practices such as hitting the time drum every half hour are less adhered to. In fact, the Mangkunegara *kraton* has become a tourist attraction and at times important visitors are allowed to view the inner bedrooms and bathrooms of the princesses.

The first thing that struck me when I entered the *pendopo* was the four beautifully-carved *soko guru* (pillars) in Joglo architecture, and the rounded ceiling composed of hundreds of *sirap* (wooden tiles) lined with copper so as to last eternally. The four *soko guru*, made of solid teak, represent the four elements of nature — earth, water, fire and wind. The ceiling, which is 11 metres from the ground, is intricately ornamented with figures of the zodiac signs harmoniously draped in Javanese style with eye-catching colours. The main motif of the painting on the ceiling is the sparkling flame inspired by the prince's collection of old Javanese miniatures called *Kumudhowati*. In the centre of the ceiling are painted the eight points of the zodiac compass, each in its own mystical colour. Yellow signifies a preventive against sleepiness, blue a preventive against disease, black against hunger, green against desire, white against lust, rose against fear, red against evil and purple against wicked thoughts. All the zodiac decorations symbolically reflect the meanings in Javanese philosophical life. The two-century-old *pendopo* is probably the biggest ever constructed in the country. It was enlarged by the late Mangkunegara VII and is carefully maintained.

On the right-hand side of the *pendopo* is the Kyai Kanyut Mesem, one of the oldest sets of *gamelan*. In Javanese, *kyai* means 'reverence' and *kanyut mesem* means 'drifting in smile'. Thus, this complete set of classical instruments, 'drifting in smiles', brings back memories of past glories of the Mangkunegara Kingdom during performances every Wednesday.

A few steps up from the *pendopo* is the *pringgitan*, the front part of the *dalem*. This is where the royal family receives guests. Sometimes the *wayang kulit* is performed in this part of the building with the screen facing inwards so that the woman attendants in the *dalem* can view from inside, while the other guests have the privilege of seeing the *dalang* operating the puppets from behind. The wall of the *pringgitan* is decorated with paintings by Basuki Abdullah, Indonesia's world-famous artist.

It was a rare privilege in the past to be invited into the privacy of the *dalem*, beautiful with its ancient Javanese architecture and eight *soko guru* — the eight pillars of wisdom. This part of the palace is used for traditional ceremonies such as royal weddings and other important festivities. On entering the hall, one is immediately attracted by two figures made of stone and seated on the floor. They represent the bride and bridegroom, called *Loro Blonyo* in Javanese. Both are dressed in traditional Javanese wedding costumes. At traditional ceremonies the guests also have to sit on the floor.

Being interested in antiques, I was captivated by the rich collection of ancient articles of cultural value arranged systematically inside the various cupboards and glass show-cases. This was a collection by Mangkunegara VII half a century ago. It includes old coins, bronze Hindu-Javanese statues, and gold jewellery from the Hindu Majapahit and Mataram periods. The gold-plated dresses for the Srimpi and Bedaya dances and articles used for ceremonial occasions are exquisite and rare. But what really stirred my imagination was the unusually big and heavy-looking gold Buddhistic rings with *mantra* inscriptions. Were they designed for giant fingers, one wonders.

There is also a complete collection of masks from various areas of Indonesia such as Bali, Madura, Bandung, Jogjakarta and Solo. An old library contains classical literary works of the late Mangkunegara, a rich source of wisdom. In the north-west corner of the *kraton* is the *pracimoyono* where Gusti Kangdjeng Putri, the Princess, has her private room. Her Highness Princess Mangkunegara personally showed us her room. It is a blend of old and modern Javanese architecture which was completed in 1921. This is where she receives her guests daily. The bathroom next door is even more interesting. It is built for the traditional way of bathing that is practised in the village. One has to descend a few steps to the well where the water is stored. Then, holding the bucket with the right hand, one has to squat down a little and pour the water over the head to cleanse the body. The long-bath from European cultures has not caught up with even the royal families of Central Java.

Both the Prince and the Princess were very hospitable. Explaining the spread of Islam to Java, they showed me a heavy wooden plaque carved with the figure of Semar. This figure was composed of a combination of Arabic characters — to show that in the early days even the Muslims respected Semar and had to use his mystical personality to spread the teaching of Islam.

Times have changed, but many old traditional ceremonies of the *kraton* are still being performed. As mentioned earlier, once a year in the month of Suro, on Friday (called *kliwon* in Javanese) the fifth day of the five days considered to have magical powers, the ceremony of Siraman is performed. It is the time when all the heirlooms inside the palace are given a holy bath. The objects, which include the golden cart used by the *pangeran* (prince) on ceremonial occasions, the many krises, the *gamelan* and the *wayang* puppets, which are kept individually in separate boxes, are all taken to the bathing site. There, before thousands of spectators, these objects are gently bathed as a mother bathes her baby. The officers who perform the ceremony are *kraton punggawa* who have fasted for one week before the holy undertaking. The ceremony is carried out solemnly and seriously. The spectators bring with them bottles and cans, ready to take away with them the water that was used to bathe the objects. They believe that the water has magical powers. They would later pour the water in their homes or over their domestic animals to free them from misfortune or disease. Some pour the water over their rice-fields for better yields.

At almost the same time, court officers fill the *encer* (water-basin) in the graveyard of the ancestors with water. The people in the surrounding village believe that if the water in the basin is not dried up, the people of Java will have ample food. If the water dries up, it is a sign of approaching famine.

Another *kraton* tradition is the beating of the *gamelan* placed on the left and right sides facing the Great Mosque. Called *sekaten*, it is held for a week in the month of Maulud, Prophet Mohammed's birthday. *Kraton* officers beat on the *gamelan* in turn, day and night. Only on Fridays do they take a rest for their prayers. This ceremony originated during the spread of Islam when it was a means to summon people to the mosque to listen to the *imam*. But now *sekaten* has become more a form of entertainment.

When an epidemic hits the village, a special ceremony is performed to ward off the evil spirit which is believed to be responsible for the epidemic. The villagers will gather and, headed by court officers, will walk barefooted in strict silence round the fortress surrounding the *kraton*. Participants have to walk throughout the night until the next morning.

When I was in Jogjakarta, I attended a Javanese funeral. It was the burial ceremony of a prominent person in the community. The deceased was a Muslim, perhaps a nominal one. However, I found the customs practised at this particular ceremony different from the usual Muslim funeral. Unlike Muslim funerals held in the Middle East or in Singapore and Malaysia, the ladies were allowed to attend the funeral procession to the graveyard. The orthodox Muslim burials which I have seen usually end with the body returning to Mother Earth naked, the mouth kissing the soil facing Mecca. In the burial which I saw in Jogjakarta, the body was lowered into the ground in a wooden coffin. There was a sweet smell of *kemenyan* prevading the air as a Muslim *imam* read the relevant passages of the Koran. The Javanese funeral ceremony was a combination of Islamic customs and Javanese traditions, yet another example of the spirit of tolerance and compromise, I thought.

13

Kebatinan— a new trend in the Spiritual Horizon

God is within you
God is everywhere
But do not think you are God.

a *Kebatinan* commandment

What is *Kebatinan*, a term which has come into prominence only during the past few years, although the principles have existed for a long time? The word *batin* means 'inner' (self) in Arabic. It is difficult to understand how and why an Arabic word was used to describe something which is entirely Javanese in origin. The word *Kebatinan* means 'to search for the inner self'. It is not a religion in the true sense of the word, like Islam, Buddhism, Hinduism or Christianity. It has no church, which it considers unnecessary. There are no scriptures like the Bible or Koran, no prophets in the same sense as Jesus, Mohammed or Buddha. It is not concerned so much with life after death, heaven and hell, or devils and angels. *Kebatinan* is a metaphysical search for harmony within one's inner self, harmony between one's inner self and one's fellow-men and nature, and harmony with the universe, the Almighty God. It is a combination of occultism, metaphysics, mysticism and other esoteric doctrines—a typical product of the Javanese genius for synthesis. It has a touch of Confucianism— in trying to harmonize one's behaviour to bring about an orderly society, and in ancestor-worship; a little bit of Taoism—in the belief in supernatural powers and communication with dead souls; a little of Buddhism—in the philosophy of contentment, not encouraging ambition; a pinch of Hinduism—in the mystic belief in reincarnation; as well as a little of the Islamic faith of surrendering oneself to God. No one can give you an official definition of *Kebatinan*. The essential, however, is peace of mind.

The Javanese mind is so flexible that nothing on earth seems uncompromisable and, given a will, everything — however contradictory — can be harmonized and syncretized. When I last visited Asia's largest Buddhist monument, the Borobudur, I asked my guide, Suharsono, a pious-looking learned Javanese, what his religion was. He replied, "I am a Buddhist." After a short pause, however, he continued, "I am also a Muslim." This took me by surprise. "How do you reconcile the two?" I asked. He answered with a natural smile, "I believe in Prophet Mohammed and Allah. But I practise the Buddhist way of life. I see no reason why there should be any conflict." Suharsono is not the only person in Central Java who is a Buddhist-Muslim. There are also hundreds of thousands of Javanese and Balinese who believe in Siva as well as Buddha and they call themselves Siva-Buddhists.

Javanese spiritualism is a never-ending source of wonder and surprise to foreign visitors who are often puzzled by numerous apparent contradictions. Most Javanese see nothing wrong or unusual in having a *dukun* exorcise evil spirits from their homes, then go on to the mosque, the church or temple to pray to their respective gods. The Javanese mind is essentially a flexible and pragmatic one as far as a person's spiritual life is concerned. The complexity is perhaps the result of the complicated cultural background and influences. But basically, Javanese spiritualism is individualistic in approach, something very Javanese, a person-to-person or person-to-*guru* relationship. Through the influence of the *wayang*, a Javanese becomes familiar with the relationship between a warrior and his *guru*, he is aware of the mystical power of communicating with the supernatural and realizes the philosophical value of self-discipline in relation to society and the universe.

The Javanese traditional spirit of tolerance allows free play for all religions. But the Javanese' latent desire of wanting to be first a Javanese provides a natural filter for the Javanese mind to accept only those qualities in 'imported' religions that can be absorbed into the Javanese culture, character and personality. One thing that hurts the feelings of a Javanese is to be called *durung ngerti*, which means 'not able to understand'. In other words, there is no point in arguing or punishing such a person since he has not yet grown up. A Javanese mother takes care not to allow her child to be excited or frightened by lightning and thunder, or be frustrated.

She makes every effort to train the child to be a real Javanese, someone who is obedient, polite, respectful to his parents and elders and has self-control and discipline over his emotions. Thus, a Javanese will always try to absorb whatever religion or culture that comes into the country and then Javanize it, accepting only those aspects that are in keeping with the Javanese character. For instance, the *Ramayana* and *Mahabharata* epics have become so Javanized in the *wayang* that Hindus from India would find it difficult to recognize their Indian origin. Similarly, orthodox Muslims from the Middle East, the centre of Islam, will find it difficult to understand the customs and religious practices of many Javanese who profess to be Muslims.

In Java today, there is a large number of Javanese who follow the Islamic faith very similar to that of the Middle East. However, there are also many who will admit quite frankly and openly that they are just 'nominal' Muslims, known as *abangan*. Dr H. M. Rasjidi, a well-known and outspoken Islamic scholar, commented in his recent book on Islam and *Kebatinan* that the population of Java generally only profess Islam but many of them are, in fact, practising *Kebatinan*, an attempt at reversion to the concept of Buddhism and Hinduism. The Islamic scholars in Java, according to Dr Rasjidi "have mostly been trained in religious schools that have worked in splendid parochialism and whose curricula are still geared to social conditions of two or three centuries ago. Thus they lack the ability to impart the spirit and sense of Islam and for that reason lay undue stress on its formalities."

Two other reasons, given by Professor M. M. Djajadiguna, another well-known scholar, for many Javanese straying away from Islamic practice and adopting *Kebatinan* are: firstly, some religious leaders were either incompetent or reluctant to summarize the principles of their religion into simple basic points which the ordinary Javanese could understand and determine their position in relation to their fellow-men and to God when facing problems of life; secondly, *Kebatinan* provides no language problem. Followers need not have to struggle with a difficult language, such as Arabic, the medium of Islam. Sometimes, unwittingly the pedantry of Islamic scholars hurts the sensitive feelings of the people when they are forced to learn Arabic.

I have met a large number of Javanese who practise *Kebatinan*; they represent a cross-section of the various schools. Normally a person who practises *Kebatinan* is rather reluctant to disclose that he is doing so if you do not know him well enough. Once the ice is broken, however, he will not hesitate to discuss the subject in great detail. Those who practise *Kebatinan* include intellectuals who have been educated in Western universities. A large majority practise *Kebatinan* as a means of releasing physical, mental and emotional tensions which they believe are the cause of ill health. Others are more esoteric and seek to strengthen their spiritual powers to communicate with souls of ancestors, spirits of deities and the cosmic world.

Generally speaking, *Kebatinan* followers believe in the existence of a super-consciousness in the cosmic world which is beyond man's comprehension, and which controls and guides man's affairs and destiny. The super-consciousness, it is believed, can be contacted through meditation. I came across a *guru* who got his disciples to demonstrate to me and a group of interested persons how they communicated with the soul of Sultan Mangkunegara. I also met a middle-aged Javanese who demonstrated to me the validity of the theory of mind over matter. He caused a cigarette to rise from a table and drop into a cup without even touching it. He later made two cigarettes fight a battle in mid-air. It was not magic but years of training in meditation. In Solo, many people have heard of a 71-year-old woman by the name of Bu Isrini, in Karang Talon. She is a well-known Javanese astrologer and a follower of *Kebatinan*. Few people have actually seen her, for throughout the year, she hides herself in her own dark room to avoid seeing sunlight. She leaves the room only once a year, on the first day of the first full moon, to receive relatives who normally come to pay their respects for the New Year. One of those who have seen her is Mr Goh Teck Suan, the *bupati* of the *kraton* of Surakarta. He says that she is bald-headed and very pale. She cures people by giving prescriptions even without seeing the patients. Another well-known *Kebatinan* follower in Central Java, Tay Chin Pok, a Chinese, could cure people when he was in a trance. He passed away recently. His grandson told me that whenever the old man went into a trance, his body would give off a rich perfume. It took more than twenty-five years of continuous meditation for his grandfather to acquire this mystical power.

In Malang, a young Chinese, Goh Boon Bee, went to Gunung Lawu and meditated for ten years after he was separated from his wife at the age of nineteen. He learnt the art of *tapa kalong*, a method of meditation in the posture of a bat. He later became a *guru*. Gunung Lawu is a mountain where many people — including high officials — still go to practise *Kebatinan*. The highest point of the mountain is called Ti Ling, which in the Chinese language means 'the peak of the king'. A place near Ti Ling is Suk Moh, again in Chinese, meaning 'the ripened touch'. Suk Moh is situated in a dangerously dark passage, and a sensitive touch is necessary to cross safely. I heard that some meditators fell to their death when visiting the spot. Nobody has yet discovered the origin of the names of these two vital spots on Gunung Lawu.

There are as many ways of *tapa* (fasting) as there are schools of meditation. Besides *tapa kalong*, there are also *tapa geni* (fire), *tapa senen* (Monday) or *tapa ngableng* (darkness) and so on. In Java, *tapa mutih* (white) means abstention from eating anything that is salted. This practice resembles that of the Taoist *ku-hung* of abstaining from grains. The Taoists try through *ku-hung* to survive on air and dew, absolutely renouncing rice and other grains. Some Taoist masters are believed to have lived on this diet for two, three or even ten years without growing pale or weak.

Fasting is one of the common methods used by spiritualists to attain discipline of the mind and body and to get rid of material and emotional desires. Many *Kebatinan* followers still keep their professed religion, but they meditate in their own way to seek spiritual and emotional relief—not in churches or mosques, but at home or in caves or mountains. Most Javanese *abangan*, the nominal Muslims, do not mind being just Muslims as long as the religion does not force them to take political sides or interfere with their *Kebatinan*. There are, however, other more militant types of *Kebatinan* followers who feel that the time has come for them to tell the world what they really believe in. This group has come out publicly to demand that *Kebatinan* be recognized legally as a separate religion. They argue that *Kebatinan*, which is an indigenous form of religious expression, is in no way inferior to any 'imported' religion, and that it should enjoy equal status as other religions such as Islam, Catholicism, Protestantism, Hinduism and Buddhism.

During my visits to Central Java, I toured a number of places where *Kebatinan* practices were being taught and collectively practised. Most of these gatherings were held very informally in private homes. One of the homes I visited was that of a Javanese Buddhist, Ananda Surjono, a middle-aged gentleman who is quite knowledgeable on spiritual matters and who is in frequent contact with those involved with similar movements throughout the country. Almost every night, the hall next to his study would be crowded with disciples of all races including hippies from Australia and sometimes from Europe. When I visited the *Kebatinan* class one evening, I saw a number of hippies, two of whom were obviously suffering from some sort of nervous breakdown and needing peace of mind. The *guru* was Pak Darno, an old man who belongs to the Sumarah school, one of the major schools of *Kebatinan* in Java. In the Javanese language, a *guru* who guides a recruit in seeking peace of mind is called *pamong* (guardian). Pak Darno is a rather shy and reserved personality. He speaks only Javanese. When all the visitors had taken their places, Surjono, who spoke English, warned that the exercise was about to begin. I noticed a sudden silence. Everyone cast his eyes downwards and relaxed. Fifteen minutes later, Pak Darno broke the silence and pointed out that the atmosphere in the class was still tense and started to give a lecture on how to relax and to seek peace and harmony with nature.

According to one of Pak Darno's disciples, Dr Hatachi of Idayu (an institute to promote research on Indonesia and named after the mother of former President Sukarno, Ida) who arranged for me to witness the group meditation, Darno is known to be able to diagnose from a distance whether a person is suffering from physical illness, emotional tension or mental disturbances. He is also able to assist the patient to cure himself through meditation.

In these sessions, the *pamong* will know the internal meditative state of each group member and is in a position to inform the member whether his meditation is right or not. The extent to which the *pamong* are capable of analysing the state of a person's meditation differs considerably. Some are only capable of saying whether it is right or wrong, whilst others can be more specific by pointing out to the person concerned where too much attention is concentrated. The principle at work is communication through vibrations called *getaran* in Javanese. The experienced *pamong* has developed the capacity of feeling the other person's vibrations like a radio receiver.

Pak Darno is a Buddhist and yet a *pamong* of the Sumarah school. He has read a lot about Confucianism, Taoism, Hinduism and other religions. He works as a peon in the Perkumpulan Masharakat Surakarta which was originally a welfare body called the Chuan Ming Kong Hui which helped the poor in burial matters. He is a simple man and leads a simple life. When we sent a car to fetch him, he preferred to ride a bicycle. Because of his devotion to the task of helping others to find inner peace without expecting anything in return, he has become a very popular figure in Solo.

According to the metaphysics of Sumarah, man is in misery the moment he is born — somewhat similar to Buddhist teaching. He is at the mercy of his passions. So long as he is unable to be rid of these passions, he has to go through misery after misery through the process of reincarnation. The reincarnation is explained this way: when one dies, the soul (*jiwa*) wanders about in the form of a spirit, carrying with it his passions. The wandering spirit with passions is always attracted towards worldly life. When such a wandering spirit meets a worldly couple having an affair, he is tempted to enter the womb of the woman and mingle with the union of semen and egg. In this way he is reincarnated. This is by far the most interesting version of the theory of reincarnation I have come across.

According to the Sumarah school, man and his physical and spiritual world are divided into three: the physical body and brain, an invisible world and a more elusive and sublime world. In the brain, the faculty of thinking has two functions — one to record memories and the other to serve as a means of communion with God. One section, which is called *sukusma*, governs the passions. The *jiwa* provides a driving force for the faculty of thinking. The invisible world, which is situated somewhere near the chest, is the *jiwa*, the unsubstantial soul, and the deeper feelings (*rasa*). The more elusive and sublime world is hidden somewhere near the anatomical heart. It contains the sublime soul, the Holy Mosque (Masjid Al Haram), the Baitullah Budi, Nur (light), and Urip (life). It is interesting to note that although this belief is contrary to the theory of the Koran, Arabic names are used.

In brief, the whole spiritual exercise of Sumarah is to help the student to liberate himself from passions so that he will reach his final destination — that is, to be one with God. Sumarah's concept of God is quite different from that of Islam. It considers God as being in every living being — plants, animals and men — as it is visualized in the Hindu-Javanese and Sumatran-Islamic mystical literature. The Sumarah theology says that man's soul is like the Holy Spirit, a spark from the Divine Essence, which means that he is in essence similar to God. In other words, man can find God within himself, similar to the 'I, God' theory found in Hindu-Javanese literature. The way of liberation is *sujud*, or thought-concentration, which is reminiscent of the Hinduistic yoga exercise.

Two of the three founder members of the Sumarah were humble folk. One of them, Pak Hardo, was a barber and the other, Pak Sukino, was a minor employee of the Jogja (Jogjakarta) Court; both were from Jogja. Only Pak Sutadi, from Solo, was a highly-educated member of the Colonial Parliament. Sumarah is the short form for Pagujuban Sumarah, or the Society of the Self-Surrenderers. During the early stages of Sumarah's development in 1935, it was a loose organization. The activity of the group was tied in with Indonesia's revolutionary struggle.

In the early days, meditation sessions of the Sumarah school involved magical practices, and the participants were divided into groups according to sex and age. The youth group was taught the *kanoman* which involved a wide range of occultism such as invulnerability to knives and guns. This was regarded as essential for youths in the struggle for independence against the Dutch. The mystical circles then were geared to fight the Dutch, who possessed deadly weapons. The other group was taught the *kesepuhan* which instilled the spirit of surrender to the independence struggle. At that time there was no formal organization of the groups.

During the revolutionary struggle around 1950, a young medical practitioner from Jogja, Dr Surono, streamlined the Sumarah movement and took over the organization. There was a shift of emphasis from *kanoman* and magic to the spirit of 'surrender to God', an attitude similar to that of Christ's 'Thy will be done'. From 1957 internal squabbles took place within the organization between Dr Surono on the one hand and Pak Sukino and Pak Hardo on the other, culminating in an open conflict in 1966 over a statement that only Dr Surono could receive true instructions from God. The conflict led to a vote of 'no confidence' at a meeting against Dr Surono. Dr Ary Murthy, an economist, became the new leader. The seat of the organization was then transferred from Jogja to Jakarta. Later, however, it was moved back to Jogja.

I was told that one of the factors that led to the split was that one of the leaders was trying to carry the message of Sumarah not only to those now living but also to the ancestral kingdom associated with sacred coastlines, volcanoes, caves, temples and graveyards.

Sumarah is only one of the streams of *Kebatinan*. There are other major *Kebatinan* schools such as the Sapta Darma, Pangestu, Subud and Majapahit Pancasila.

Sapta Darma was founded by Harjosapura, a barber from a village called Para in East Java. Believers of Sapta Darma say that the concept of Sapta Darma was revealed to the founder on the night of 27 December 1952. They even remember the time, which was, according to them, one o'clock. According to Sri Pawenang, the present leader, Sapta Darma *Kebatinan* was a product of the Indonesian Revolution. It was God's wish to provide the Indonesian people with a new spiritual approach in their search for peace of mind and happiness at a time when they were undergoing a mental and spiritual crisis. Sapta Darma believers are convinced that one of these days, *Kebatinan* will become a recognized religion in Indonesia. In December 1955, the founder of the movement was consecrated and given the name of Sri Gotama. He was further bestowed the title of *Panuntun Agung* (the Exalted Leader), so the official title of the leader has now become Panuntun Agung Sri Gotama. When he died in December 1964, Sri Gotama was succeeded by a woman then studying law at the Gaja Mada University in Jogjakarta.

Like Sumarah, Sapta Darma is also a training school for *sujud* (meditation). The origin of Sapta Darma is described in a small booklet entitled *Wwarah Agama Sapta Darma* written by Sri Pawenang. A retired journalist by the name of Bratakesawa has also written a book *Kuntji Swarge* (The Key to Heaven) in the form of a dialogue between a teacher and his disciple, which propounded further the theory of Sapta Darma. It was an attempt by the author to have Javanese mysticism founded on the Koran. It deals with God, death, the way to search for God and other esoteric matters.

A significant aspect of the Sapta Darma doctrine is the use of Semar, the guardian spirit of Java, as its main symbol. Semar is seen carrying in his left hand a symbol of his exalted feeling. In his right hand he holds a weapon signifying that he possesses magical powers. Semar wears a five-pleated gown symbolizing Pancasila, the five principles of State. The idea is that constant meditation should bring one in touch with Semar. But to get in touch with Semar is not easy as indicated in the Sapta Darma symbol. Semar is seen surrounded by various shades of colour — starting from a greenish square, to a brown triangle, then a layer of black, red, yellow and finally white where Semar is seated. One has to pierce through the different layers or obstacles through meditation before one can reach Semar to find peace and tranquillity of mind.

The theory and practice of Sapta Darma meditation resembles that of Kundalini, the awakening of the serpent power in man, practised very widely in South India. It involves generating vibrations in the twelve *chakra* (centres of power) of the body. The *chakra* that controls passion is situated in the navel and is termed Majankara, representing the monkey characteristic in man — mischievousness and the animal desire for teasing and seducing. The power that is situated in the vertebral column, just as in Kundalini yoga, is called Nagatuhun, the dragon of the soul. It has the characteristics of the serpent for it is poisonous and complicated, but extremely powerful when awakened. It seems to me that Sapta Darma is a combination of Hindu yoga, the Islamic Koran and Javanese mysticism. The aim of Sapta Darma is the same as that of Sumarah — that is, to liberate men from the grip of his passions.

I first learnt about Pangestu from a general when he visited my office in Jakarta in connection with his visit to Singapore. We were talking generally about *Kebatinan* and he admitted that he belonged to the Pangestu school. Pangestu was founded in Surakarta sometime in May 1949. The doctrine in its 'Holy Scripture', the *Serat Sasangka Djati*, is believed to have been revealed to one Sunarto Mertowarjoyo in 1932. Later it was put into writing by R. T. Harjoparakoso and R. Trihardono Sumodiharjo Pangestu. It describes the way to attain *wahyu*, the blessing of God. It is a general belief of the Javanese that only people with *wahyu* can become rulers. When Sukarno's power was on the decline, it was interpreted as his having lost his *wahyu*.

The Pangestu scripture consists of seven parts: the Hasta Sila (the eight forms of good behaviour), Paliwara (the great prohibitions), Gumelaring Dumadi (the unfolding of creations), Tunggal Sabda, Dalan Rahayu (the way of salvation), Sangkan Paran (origin and destination) and Panembah (adoration). Pangestu is indeed a modern, organized, mystical school and has many followers among the intellectuals. In 1956 Dr Sumantri Hardjoprakoso wrote a dissertation in Dutch on this mystical school entitled *The Indonesian Concept of Man based on Psychotherapeutics*. In it, he attempts to give scientific meaning to its mystical doctrines.

Another school which is rather popular among Europeans is the Subud, which has branches all over the world. It has a more pragmatic approach to modern problems, for the organization also indulges in business enterprises to increase its funds. It has its meditation centre in the form of a huge housing complex on the outskirts of Jakarta. Many Europeans and Americans from abroad stay in the Subud centre when they are in Jakarta; they are often members of similar organizations in their respective countries. During their stay, they undergo training in meditation under a panel of *guru* who were trained by Pak Subuh, the founder of the school who is now over 70 years of age.

Subud is the acronym of the words *Susila*, *Budhi* and *Dharma*. *Susila* refers to the good character of man. *Budhi* means 'the force of the inner self'. *Dharma* means 'trust in God'.

Subud, therefore, is the symbol of a man who has a calm and peaceful inner feeling and who is able to establish contact with the Great Holy Life Force. The aim of Subud is to attain perfection of character according to the will of God. Subud does not consider itself a religion or a teaching in itself, but merely the spiritual experience of awakening by the power of God, leading to spiritual reality, free from the influence of passion, heart and mind. According to Subud theory, unless passion, heart and mind are separated from the inner feeling, it is impossible for the inner feeling to establish contact with the Great Life Force which permeates everywhere. By separating passion, heart and mind from the inner feeling, one is able to distinguish between the various kinds of life forces in man. This will eventually lead to the realization of one's true self and the elimination of the false one. The Subud school believes that as chemistry can extract iron, tin, gold, silver and other materials from a lump of earth, man's mind and heart can draw out similar vital forces, the chemistry in the spiritual realm, through God whose power reaches far beyond the power and ability of man.

The latest entry into the *Kebatinan* mystic world is a school called Majapahit Pancasila founded by a 50-year-old Javanese mystic, W. Hardjanta Pradjapangarsa. He lives in a dilapidated shop-house in a back lane behind the Surakarta *kraton*. When I visited him one sunny day, he was discussing his theory and method of practising the Kundalini yoga with some of his disciples, some of whom came from Australia and others from as far as Bonn. Wearing a *blangkon* (headgear) and the traditional Javanese sarong, he sat in a squatting position on a rickety chair. Piles of books and files filled his simple wooden cupboards in a rather disorderly fashion. The old junk-store look of his house only helped to strengthen my impression of Hardjanta's simplicity and humble way of life. He goes barefooted and meets and helps anyone who comes in search of the secret path of Kundalini, the serpent power which makes one permanently young and strong, physically and spiritually.

Hardjanta has never stepped into a university nor does he claim to be a scholar. He is an autodidact — a person who is self-taught. He has never been to an English school and yet he writes beautiful English and is able to expound his theory clearly in that foreign language. He is popular among the European and Australian seekers of mystical knowledge, probably because he is conversant with the English language.

Hardjanta's emblem for Majapahit Pancasila reflects a syncretism of many sources of wisdom. At the base curl two serpents — one *ying* (female) and the other *yang* (male) — and above the serpents stands the *garuda* bird. The bird represents power arising from the awakening of the serpent power of the Kundalini practice. Above this stands the figure of Vishnu representing eternal wisdom. This emblem is carved in cement and prominently displayed outside Hardjanta's humble dwelling.

Originally, it was the intention of Hardjanta to proclaim Maja-pahit Pancasila a new religion. However, under certain rules promulgated in Indonesia in 1967, when the Pancasila Democracy was implemented, one of the principles of which is 'Belief in one God', no new religion would be tolerated apart from the official religions already in existence, such as Islam, Hinduism, Christianity, Buddhism, Confucianism, Taoism and other world-recognized religions. So Hardjanta finally got his school registered under the Hindu-Dharma religion.

Hardjanta's Majapahit Pancasila is perhaps the only school of *Kebatinan* which uses Kundalini yoga as the means of attaining spiritual enlightenment and mystical powers. It is one of the highest forms of yoga, with a strong influence of Tantrism from Tibet. Kundalini is a sort of mystical force — in the form of mercury coiled like a serpent and hidden in a tiny spot at the end of the vertebral column of the human spine. Through meditation or other methods, the power is awakened and is brought through the spinal canal to the 'third eye' (between the two eyebrows) and the top of the head called the 'wisdom eye'. As it rises to the top, it vitalizes the six centres of power called *chakra* along its invisible course to the brain. Those who have mastered Kundalini yoga possess super-energy beyond the reach of ordinary souls.

There are many methods of awakening the Kundalini power in a person. In ancient days, the secrets were carefully guarded, and disciples had to undergo years of apprenticeship before the *guru* would divulge the secrets. Kundalini was also practised by ancient Egyptians in the temple of Luxor. In India there are hundreds of Kundalini schools under the name of Universal Peace Sanctuary; it has a branch in Singapore, too. Disciples of Kundalini are first initiated by the *guru*, who is known as Paranjothi Mahan, using his mystic first finger. The whole initiation process involves three stages which are carried out within an interval of three weeks.

In Solo, where Hardjanta's Kundalini practice is becoming popular, particularly among Westerners, the method of initiation is rather different. Hardjanta uses the power of the sun to initiate his disciples. At the back of a compound of *sawo* (a kind of tropical fruit called *ciku* in Malay) trees I saw a number of disciples, with their eyes blindfolded with black cloth, lying on the ground with their faces to the sky. It was midday and the blazing sun pierced through the *sawo* trees casting menacing rays on the disciples who were supposed to keep their blindfolded eyes on the sun between 11.30 a.m. and 1.30 p.m. The exercise was supposed to go on for 40 days in order to awaken the serpent power of the spine.

In the presence of Hardjanta, I interviewed a young Australian Air Force man who had taken leave from Butterworth airfield in Malaysia, where he worked as a pilot, to come to Solo to look for the secret knowledge of Kundalini. He had become interested in Indian mysticism because he had fallen in love with an Indian girl from Kedah. Seeming excited and agitated, the frank and outspoken Australian told us of his six-day experience in the sun-gazing Kundalini initiation. "I cannot stand it any longer. I will go mad if I continue," he said. "What is the reason?" asked the *guru*, who was taken aback by the comments of the Australian. The young man replied that there were many ants crawling on his head and legs during the meditation and he could not bear it any more. "Why not put some kerosine around you to keep away the ants if they are the only obstacles?" suggested the *guru*. The young Australian, appearing rather flabbergasted, went on to tell of his other frightful experience. "I cannot sleep at night. Whenever I close my eyes, even in the daytime, I see little blue devils about the size of the thumb dancing in front of me and coming towards me. As they approach they seem to grow larger and larger." He also mentioned other fantastic visions which had haunted him in his sleep. Hardjanta explained that these were the effective result of the meditation and that they were the cosmic visions which were hidden from the ordinary eye. He tried to persuade the Australian pilot to complete the forty-day meditation for it would mean much for those who could succeed. According to Hardjanta, anyone who had mastered the sun meditation would be invulnerable to external attacks by knives, daggers and other weapons, and nobody could harm him. He would also have supernatural powers and wisdom. But to complete the initiation required patience, faith and perseverance. Not everyone could succeed. Hardjanta had several young Javanese disciples who were undergoing Kundalini initiation which was not confined to sun meditation only. Each disciple had to soak himself inside a bathtub filled with cold water up to the neck. He had to hold his navel with his left hand and touch the back of his shoulder with his right hand. This method of meditation was called the moon meditation. It would result in clarity of mind and the development of extra-sensory perception.

While we were discussing mysticism, a Polish couple hurried in and were whisked away by a young tutor. I was told that the couple wanted to get their 'third eye' opened within three days as they were in a hurry to leave. For such emergency cases, Hardjanta said, special intensive methods had to be used. I did not press him to explain the method.

The word 'Majapahit' is used for his philosophy and religion because it was the name of the strongest and most famous empire in the history of Nusantara (Indonesia). Hardjanta said one of his aims was to revive Hinduism in its true form and to bring back the glory of Hindu practices.

There are hundreds of other *Kebatinan* schools which could take up enough space for a separate book. The ones I have mentioned are those with large followings. Owing to the mushrooming of *Kebatinan* schools and practices, the Office of the Public Prosecutor has set up PAKEM, a body in charge of supervising religious schools in order to keep them under control. The PAKEM — *Pengawasan Aliran Kepercayaan Masjarakat* meaning literally, 'Authority for the Supervision of Social Beliefs' — sees to it that *Kebatinan* schools or Islamic mystical brotherhood (*Tarakat*) minority religions, soothsayers and traditional healers do not abuse their powers or carry out undesirable activities. Undesirable practices, which are commonly known as *klenik*, are those that lead people astray by inciting them to break the law and disturb social order, by ridiculing or insulting other established religions, or by involvement with the communists. The fear is that some of these schools may be exploited by political adventurers which may endanger peace and security. There was an incident in March 1967 in Central Java, where the Mbah Suro Incident resulted in the death of more than 80 people and the near-obliteration of the hamlet of Nginggil. It was caused by the outlawed Indonesian Communist Party (PKI) which had infiltrated and subverted a fanatical pseudo-religious sect. The incident was precipitated by the defiance of the mystical adherents of Mbah Suro who believed in their invulnerability to guns and pistols. At the time of his death, Mbah Suro was identified as both a *dukun klenik* and a dupe of the PKI.

Meanwhile, the leaders of the different *Kebatinan* groups such as Sumarah, Sapta Darma and Pangestu have been active since 1965 to bring together all the assorted contemporary mystical groups into a congress called the BKKI (*Badan Kongress Kebatinan Indonesia* or 'The People's Congress of *Kebatinan* of Indonesia'). This Congress has held several meetings and seminars since its foundation. The Congress, under the leadership of Mr Wongsonegoro, a lawyer, has been striving hard to get *Kebatinan* recognized as one of the official religions of the country. Since the conference of mystical groups held in Jogja in December 1970, a Secretariat called *Kerjasama Kepercajaan Kebatinan Kejiwaan* (A Joint Secretariat for the Promotion of *Kebatinan*) has been formed for this aim. As a result, the recent Parliamentary Session has given recognition to the practice of *Kebatinan*. This newly-gained status has given its leaders the impetus to come to grips with some fundamental problems of properly defining their objectives and practices to the public. In the process of adjusting to changing conditions, each group is seriously examining itself in relation to the larger group as a whole and in relation to society. For instance, there is increasing emphasis on meditation in daily life as opposed to the esoteric aspects of the movement. The implications of 'surrender through meditation' is being more clearly defined as a comprehensive philosophy of life and action.

Another aspect of the changes in theory and practice involves an attempt to synthesize the adaptable concepts of other religions such as Buddhism, Hinduism, Islam and Christianity. Meanwhile, the BKKI has yet to develop into an effective organization. It has so far gathered together more than 85 *aliran* (schools) and a number of individual mystics at its Congress, whilst there are some 1,000 *aliran* in Java alone.

The struggle for recognition marks the beginning of an epoch in the history of religious beliefs in Indonesia and will have far-reaching effects on the future development of the country.

14

Sports
and
Recreation

In Indonesia, games and dances are part of the way of life of a people who are by nature artistically and culturally inclined. It would be difficult for anyone, be he a foreigner or even an Indonesian from any one of the 3,000 islands, to appreciate fully the Balinese, for example, if he has not seen a cockfight, a Barong and Kris dance, or the Kecak (monkey) dance, and try to understand their history and background. The games and dances of Indonesia are as varied and colourful as the multi-racial and multi-religious people.

Certain arts such as the *adu jangkrik* (cricket fight) or *bersilat* (art of self-defence) are popular throughout Indonesia. Each province, however, has its own form of recreation with peculiar characteristics for which it is known. The Madurese are famous for their bull-race, known as *karapan sapi*, which faithfully depicts the ruggedness, bravery and impulsiveness of the Madurese people. The Torajans have bull-fights as part of the entertainment before funeral rites are performed. Every Minangkabau knows the legend of the bull-fight from which the tribe derived its name. In West Java, *adu dombak*, the ram-fight, has become a weekly sport for the villagers.

In a country which is blessed with fertile soil and rich natural resources, life is less of a painful struggle and the people have more leisure hours to experience harmony with nature and to enjoy a more gracious life. As Indonesia is predominantly an agricultural country, most of the games and recreation have their roots in nature and in many cases are associated with supernatural powers.

It would be difficult to cover all the games and recreation of such a vast country like Indonesia. What I am trying to do in this chapter is just to give an outline of the games and dances which are well known in some parts of Indonesia I visited.

Indonesia is a land of colourful dances. Every province has its own peculiar style and rhythm of dancing. The slow and gentle movement of the Javanese dances is quite different from the swift and abrupt motions of the Balinese dances or the gay and quick tempo of the Minangkabau dances. Generally, however, the dances of each province can be divided into two categories: the court or *kraton* classical dances and the folk-dances. I took a fancy to folk-dances, particularly those with a touch of mysticism. The Kuda Lumping dance of Central Java is one of them. It is a popular street dance enjoyed by the commonfolk in Solo, Cirebon and other parts of Indonesia. I first saw a Kuda Lumping dance in the courtyard of a batik factory owned by enterprising Mr Goh Teck Suan, the *bupati* of the *kraton* of Surakarta, who now bears the Javanese name of Hardjonegoro. He had been appointed *bupati* because of his contribution to the promotion of Javanese culture. The dance was especially arranged for me as he had heard that I was keen to see it. The troupe came from the village of Ponorogo, the birthplace of the Kuda Lumping dance. It comprised two drummers, a gong attendant and two female singers. One of the singers wore man's clothing, a moustache and a pair of dark glasses.

The performance was held under the glaring eyes of a stone statue of Bima, the hero much respected by the audience of the *wayang kulit* for his bravery. He was holding his vital organ which he had used, as a legend says, to widen a river in Central Java. The players first paid respect to the brave hero; then the singing started, accompanied by drums and gongs. After the prelude, the two women who were singing, 'mounted' bamboo horses which had only a head and tail. When the tempo of the drums and gong gathered momentum, the drummer suddenly made a sommersault and took over the saddle from one of the ladies. The new rider soon went into a trance, riding the horse furiously as he was whipped from behind by his colleague. When he was tired, he drank water from a bucket like a horse. He then knelt down like a horse to eat raw paddy, and at times the lady fed him. Then came the exciting moment when he started to chew and swallow electric bulbs and broken glasses. I noticed he was bleeding from the mouth, for some glass had cut his lips. But this did not deter him, for he continued to eat the glass until not a single piece was left. Having completed the first act, the drummer, still in a trance, transformed himself into the *Setan* (Devil) of the forest by putting on a red mask with white eyes, white eyebrows and a black moustache. With his protruding white eyes and a long, red nose, he was looking around for weaker animals to devour. Having found nothing, he turned himself back into a horse and started to rip the husk off a coconut with his teeth. While he was doing this, the two ladies sang light-hearted children's songs. The man-horse was delighted with the songs and started to dance merrily, holding the coconut in his hands. Not contented with the coconut, he started to swallow the flames of fire whilst the ladies sang 'Hello, Hello Bandung', another light-hearted song. When he became completely exhausted, he fell to the ground and then woke up as if recovering from a nightmare.

During the dance, when the rider was at the height of the trance, Hardjonegoro politely asked whether I would like to go into a trance too. Perhaps that was meant to convince me that the trance was real and that, if I disbelieved, I had the opportunity of experiencing it personally. I rejected the offer with a polite smile. When the dance was over, I asked how and what spirit had taken hold of the rider. What was the historical background of the Kuda Lumping dance? Was it the music that had hypnotized the rider? The answers to my questions were rather vague. The exercise apparently was not connected with any known deities. It was just a matter of practice: the man got into a trance and behaved like a horse. It seems the performers know how to get into that state of mind. It is a secret passed on to them for generations. And they see nothing remarkable about it.

For the horse dance which I saw in Bali, more elaborate preparations were made. In the Sanghiang Jaran dance, the priest prayed before the dance to seek permission from the spirits. The dance was performed in front of a temple, under a banyan tree. The dancer, wearing white shorts and a sarong, rode a hobby-horse decorated with leaves which formed the head and tail. He trotted around in a circle until he went into a trance. When he became one with the horse, he pranced, galloped and kicked about like a horse, climaxing by jumping into a bed of hot, burning coconut husks. The fire-walking continued until the last trace of fire was extinguished by the feet. When the job was done, the dancer suddenly collapsed unconscious for a few minutes. He soon regained consciousness, but appeared pale and exhausted.

Dances in which man takes on the role of an animal are common in Bali. The inspiration could have been derived from Panji stories. In a village near Selat, in the eastern part of Bali, the villagers are fond of performing folk-dances in which a performer suddenly goes into a trance and takes on the role of a pig, a monkey, a puppy, a snake or a turtle. They have different names for such dances: the snake dance is called Sanghiang Lelipi; the puppy dance, Sanghiang Kuluk; the pig dance, Sanghiang Celeng; the monkey dance, Sanghiang Bojog; the turtle dance, Sanghiang Penyu, and so on. The dance is named after the animal and is prefixed by the word *Sanghiang* which means 'spirit of god'. The people from time to time invent new dances according to their inspiration. When Sanghiang Bojog is performed, the man dresses up as a male monkey with a long white tail, using the fibre of white sugar-palm and covering his jaws with bamboo shavings. The female monkey is black, with a shorter tail. Before the performance, the two sit together in front of the temple to be sprinkled with holy water. Holy hymns are sung until they fall into a trance. Suddenly both of them simultaneously jump up, climb up trees, swing from one branch to another, and perform various acrobatic feats like real monkeys. They cry like monkeys, and the crowd makes fun of them by shouting, "Nyoet, nyoet". It is really fun for them. When the time comes to stop the show, the organizers always have difficulty capturing the human monkeys. Both are again sprinkled with holy water, and they return to the world of humans, completely exhausted.

Similarly, in other dances the performers would behave exactly like pigs, snakes or turtles. I am told that in the Sanghiang Lelipi, the snake dance, the grass which is necessary to dress up the performer has to be fresh grass stolen without anyone's notice, and it must not have been previously stamped on or eaten by a cow or any other animal.

In certain areas, almost every household has one form of Sanghiang performed seasonally under the moonlight. The performances are still spontaneous and as such, are not commercialized.

Folk-dances of this kind, in which the performers go into a trance, can also be found in other parts of Indonesia, such as the Ma'anjan dance of Central Kalimantan and the Ahmad Rifai dance of Minangkabau, which also have strong mystic influence.

The Tanrik Behalai or Ma'anjan dance of Central Kalimantan is a performance usually carried out in connection with the celebrations of Siva, to illustrate the dramatic climax of the abrupt transition between life and death. It is a sort of mock battle which begins after an offering is made to the forested cremation site in a final tribute to the spirit of the dead. Some of the participants would act as invaders and others, defenders of the ceremonial hall. The tinkling sound of the *gamelan* gives the signal for combat when both parties emerge from the forest. The frenzied yells of the participants soon drown the *gamelan* music. The raiders hold aloft shields and ancient skull fragments, relics of bygone headhunting days. As the dance gathers momentum and reaches the height of emotional ecstasy, one of the dancers would suddenly go into a trance.

In the Minangkabau land of Sumatra where the Islamic religion predominates, trance dances are also performed, though not as commonly as in Central Java or Bali. In the village of Mandiangin, one could see the dance of Ahmad Rifai performed in an open space behind the mosque. The dance, which was named after the spiritual leader who was an early North Sumatran mystic, has become extremely rare. The dance had to be performed under the supervision of a *Khalifah* (teacher), for it involved the dancers piercing their own bodies with iron awls called *dabuih*. The dancers had first to undergo long years of training in esoteric practices. They also had to fast for twenty days before they qualified to be true followers of the *Khalifah dabuih* to perform the dance.

This dance bears a similarity to the Barong and Kris dance which most visitors to Bali would have seen. At the end of the Barong dance, young dancers stab their own chests with krises. The Kris dance is part of the Barong and Rangda drama which depicts an eternal fight between good and evil, the Barong representing good and the Rangda, evil. In some cases, the dancers who, in a trance, perform the *ngurak*, the act of self-stabbing, lose consciousness and have to be carried away.

There are so many trance dances in Bali that it would take years to see them all. Bali is a country of trance. Men, women, and even children like to go into a trance. In the case of children, they perform the intricate Sanghiang Deling dance without even being trained. The Balinese feel a sense of pride when they are able to go into a trance — it has become a status symbol, so to speak. According to their beliefs, the gods who dwell in high places would come down at festival time to inhabit shrines and temples. There they enter the bodies of chosen humans. Thus, there is a sense of satisfaction accompanying this 'rise in status'. A trance may also have the effect of relieving one's emotional tension.

Some Western psychologists believe that the state of trance is an essential part of the Balinese social organization, for without it, life might become too fixed and rigid. The trance makes a temporary change possible and helps to relieve tension. The act of being in a trance has become so institutionalized in Bali that the ability to get into a trance is often considered an honour. The entranced are regarded as the chosen ones who can speak to God.

In Central Java, children become acquainted with mysticism at a tender age before they are further influenced by the shadow-play. They play the game of Nini Towok or Sintren, a sort of encounter with supernatural powers through the medium of a coconut shell. A *tempurong* (coconut shell) with a stick handle is brought to a graveyard in the early hours of the morning. It is brought back the same evening and stuck on a round bamboo filter called *lambung*. On one side of the *tempurong* is painted the face of a human, with eyes, nose, mouth and ears. A rattan basket is put below the *tempurong* and covered with clothes. The children gather and start to sing songs, accompanied in some cases by *gamelan* music. The game is often played under a banyan tree. As the songs and music gather momentum, the doll begins to dance. In some cases the children hold on to the doll, and in other cases the doll is held by a number of strings pulled from all sides.

A Javanese friend of mine, who was very fond of this game when he was young, said that sometimes it was quite difficult to call off the game for the doll refused to halt. Javanese children take it for granted that the doll would dance of its own accord and believe that a supernatural power enters the body of the doll to amuse them.

Another game which Bali is known for is the cockfight which, incidentally, has been banned in other parts of Indonesia. The cockfight was once part of a religious ceremony of the Balinese Hindu-Dharma group. It was usually conducted near a temple; the blood from a wounded or dead cock helped to purify the earth and to pacify the hungry evil spirits. It was so important a part of Balinese culture that the rituals and rules of a cockfight and of keeping a cock were contained in old *lontar* exclusively devoted to the art. The *lontar* mentions, for instance, that cockfights should not be held on certain days of the week for religious reasons, and that on certain days the white cock must never fight the red cock. The villagers in Ubud believe that a white cock will always win at its first appearance, whilst other villagers believe in the superiority of the red or brown cocks. These are mere superstitions and not rules, but they are all mentioned in the *lontar*. There are even rules on how a spur should be tied to a cock's leg.

I saw my first cockfight in Bali in 1955 after an exhausting week of reporting in Bandung where the Afro-Asian Conference was held.

Since then I have seen several cockfights, all of them in Bali. It is usually a man's affair, for the womenfolk are too busy with the farm, housework, and attending to the temple gods. It is actually taboo for women to attend a cockfight. In Bali, it is a common sight to see the men nursing their roosters and the women either on the farms or in pairs or threes delousing each other's long black hair. The men are often preoccupied with stroking the feathers of their beloved birds and feeding them with rice, small frogs, snails, or before a battle, chopped chilli — for hot food would stimulate their fighting spirit. They also bathe them in water mixed with onions and herbs, and then massage them with fresh cow dung and nutmeg juice, and shine the feathers before taking them to the *wantilan*, the cockpit. The cock owners also remember that the birds must pass the heat of the day in the shade. They also take them for evening walks or cradle them like babies and even talk to them in endearing tones.

The cockfight in Bali, like many other games, goes with gambling, a habit which was perhaps an offshoot of divination. The cockfight which I remember vividly was between a red cock and a black one. It lasted for only a few seconds of the first round, although a normal fight is a match of five rounds. First, the jurymen weighed the birds and examined the spurs to see that the birds were equally matched. While this was going on, the betting started. There was general excitement as betters shouted and waved bundles of rupiah notes in the air. The owners held their birds as they squatted at the edge of the ring. When the gong was struck, the shouting ceased and the air became silent and tense. The birds were let loose. I saw the red cock stretch its wings, jump into the air with folded feet, and then, in a lightning strike, plunge its spurs into its opponent. Feathers scattered as from an exploding pillow. Blood dripped from the staggering black cock. It stumbled and dropped dead. In a Balinese cockfight, the decision of the judge is final and is never disputed. All bets are honoured as soon as a fight is over. The cockfight is indeed a demonstration of the honesty of the Balinese who are most law-abiding citizens.

Cockfighting must have been popular throughout Java in the feudal days of the Javanese kingdoms. Among the many Indonesian folk-tales is one called 'The Cock of Panji Laras'. There was once a mighty king of Banten who had a son. The son was so addicted to cockfighting that his father drove him away from the palace. He roamed about in the forest until he met a beautiful girl whom he married. Two months before their first child was born, he heard that his father was seriously ill. So he returned home, just in time to inherit the kingdom. Meanwhile, his wife was left to fend for herself. Before the child was born, a strange bird flew over the house and dropped a chick into the lap of the pregnant woman who was bemoaning her future. She took good care of the wounded chick. When a baby boy was born, the chick became the child's companion and he did not know who his father was. The chick turned out to be the best fighter in the country and on many occasions defeated the birds of the king who was still addicted to cockfighting. Out of curiosity, the king traced the owner of the champion cock and discovered that he was his own son, Panji Laras. The king then took Panji Laras and his mother to the palace. Amidst great rejoicing, the faithful wife was crowned his queen. When the king died, Panji Laras succeeded him to the throne.

Another game which is not only popular in Bali but all over Indonesia is cricket-fighting. Crickets are called *jangkrik* in Bahasa Indonesia. Mention *jangkrik* to any Javanese and invariably you will find him smiling nostalgically as he recollects his childhood days when he enjoyed the game of *adu jangkrik*. I have asked several diplomat friends of mine from Vietnam and Thailand, and they confessed that when they were kids they, too, indulged in the game. Strangely enough, cricket-fighting is seldom heard of in Singapore and Malaysia. I only recall friends catching crickets to feed their birds.

It is difficult to trace the origin of the *jangkrik* fight. According to Chinese chronicles, as early as the T'ang dynasty, some emperors gambled with crickets, a game termed *shi shuai* in Chinese. It seems that one of the Chinese emperors was so enthralled by cricket-fighting that he neglected his kingdom. One day when his enemies marched into his palace, his eyes were fixed on his crickets, so he shouted loudly to the intruders who had occupied the palace, "Don't disturb me, my pet is winning." His cricket won the game, but he had lost his empire.

There are many stories about *jangkrik* in Chinese history. An emperor once ordered his army to look for *jangkrik* which took their nap on the forehead of poisonous snakes inside hilly caves. In Indonesia, it is generally believed that the *jangkrik* that are found near graveyards have magical powers and are potential money-spinners.

In Indonesia, the fighting *jangkrik* are put in a bamboo container called a *bungbung*. It is a cylinder about 18 centimetres long and four centimetres in diameter, closed at one end and with a small window at the other. It is inside this container that two crickets are put to fight, viewed eagerly by the owners through the small window. *Jangkrik* vary in size and colour. Some are a pale golden brown and others, black. The black ones are generally believed to be stronger. *Jangkrik*, unlike fighting cocks, need to be provoked before they fight. Some people use brushes to tickle them. Others feed them with chilli and pepper, or even slice their forehead to make them lose their temper. The game of *jangkrik*-fighting is normally played by children, mainly boys who have dared to search the undergrowth to find their specimens.

For girls, a game called *congklak* in Sumatra, and *dakon* in Java, is popular throughout Indonesia. A boat-like wooden board with a large hole at each end is used. On both sides of the 'boat' are five, seven or nine smaller holes. Each hole is filled with seven beans, pebbles or seashells. With her little fingers, a girl collects the beans from one hole and proceeds to drop one into each of the next consecutive holes. The aim is to collect the most beans in your large 'storehouse' or hole at the far end of the board. When the last bean reaches a hole which is empty, and the opposite hole of the opponent is filled with beans, it *tembak* (meaning 'shoot') and reaps the harvest. If the bean reaches a hole which is empty but is surrounded on both sides by a rich store of beans, it *pikul* (meaning 'carries on the shoulders') and again reaps the harvest from both sides. The terms used in the game seem to suggest that it was originally an agricultural game. In the olden days, it was an ideal game for ladies-in-waiting at the *kraton* to while away time as they waited for the princess to dress up for ceremonies. It is a game of patience as well as skill. A girl with mathematical talent has an advantage, for the rules enable her to determine in advance whether she will win or lose before selecting an odd or an even-numbered pile of pebbles.

It is interesting to know that the *dakon* is also popular in Arabia, India and many other places which Arab traders visited in the past. In Sri Lanka it is known as *chanka*, in the Dahomeans, *maji*, and in the West Indies, *wa wee*. According to some experts the game was of central African origin. It gradually spread from the interior to the edges of the continent where the Arabs picked it up and transmitted further to those places where they established their business contacts. Some tribes in Africa who play the game believe that a *dakon* board must be made by a man who has lost a wife or who is old. They also believe that the board, which they call *adjiboto*, has some connection with the spirits of the dead, and it may be dangerous to meddle with such a game. A good board must at first be roughly hewn and must gradually become smooth and polished through use.

The popularity of folk games and dances, such as the *dakon* and Kuda Lumping in Central Java, reflect to a certain extent a life of ease and the love for peace, quiet and serenity, and the mystical nature of the people of that region. The common Javanese saying often heard in Central Java is *alon alon asal kelakon*, which has almost the same meaning as 'slow and steady wins the race'. The Javanese do not like to rush or to be rushed. The feeling of excitement is viewed as a disaster. From childhood, most Javanese are trained to control their emotions. Thus, games of excitement do not easily flourish. The highest peak of excitement which Javanese children can reach is to peep through the *bungbung* to see the tiny insects, *jangkrik*, fighting their miniature war in an unobtrusive surrounding.

Less than half an hour's boat ride from the eastern tip of tranquil Java is an island where excitement is a key factor in a game or sport called *karapan sapi*, the famous bull-race of Madura. It is perhaps the only one of its kind in the world.

We have heard of the bull-fights of Spain or Mexico which have become world famous. Horse-racing or greyhound-racing have also become common sports in many countries, both in the East and West. A bull-race is, however, rarely heard of in any other part of the world besides the tiny island of Madura. The Madura bull-race season comes annually in August. The game originated in the olden days when rice was scarce and the Madurese had to prod the bull on, as if in competition, to plough the not-too-fertile land faster. This habit of prodding on the bulls gradually developed into a game of fun and sport. At harvest time, the Madurese farmers had time to spare, so they got the bulls out of the rice-fields onto the open turf land, and a game was readily created for the recreation and entertainment of the people. Today, the Madura bull-race has become the most popular sport and entertainment not only for the Madurese but also for thousands of visitors from all over Indonesia and abroad.

I had heard of the Madura bull-race for some years, so it was one of those things which I had longed to see. The invitation to the bull-race from the former Governor of East Java, Mr Mohamed Noor, was perfectly timed. I was then in the mood to relax, for I had just returned from Singapore after President Suharto's official visit.

The trip to Madura was a tedious four-hour drive from Surabaya. The soothing music emanating from the cool air-conditioned luxury bus, however, made the long journey less uncomfortable. The bus, belonging to the East Java provincial administration, was evidence of the slow but steady progress made by the authorities in rural communication. Overloaded lorries, cars, bicycles and passengers jammed the old-fashioned ferry-boat which took us across the narrow Straits of Madura. All the traffic seemed to be heading in the same direction—the village of Pamekasan where the bull-race was to be held.

When we reached Pamekasan, the whole town seemed to be deserted. The villagers had packed the stadium which was a spectacle of colour. The air was filled with excitement and festivity. The buzzing voices intermingling with tinkling ice-cream bells conspired to gear the bulls into a frenzy. About a hundred of them, yoked in tandem, were snorting at the crowd in the open field. Wearing fancy halters, each pair of bulls trailed a long harrow-like rig meant for the jockey to ride on. They were made to parade the arena to the blare of flutes, drums, gongs and *gamelan* music. Proudly, they displayed their dazzling gilt and tinsel leather bibs, tasselled horn-sheaths and golden studded harnesses all gaily bedecked with fresh flowers. Above each pair of bulls was perched either a colourful, tasselled parasol or a flag. Each bull also had a large bell dangling from its yoke, making sharp jangling sounds that seemed to compete with the *gamelan* music.

The bull parade ended and the crowd's excitement mounted. Racing fans began to bet. Suddenly a trumpet sounded. The first race was about to begin. The handlers prodded two pairs of bulls into position. Several strong-armed youths used all their might to hold back the bulls which were apparently feeling the effect of the rum, beer and raw eggs which they had been fed with earlier. The jockeys bent low on their rigs waiting for the signal. The red flag dropped and the two pairs of bulls jolted into motion. The crowd roared. Fans shouted the names of their favourite bulls as the jockeys prodded the animals from behind with pointed sticks. Suddenly the noise rose in crescendo as one pair of bulls made a zigzag and then plunged headlong into the yelling crowd which scrambled in all directions. The other pair of bulls headed straight for the finishing line and the audience screamed with excitement. The race was over for the first four bulls and two jockeys. But not for the younger spectators, who often gathered near the winning-post. For them, the excitement was not so much to see which bulls won, but to get the thrill of scampering away from charging bulls. Some even tried to climb onto charging bulls after the race. Gambling with death is the surest way to gain real excitement.

The famous bull-race of Madura is an annual excitement for the Madurese.

Ram-fighting is a very popular form of entertainment in the villages of West Java.

Sometimes death triumphed, for on several occasions one or two of the spectators were stampeded to death.

Unlike conventional horse-racing or greyhound-racing where there are proper race-tracks, the Madura bull-race is held in a stadium where there is really no clear dividing line between the racing area and the spectators' area. There is no enclosure or fence to separate the two. The only line visible in the field is the finishing line drawn with white lime.

The area of the grassy turf which holds both the bull-race and the spectators is about 130 metres by 40 metres. The bulls are supposed to race for 100 metres. Normally 30 pairs of bulls are put to race. The best time recorded so far is nine seconds, faster than man's world track record. The winners are always the pets and pride of the village. When the victorious bulls parade back to their home-town, there is great rejoicing and a feast is usually thrown to celebrate the occasion. Every member of the village feels a sense of pride when their bulls win a race. The love for the bulls has developed a tradition not to kill any bulls which have won a bull-race. It has, therefore, become a superstition that if champion bulls are slaughtered, bad luck would befall the village.

The village of Sumenap is reputed for its champion bulls which are well known for their stamina and swiftness. Nowadays, bull-races are becoming increasingly popular in Madura; the sport reflects the general ruggedness and impulsive character of the Madurese.

Another place where youths are trained to be rugged is Nias, an island at the northern tip of West Sumatra. The village youths have to jump over a tall, solid hurdle of stone to prove their strength and manhood. On the prescribed day, when they are ready, the villagers, old and young, watch the boys leap, one after another, from a well-worn boulder at the foot of the hurdle, sail over its top with feet forward and then land on rough, heavy paving stones with resilient bare feet, again and again. This famous custom is called *fahombe*, and often serves as an introduction to a community whose greeting is *jaho*, meaning 'strength'.

There are times when a less rugged youth fails to scale the stone hurdle and breaks his leg or is wounded when he lands on the rough stones. There is no room for self-pity or sympathy from relatives or friends. He has to try again in order to prove his manhood and to show that he is strong enough to protect a beautiful bride. These are signs of a Spartan society which still exists in both Madura and Nias.

The only place in Indonesia where bull-fights are still performed as a ceremony is Toraja. There the bull-fights have become part of the burial ritual. Before the bulls are slaughtered to feast the guests who have come to mourn the dead, they are put to a fight in an open field. No stadium is necessary; nor are there any rules or any referee. It is just a sort of game to amuse the guests who have come from faraway villages. In Toraja, funerals are always held after the harvest. This is the time for the farmers to rest. The bulls which are put to fight in Toraja are less fortunate than those in Madura, for winner and loser face the same fate — the winner has only the privilege of surviving a little longer than the loser. They all end up as *papiong*, a typical Torajan dish which is a mixture of blood and beef, cooked inside hollow bamboo over a hot charcoal fire.

The bull-fight could have been a popular sport in ancient days. The tradition must have died out, as the destruction of bulls meant fewer cows for the farm. It is difficult to ascertain whether bull-fighting existed on a large scale in the past. The only written record is in the form of a folk-tale, telling the origin of the word 'Minangkabau', the name of an area and its people who have become famous throughout Indonesia and overseas for their *nasi padang* restaurants.

It seems that about 600 years ago, a king of Java wanted to conquer West Sumatra and sent a messenger there to advise the people to surrender. The people, however, proposed a bull-fight as a way to avoid bloodshed. The deal was that if the Javanese bull should win, the Sumatrans would surrender. When the time came for the bull-fight, the people of West Sumatra selected a tiny calf to fight the huge Javanese bull. It took the audience as well as the big bull by surprise. The calf, which appeared helpless, ran straight to the large bull and pressed his nose against the underside of the bull searching for milk. Soon the bull was seen running away roaring with pain. Blood began to drip from its stomach while the little calf was still chasing after it for milk. When it finally dropped dead, the people of West Sumatra shouted, "*Minangkabau, minangkabau!*" meaning "The buffalo wins, the buffalo wins!" (*minang* means 'victory', and *kabau*, 'buffalo' or 'bull').

According to the story, the owners of the calf fastened sharp pieces of iron to the tips of the calf's horns. The calf was kept away from the mother buffalo for three days and was therefore half-starved when he was put into the arena. He went straight to the bull from Java, thinking that it was the mother. When he searched for milk, the sharp-pointed pieces of iron on his horns pierced the belly of the big bull.

For hundreds of years the roofs of the houses in West Sumatra have been built in the form of buffalo horns, and the people in that part of the country call themselves and their land Minangkabau.

Nobody can really tell whether it was a true story or just a legend. But it may be a clue that bull-fights existed a long time ago. Historically, the kingdom of Malayapura in Minangkabau was founded by Adilyawarman, a prince of Majapahit. In 1365 it was registered as a dependency of Majapahit. The name 'Minangkabau' was said to be a combination of the words *minanga* (a river in that region) and *kempar* or *kerbau* (buffalo). The legendary bull-fight also reflects the sharp wit, shrewdness and gift for diplomacy of the Minangkabau people, and their desire for peaceful settlement to avoid bloodshed.

The Minangkabau people like to emigrate for better fortunes. They call this *merantau* (moving out). They are gifted in commerce and trade. Of the petty traders in Jakarta, nearly 70 per cent are Minangkabau. In every village throughout Indonesia and in every city of South-East Asia, you will find *nasi padang* restaurants selling the typical food of Minangkabau.

As Bali is well-known for its cockfight, Madura for its bull-race, Toraja for its bull-fight, and Central Java for *jangkrik* fighting, West Java is a land of the ram-fight, known as *adu dombak*. Ram-fighting has been a tradition in West Java for hundreds of years. It has become so popular a folk game that every village has its own ram-fight society. The societies are so well organized that their influence has extended from the grass-root level to the provincial level. The West Java provincial administration has now a Provincial Federation of Ram-Fight Societies, called the Persadom (Persatuan Dombak Adu Dombak). Visitors can easily see a ram-fight on any Sunday in one of the villages of West Java. Once a fortnight, a tournament is held at village level. The best rams are chosen for the grand show of the provincial ram-fight tournament which the Governor attends. I was told that the West Java Governor himself has a strong ram of which he is very proud.

I saw a ram-fight one afternoon in Cikalong, a village about two hours' drive from Jakarta. Like other villages, Cikalong also has a community ram-fight shed constructed of wooden poles with an *atap* roof (thatched with palm leaves). There are no walls, only pillars. The sound of drums and gongs played by little children attracted us. A small crowd had gathered to watch the show. No tickets were sold as it was part of village recreation. It is a weekly affair. I saw two rams, one brown and one white, being dragged to the centre of the shed. The rams seemed to nod at each other and then retreated simultaneously to a distance of about ten feet apart. They stared at each other for a few seconds, lowered their horns, charged, and then there was literally a head-on clash. The horns banged, followed by the sound of the gong. A second retreat took place, then another clash, accompanied by drums, gongs, and hand-clapping. At the end of the third bang, the white ram appeared dizzy and stayed put, apparently unable to retreat for another charge. The crowd booed and shouted the name of the ram, provoking it to continue the fight. The owner went forward, took hold of the ram and started to massage it from head to tail, including its testicles. He lifted its front legs and then the hindlegs. Minutes later, the fight continued, but the white ram was too weak to take on any more clashes and ran away.

At the Cikalong ram-fight I saw no betting, but was told that betting was more rampant at the district and provincial ram-fights. When a ram is killed in the fight, the earnings from bets go to buy the owner another ram. This, the organizer explained, was in the spirit of *gotong royong*. After all, it was more for fun than for gambling. The objective was to encourage farmers to rear a better and stronger breed of ram.

The West Javanese ram is an unusual type of animal. It has the face of a timid sheep. The long curling horns look like screw-drivers. The body and hips resemble an Alsatian. It has woolly fur on its head, but its coat is well-cropped at the back. A good fighting ram can fetch a price as high as half a million rupiahs (about US$1,000). Like the heroes of the bull-races of Madura and other game fights, the champion ram also becomes the pet of the village, especially the children. At the time I saw the ram-fight, the village of Cigarut was producing the best breed of rams. Once a year, handsome prizes are presented to the village which produces the best ram. This is decided by the Provincial Ram-fight Federation.

The well-organized ram-fights of West Java reflect the thriving spirit of *gotong royong* in the tightly-knit village community. Ram-fights are always held in an atmosphere of fun and gaiety, truly revealing the temperament of the people in that region.

Indonesia is a land of games and dances. The ones I have covered are just a few which I happened to witness. The list does not include games which are universally known, such as bridge, chess, mah-jong, dominoes, table-tennis, badminton, football, or horse-racing which are also popular in the country. Indonesia is a paradise for those who have an interest to·look into the social and cultural impact of games and dances on the people. This chapter has merely scratched the surface of a broad and interesting subject.

Glossary

abangan: nominal Muslims; those influenced by pre-Islamic beliefs.
adat: customary law.
adu dombak: ram-fight.
adu jangkrik: game of cricket-fighting.
air mata duyung: mermaid. It literally means 'longing tears'.
alat: instrument or weapon.
aliran: streams; trends.
alon alon asal kelakon: literally means 'go slow so long as the target is achieved'; equivalent to the proverb 'slow and steady wins the race'.
angklung: West Javanese bamboo musical instrument.
ayase: Papuan headhunter's song.
banci: one who is neither male nor female.
barong berutuk: the name given to boys who, in ancient times in Trungen, performed a dance semi-naked and whipped anyone they came across in the temple grounds.
Batara Tunggal: the supreme god of the Baduis.
becak: trishaw.
Bedaya: dance performed at Javanese royal weddings.
bersilat: art of self-defence.
Bharatajudha War: war between the Kurawas and the Pandawas leading to the extinction of the Kurawas.
Bhinneka Tunggal Ika: 'Unity Through Diversity', the national motto, which is inscribed on the Indonesian state crest.
blangkon: Javanese headgear.
blencong: the oil-lamp lighting the wayang.
bombo: Torajan name for 'personal spirit'.
boru: the name of a leg of the *dalihan natolu* of the Bataks. In the hierarchy system of the Bataks, this represents the family of the bride-groom.
bungbung: bamboo container for crickets.
bupati: official title of the officer in charge of palaces in Central Java.
buyut: taboos or prohibitions of the Baduis.
candi: ancient monuments.
cempaka: name of a flower; gemstone with the colour of the flower.
cenderawasih: bird-of-paradise.
chakra: Hindu name for the centres of power.
chayanataka: a kind of shadow-play performed in India in ancient times.
chiam-si: Hokien name for a fortune script obtained from the Klenteng Sampo.
cinde: red cloth worn on the ankles of dancers.

Glossary

congklak or *dakon:* Sumatran name for a game for girls, in which a boat-like wooden board and beans or pebbles are used.

dalang: the man who manipulates the shadow-play puppets and narrates the story.

dalem: inner chamber of the palace.

dalihan natolu: three-legged earthen burner for cooking. The term is used also to describe a sort of clan system of the Bataks which stipulates the hierarchy of inter-family relations.

dangka: square wooden containers for making rice-flour.

demisori: rice bed used at royal weddings for the bride and groom to sit on.

dodot: long piece of cloth wrapped round the hips of puppets representing kings, princes, and ministers.

dongan sabutuha: the name of one of the three legs of the *dalihan natolu.* In the hierarchy system of the Bataks, the term refers to relatives and friends.

dongeng: legends.

dukun: medicine man, magician, healer, seer.

durung ngerti: Javanese term for 'not being able to understand'. (It is used in a derogatory sense.)

fahombe: a custom in Nias where boys are required to jump over a stone hurdle to prove their manhood.

gamelan: Javanese instrumental orchestra.

garuda: Indonesian name for a kind of mythological bird.

gedebok: the banana stem used to support shadow-play puppets.

gotong royong: spirit of mutual help.

grinsing wayang: the flaming heaven of the ancestors.

guci: Balinese name for 'old porcelain'.

gunungan: large mountain-shaped leather puppet, used to begin and end a shadow-play.

guru: teacher.

Gusti: Lord.

haji: a Muslim who has been to Mecca.

holim: Dhani word for the covering worn by Dhani men over their penes.

horas: word of greeting used by the Bataks.

hula-hula: the name of a leg of the *dalihan natolu.* In the clan hierarchy system of the Bataks, the term refers to the family of the bride.

huma serang: Badui sacred plot of land where the rice grown is normally reserved for harvest festivals.

imam: Muslim religious leader or teacher.

jao: long chains of cowrie shells, formerly used as currency by the Dhani people to purchase pigs.

jaro: administrative heads of Badui villages on the outskirts of Badui Dalam.

jiwa: soul.

kamandak: Javanese archaic musical instrument played only on royal occasions.

kandang or *rebab:* Javanese violin.

kanoman: a kind of training of the Sumarah school of *Kebatinan*, which involves a wide range of occultism.

kapur: limestone powder.

kapur barus: sort of camphor used for mummification.

karapan sapi: bull-race.

karbere: club used by the *koreri* supporters against their enemies.

Karia Taur Agung Ekadasa Rudra: 'The Great Ceremonial Offering to the Eleven *Rudra*'. This grand festival is held in Bali once in a hundred years when a communal cremation is performed.

kayob: a song of lament for the dead.

Kebatinan: Javanese spiritualism.

Kecak: Monkey Dance.

kecapi: Sundanese stringed musical instrument.

kemenyan: incense.

kerbau: buffalo.

kesepuhan: a kind of training of the Sumarah school of *Kebatinan*.

Khalifah: teacher.

klenik: undesirable practices which lead people astray.

klenteng: temple.

kliwon: Friday, the fifth day of the five days in the month of Suro which are considered to have magical powers. On this day all the heirlooms in the palaces are given a holy bath.

komkom: fresh flowers soaked in water.

koreri: literally means 'we change'. It was the name of a religious movement of the Biak people who believed in the resurrection of the dead.

koteka: horn-shaped covering worn by Dhani men over their penes.

kraton: palace.

kraton punggawa: palace officials.

kris: dagger.

kui-aha: feast-house of the Marind Anim, a headhunting tribe. It is used for festivities following a successful headhunting expedition.

kuku pancanaka: thumbnail.

kupeng: Balinese headgear.

kupeng: ancient Chinese coins used as spiritual currency.

Kurawas: collective name for the 99 sons and one daughter of Prince **Drestarata**.

kyai: mystic; **Muslim scholar or sage**.

Kyai Kanyut Mesem: one of the oldest sets of *gamelan*.

lakon: drama; stories.

laksa: Badui festival when *laksa*, a kind of compressed rice-flour, is distributed to everyone who has helped with the harvesting.

lambung: round bamboo filter.

Legong: a traditional Balinese dance.

leyak: witchcraft.

lingga: symbol of the male organ.

lontar: ancient writings on palm leaves.

Glossary

Loro Blonyo: stone statues representing a bride and bridegroom.

Lubang Buaya: 'Crocodile Hole', the place where the six generals and a soldier were thrown after the Gestapu coup of 30 September 1965.

lumbong padi: Torajan storage-hut for padi.

Ma Parempe: the Torajan ceremony of bringing the dead to the cut-rock grave.

Ma'badong: Torajan hymns.

Mahabharata: one of the two classical Indian epics.

mantra: mystical chants.

merah putih: 'red and white', the Indonesian flag.

meru: pagoda used by the Balinese as contact points for dialogue with the souls of their ancestors.

moksa: the ability to make oneself disappear.

musika: small pink precious stone the size of a pomegranate seed. The Trungenese put this into the mouth of a dead person before burial. They believe that it helps to preserve the body.

Naga banda: a wooden dragon used to contain the king's body for cremation after death.

Nasakom: acronym from Nationalism-Religion-Communism.

nasi padang: the typical food of Minangkabau.

nayak: Dhani word meaning 'thank you'.

ngurak: act of self-stabbing.

nirwana: heaven.

padma: lotus.

pahlawan: national hero.

pakem: handbook of the dalang.

paleton: musical instrument.

pamengku: caretaker of the temple.

pamong: guardian or *guru* who guides a *Kebatinan* recruit.

panakawan: servant clowns.

Pancasila: the five principles of democracy of the Indonesian nation.

Pandawas: collective name for the five sons of King Pandu — Judistira, Bima, Arjuna, Nangkula and Sadewa.

panglima besar: military commander-in-chief.

pantun: short verses.

papiong: typical Torajan dish made from a mixture of bull's blood and beef, cooked inside a hollow bamboo over a charcoal fire.

Patih: military commander to the king.

pendopo: entrance or front porch of a temple.

peranakan: born locally.

petinggi: chief or head of Tenggerese village.

pinang: areca nut.

pis Arjuna: coins of Arjuna, the hero of the *Mahabharata* epic. The coins can bestow to the possessor the magical abilities of Arjuna.

pis bolan: coins which are supposed to bring luck in affairs of love.

pis Hanuman: coins of Hanuman, the Monkey-god. They can bestow the magical qualities of Hanuman on the possessor.

pis Kresna: coins of Kresna. They can bestow magical qualities of Kresna.

piupiu tanggule tree: a kind of tree that bears juicy fruit. The trunk is covered with long thorns.

pracimoyono: part of *kraton* where the princess has her private room.

pramana: inner soul.

prasasti: inscription.

pringgitan: outer chamber of the palace.

pujangga: poet of the court.

pungpuhanam: small bamboo cottage where Goddess Dewi Sari dwells.

pura: temple.

pusaka: heirloom.

Putri Cina: Chinese princess.

pu'un: top chieftains of the Baduis.

raksasas: giants.

Ramayana: one of the two classical Indian epics.

rasa: deeper feelings.

Ratu Adil: the Just King.

Romo: term of respect for an elderly Javanese sage.

ronggeng: a dance.

rudra: guardian spirits of the eleven points of the Balinese compass.

Sanghiang: spirit of God; a deity.

sawo: a juicy fruit, called 'ciku' in Malay.

sekaten: the custom of beating the *gamelan* in the *kraton* continuously for a week in the month of Maulud, Prophet Mohammed's birthday.

Selawi Negara: stories of the 25 ancient kingdoms of the Baduis.

Setan: devil.

Singa-Kaang: a coffin in the shape of a flying lion, used in the cremation of heroes when they die.

sirap: wooden tiles.

sirih: betel leaf.

soko guru: pillars.

songkok: turban; velvet cap worn by male Muslims.

Srimpi: a dance.

sujud: way of liberation by meditating.

sukusma: part of the brain governing the passions.

sulut: musical instrument.

sumana: consciousness.

Sunan or Susuhunan: Prince.

tandu: sedan chair used in royal weddings to carry the bride.

tapa: fasting and meditation.

tapa geni: fire meditation.

tapa kalong: meditating in the posture of a bat.

tapa ngableng: meditating in darkness.

tapa mutih: abstaining from eating anything that is salted.

tapa senen: fasting on Mondays.

tapak jalak: gemstone with the design of a bird's footprint.

tedong: an albino breed of bull. It has white skin with black spots and stripes and is used by the Torajans in their funeral rites.

tempurong: coconut shell.

To Mebalam: the expert who knows the secrets of embalming the dead.

tokoh or *sin kheh:* terms given to the Chinese who are comparatively recent arrivals from China.

tongkat: walking stick.

tongkonan: Torajan community house, which is used as a death-house.

topeng: mask.

tuak: a kind of liquor made from palm seeds.

tugu: special houses built by the Bataks for preserving the ashes of the dead of each clan.

tukang: artisans.

tukang melak: master of ceremonies.

tumbukan: when one reaches the age of 48, 56 or 64 according to the Javanese eight-year cycle.

tunggal panaluan: a carved walking-stick which is used as a symbol of great honour and authority by the Bataks.

turun: to descend.

ulos: Batak name for a piece of cloth used to wrap new-born babies. It is also used in a marriage ceremony when it is placed on the shoulders of the bride and groom to bless them with harmony, unity and fertility.

undang mantu: the custom of 'inviting a son-in-law'. The term is used for the interval between the wedding day and the fifth day after the wedding ceremony when the marriage is consummated.

wahyu cakraningrat: Javanese term for a blessing given by God to a ruler of the country.

Wali: Muslim saints.

wangkang: Balinese name for porcelain plates.

wantilan: cockpit.

waringin: banyan tree.

wayang: puppets.

wayang golek: puppet-show using three-dimensional wooden puppets resembling human beings.

wayang kulit: shadow-play.

wayang madya: puppet-show performing stories from the *Book of Hajipamasa* which contains mythical stories and tells of the coming of the Hindus to Indonesia.

wayang menak: wayang performances about Amir Hamzah, uncle of Prophet Mohammed.

wayang purwa: images or shadows of Javanese ancestors drawn on *lontar* (palm leaves).

wayang suluh: shows relating contemporary history and propaganda. The puppets are made of leather but have human profiles.

wayang topeng: dance-drama based on stories of the Panji cycle, performed by people wearing wooden masks.

yoni: symbol of the female organ.

Index

Index

Index

Index

The Author

Lee Khoon Choy had 14 years of journalistic experience before he entered politics in 1959. His interest in Indonesia began in early 1955 when he covered the Afro-Asian Conference in Bandung as a journalist. Later, he visited Indonesia as a politician for short periods, and then stayed for $4\frac{1}{2}$ years as Singapore's Ambassador to Indonesia from 1970. Before his Indonesian assignment, he was Ambassador to Egypt, concurrently accredited to Lebanon, Pakistan, Yugoslavia and Ethiopia. He has served as Parliamentary Secretary for Education; Minister of State for Culture; Minister of State to the Prime Minister's Office and is now Senior Minister of State for Foreign Affairs.

For his contribution to the promotion of better understanding between Indonesia and Singapore, he was awarded the Bintang Jasa Utama (a first class meritorious medal) by President Suharto in 1974.